Winning Secrets
of Online Poker

Douglas W. Frye and

Curtis D. Frye

THOMSON

COURSE TECHNOLOGY

Professional ■ Trade ■ Reference

ISBN: 1-59200-711-2

Library of Congress Catalog Card Number: 2004117708

Printed in the United States of America

05 06 07 08 09 BH 10 9 8 7 6 5 4 3 2 1

General Manager and Publisher of PTR:
Stacy L. Hiquet

Associate Director of Marketing:
Sarah O'Donnell

Marketing Manager:
Kristin Eisenzopf

Manager of Editorial Services:
Heather Talbot

Acquisitions Editor:
Mitzi Koontz

Senior Editor:
Mark Garvey

Marketing Coordinator:
Jordan Casey

Project Editor and Copyeditor:
Kim V. Benbow

PTR Editorial Services Coordinator:
Elizabeth Furbish

Interior Layout Tech:
Danielle Foster

Interior Designer:
Mike Tanamachi

Cover Designer:
Nancy Goulet

Indexer:
Kelly Talbot

Proofreader:
Gene Redding

THOMSON

COURSE TECHNOLOGY

Professional ■ Trade ■ Reference

Thomson Course Technology PTR,
a division of Thomson Course Technology
25 Thomson Place
Boston, MA 02210
http://www.courseptr.com

This book is dedicated to our parents
David and Jane.

Acknowledgments

Doug Frye

I would like to thank Mitzi Koontz, our acquisitions editor, for her belief in this project and for her hard work in helping make it a reality. Kim Benbow, our friendly, intelligent, and always responsive copy editor, was forced to figure out what the heck we were talking about, but she was without fail able to steer us toward lucidity. Our long-term involvement with the game took us into "poker-speak" at times, and her feedback brought us back to proper English. That being said, Curt and I had final say over what ultimately went in and how it was worded, so as much as we would love to shift the blame for mistakes, the blame is 100 percent ours.

My deepest appreciation goes out to the folks at StudioB for their strong representation. Neil Salkind has played a major role in getting Curt's talents and ability recognized and rewarded with consistent work. He, and recently Laura Lewin, have worked diligently to help me establish a foothold in the writing business. They are unfailingly professional and nice folks to boot. Thank you.

I would next like to note the role Wilson Software's products have played in my game's development. Their software has helped me weed out many imperfections in how I play; any remaining shortcomings are solely my fault. They graciously provided the most recent versions of their products to us for use with this book, but it is important to note that we chose them as the company whose products we would use only after having paid full price for many of them over several years before this book was conceived.

I can't fail to mention several of the closest poker friends I've made over the years. Johnny, Robin, Tina, Jae-gor, Kim, Steve, Heather, and Larry—it's been great getting to know you. I've met a lot of good and friendly dealers and floor people over the years as well. It's a stressful job, I know.

Finally, thanks to my twin brother and co-author Curt for everything, but for this book especially. He helped get me through my first major writing project with no permanent damage.

Curt Frye

First off, I'd like to thank Doug for coming up with the idea for this book. Good ideas often seem obvious in retrospect, but I'm surprised no one had ever gone beyond the basics of tracking your poker results or how to use the Wilson Software Turbo Poker series to test your strategies. I'd also like to thank Mitzi Koontz, our acquisitions editor, for putting her faith and her company's money into this project. Kim Benbow did a great job editing our text: tweaking here, querying there, and helping to fix the inevitable repetitions that crop up when two writers work in parallel. Thanks also go out to Mike Tanamachi for his interior design and to Danielle Foster for the interior layout.

I'd also like to thank my agent, Neil Salkind, and David and Sherry Rogelberg of StudioB. They've helped my writing career take off.

Contents at a Glance

Contents

Part III

Contents

Part IV

Introduction

What You'll Find in This Book

Our goal is to show you how to be a better poker player, *regardless of how you want to play the game*. If you only want to play good cards and never take any risks, you can play that way. If you want to be a wild man who always stays in for the last card in a hand, where you only have a 5 percent chance of winning, you can play that way. For that matter, you can write out a list of strategies and tactics, and then roll dice to determine your next action. We don't care what you do, as long as you don't throw away a winning hand after the last bets are down. That would break our hearts.

Who We Think You Are

We wrote this book for the beginning poker player, but we realize that a lot of poker players buy many of the books that come out in the hope that they can glean any advantage from the material. To that end, we included a fair amount of advanced material with instructions on how to analyze your performance in general and specific game situations in particular. We do assume that you're familiar with the Internet and can install software on a computer, but that seems like a pretty safe assumption, considering you saw the book's title when you picked it up.

Conventions Used in This Book

- ✦ We display new terms in *italics* and define the term in the text.
- ✦ We abbreviate non-numeric cards with the first letter of the card's name, so A means Ace, K means King, and so on. We abbreviate spot cards with the number of spots on the card, so Nines are 9, Eights are 8, and so on. The exception is the Ten, which we represent with the letter T.
- ✦ We use symbols to designate suits, so expect to see lots of ♣, ♥, ♠, and ♦ throughout the text.
- ✦ An "s" after the cards in a hand means the cards we discuss are *suited* (or all of the same suit), but the suit doesn't matter (e.g., AKs can mean A♠ K♠, A♥K♥, and so on).
- ✦ An "o" after the cards in a hand means the cards we discuss are not suited, and that the suits don't matter (e.g., AKo can mean A♠K♥, A♥K♠, and so on).

How This Book Is Organized

We've broken our coverage into a number of topics, each of which has its own chapter.

Part I tells you everything you need to know to get started playing online poker.

Chapter 1, "So What Is This Online Poker Thing?" provides a quick introduction to on-line poker, how it affects your life, and whether it's legal or not in the United States.

Chapter 2, "Getting Started," presents the mechanics of online poker, lists the hardware requirements for popular poker software, and shows you how to deposit money into an online account. Credit card companies don't allow United States residents to transfer money to most gambling sites, so you may need to go through an alternative funding source.

Chapter 3, "The Mechanics of Online Poker," reviews the basics of poker, the actions you can take, and how the games are designed to stimulate action.

Chapter 4, "Games You Can Play," expands on the material covered in Chapter 3 by describing the games you can play online, from the old standard seven-card Stud to the hottest game in the poker world, Texas Hold 'em. Those basic games have variations, such as dealing you more hole cards or letting you play for both high and low hands; we'll cover them all.

Chapter 5, "Cash Games versus Tournaments," describes the differences between tour-nament and cash game play. You may have read that the best tournament players are wild and aggressive cash game players who can throw away their money. That stereotype is true to some extent, but you have to remember that the best tournament players are used to playing hands that could cost them $100,000 or more if they lose, and even smaller tournaments can have a $10,000 difference between the prizes for first and second place. Risking that much money is a lot more stressful than taking a shot at a $400 pot in an online game, where all bets and raises are $10 in the first two betting rounds and $20 in the final two rounds.

Chapter 6, "Playing the Game," introduces online poker rooms and shows you the in-terfaces you'll use to play at the most popular sites. Many of the sites use a variation on the same software, so you won't be at a loss when you log on and put your money at risk. Even so, there are options you can use to speed the game along, to take a break without risking any money while you're away from your computer, and to protect your interest in a pot if your Internet connection drops in the middle of a hand.

Chapter 7, "Cheating," covers cheating, which is a serious consideration when you play poker online for real money. There is no way to tell if two or more players at your table are using their cell phone company's generous gift of unlimited weekend minutes to share their cards, but does it make a difference if one of the players folds early and is no longer in the hand? It can—that player's cards aren't available, and knowing that your full house can't be beaten by a higher full house because the required cards are out of play could make a big difference in how you play a hand.

Part II covers the games you play from the first round of cards to the last round of betting.

As **Chapter 8, "Starting Hands,"** explains, the first decision you need to make is whether the two, three, or four cards you start with are worth risking money over. You might not have a choice of whether to throw in your first few dollars, but you can sure choose whether to toss any more cash on the fire if someone else raises or whether to put in a raise yourself if the situation warrants. And, for you more aggressive players out there, the cards you hold don't always drive that decision.

Chapter 9, "The Flop," Chapter 10, "The Turn," and **Chapter 11, "Playing the River,"** take you the rest of the way through your hand, pointing out traps you can fall into, traps you can set, and how to make sense of your opponents' actions. We'll also show you how to analyze your chances of winning a hand and determining whether or not there's enough money in the pot to make it worth your while to call. You can set your own pain threshold there, too.

Part III is all about the data, baby.

Chapter 12, "Evaluating Your Play Using Spreadsheets," introduces a basic system for tracking your results by hour, game, session, and location. Want to know if you do well at certain times of the day but do poorly at others? Are you the sort of player who always loses at the start of a session but usually comes back at the end? You can only find out if you keep track of what happens as it happens. Then we'll show you how to use Excel (or another spreadsheet program) to find deeper meaning in your data, using advanced statistical analysis techniques.

Chapter 13, "Analyzing Your Game Using Poker Software," introduces PokerStat and PokerTracker, two programs that expand on the basic results tracking system and get into the type of hands you call with, when you tend to fold or hang on, and what percentage of showdowns you win. Some online card rooms give you other information you can use, such as how often you fold during a particular betting round. We'll also show you how to perform post-game analysis using the Wilson Software product line—there's a lot you can learn from the computer, and a lot more you can figure out when you combine computer analysis with your own take on what happened at the tables.

Finally, in **Part IV**, we show you how to maintain control over your environment and yourself. Discipline is the most important element of poker, regardless of where you play.

In **Chapter 14, "Turning Data into Discipline,"** we demonstrate how a lack of discipline can impact your bottom line. You can learn some rather stark lessons when you stray from your game plan, so pay attention to what we have to tell you.

Chapter 15, "Maintaining a Stable Playing Environment," shows you how to establish an optimal playing environment, depending on your threshold of distraction.

Finally, in **Chapter 16, "Conclusion,"** we dispense a few final words of wisdom and summarize what we want you to take away from the book. Yes, there is a method to our madness; your madness should have a method as well.

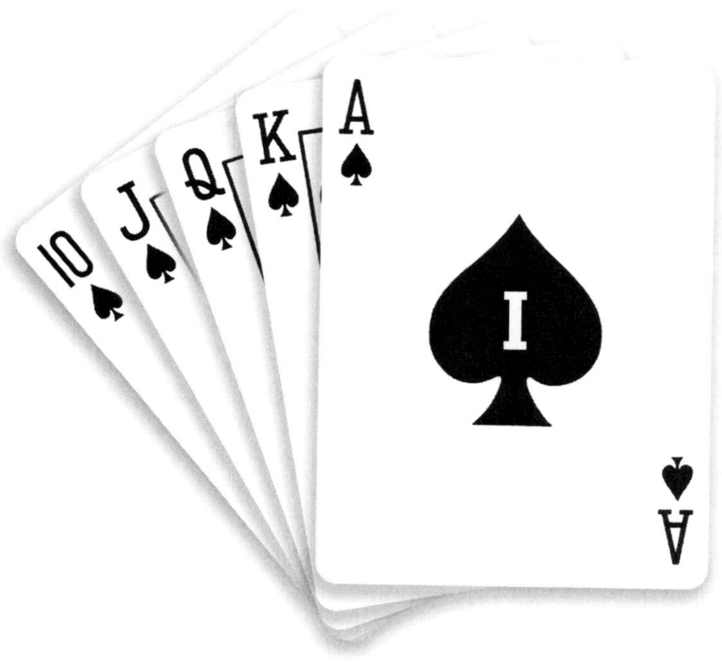
10
J
Q
K
A
I

So What Is This Online Poker Thing?

Playing poker online is a blast. No one can tell you how to dress, that your music is turned up too loud, or that your play fails to meet a certain minimum standard. More specifically, if someone does try to tell you anything you don't want to hear, you can muzzle the moron with a few deft mouse clicks. Online poker has come a long way since the early days, but you'll appreciate the game more if you know from whence it came.

A Potted History of Online Poker

The first true Internet poker game, which started in 1994, was run on an Internet Relay Chat (IRC) server, irc.poker.net, where a software program administered Omaha, Hold 'em, Stud, and Draw games. IRC was a precursor to instant messaging and was text-only at the time, but Greg Reynolds wrote a graphical front end named Gpoker that interpreted the text into graphics and let you play without memorizing dozens of commands for the games. You can still find information about the IRCBot dealing program and Gpoker at www-2.cs.cmu.edu/People/mummert/ircbot.html, but even Reynolds' graphical interface couldn't keep the IRC server from being overtaken by World Wide Web sites with more attractive designs.

> ### ♠♥♣♦ Note
>
> If any readers were on IRC poker from 1994–1995, Curt played under the user names cfrye and wildcat.

If you were a hard-core tournament poker player, you could also play in the World Rec.Gambling.Poker Tournament (WRGPT), which was run by e-mail. Most of the Web pages about the tournaments are lost to antiquity, but you can still find Curt's table assignment for the second round of WRGPT 5 at http://www-2.cs.cmu.edu/afs/cs.cmu.edu/usr/sippy/www/Poker/Assignments/B.html. No, he didn't finish "in the money" in WRGPT 5, 6, or 8 (whatever that means in an online tournament played for etherbucks and pride), but he did have fun. Ron Duursma wrote the e-mail server program that made it possible for hundreds (and later thousands) of players to share their love for poker, regardless of the time zone they called home. If you're curious to see what the players went through to have some fun over the Internet, Ron's instruction manual for using the e-mail server is still on the Web at http://www-2.cs.cmu.edu/afs/cs.cmu.edu/usr/sippy/www/Poker/rules.server.

The Web became popular in the mid-1990s, so it wasn't long before the gambling community offered ways for Internet users to play for real money. Internet Casinos, Inc., launched their first Web casino on August 18, 1995; they offered 18 casino games, but poker wasn't one of them. The first online card room, Planet Poker, opened for play money games in August 1997, before turning on the taps and enabling players to play for real money on January 1, 1998. Since then, dozens of online poker rooms have appeared and disappeared (one online resource lists 209 online card rooms as of this writing), but a few rooms have flourished and continue to draw new players.

Online Poker Is Taking Over

Poker, particularly Texas Hold 'em, has exploded in popularity over the last three years. You can find Late Night Poker on the air in England, the World Poker Tour on the Travel channel in the United States, and even ESPN, a sports-only network based in the U.S., has expanded its World Series of Poker coverage to include the Razz, Stud, Omaha, and other tournaments in addition to the $10,000 buy-in main event. Dan Goldman, the vice president of marketing for the popular online poker room PokerStars, said in a September 2004 interview that his best guess was that between 50 million and 60 million people worldwide play poker at least once a month.

How many people play online poker? It's hard to tell, mostly because it's difficult to associate an Internet identity with a person's real name, but online card rooms do note the number of players on their sites. Figure 1.1 shows what that note looks like on PartyPoker.

PokerPulse, a Canadian site that tracks the player and wagering statistics published on the most popular online card rooms' home pages, estimated recently that during one 24-hour period 7,341 players played for real money in online tournaments, 7,072 players wagered real money in *ring games* (games that continue at the same limits and without eliminating players from action when they lose a set amount of chips), and that more than US$141 million was wagered in online ring games during that 24-hour period. That's a lot of poker hands and a lot of money changing hands! You can find out how many people are on the most popular sites or view the free industry-wide statistics for the last 24 hours at www.pokerpulse.com.

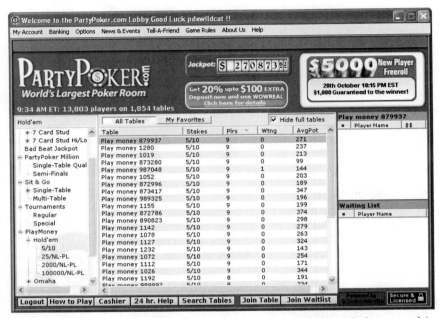

Figure 1.1 Online poker sites like to advertise how busy they are (at least, the busy ones do).

Positives, Negatives, and Legalities of Online Poker

There's a lot to be said in favor of playing poker online, but there are pitfalls you need to avoid. You might expect that we wouldn't try to talk down the subject of our book, but when you're putting money on the line, you need to go in with as much knowledge as you can so you don't get caught up. But there are good parts to the ride, too. Over the next few pages, we'll cover

✦ Reasons to play poker online

✦ Reasons not to play poker online

✦ Legalities of online poker

Reasons to Play Poker Online

But why should you play online poker? It does seem odd that folks are willing to put their money in the hands of a privately held company based in the Dominican Republic, Costa Rica, or Antigua and engage in a game of chance with faceless players from around the globe who may or may not be using their wireless phone company's unlimited nighttime calling plan to conspire against you. Then again, playing online has its advantages, not the least of which is that you can play from home, where you set the rules. You can smoke or not, eat at the table, wear whatever catches your fancy, and listen to music without wearing headphones. You can also find games at any time of the day or night. Curt is a night owl who's often up until 3:00 AM or later, which means that he hits the sweet spot for mid-day players in Great Britain, Germany, Sweden, Norway, Denmark, and Finland. Doug is more of an evening player, so he often shares tables with players from the eastern part of the United States, early starters on the Pacific coast, and the late-night players from Europe and Scandinavia. To top it off, you can leave a game whenever you want to. It's not uncommon for someone to log on and play for 15 minutes to kill time before their favorite television show comes on, so leaving abruptly doesn't raise eyebrows the way it might if you drove for an hour-and-a-half to a brick-and-mortar casino, won a few hundred dollars in a nice little rush, and shoved off before your first drink arrived.

There are also procedural benefits to playing poker online. For example, the limits can be much lower than in a physical casino. Believe it or not, you can play for as little as two cents a bet—yep, that's $0.02. Online casinos also tend to take a bit less money out of each pot (the *rake*) because they don't have to pay for dealers, cocktail servers, floor personnel, or carpets. Also, because the cards are shuffled within a second after a hand ends, you will often get in 30 or more hands per half hour, as compared to 20 hands per half hour in a traditional casino. When you're a favorite to win money at your table, you want to play as many hands as you can. Yes, the rake grinds away at everyone's bankroll, taking a few dollars out of circulation every time the cards are dealt, but with some good play on your part, you can get your share of the loot. As poker genius Mike Caro says, the chips flow clockwise around the table and eventually end up in the good players' stacks. If you're good at making good decisions quickly, you can play at multiple tables simultaneously and increase the number of chips coming your way.

Finally, the number of aggravations that make a game a struggle goes down when you play over the Internet. Online dealers don't make mistakes, and the other players can't fold out of turn, reach for their chips while watching for your reaction, or talk trash without your permission.

Reasons Not to Play Poker Online

With that sort of build-up, you might think that online poker is the universe's gift to gamblers. In many ways it is, but online poker does have its downside. For example, always being able to get into a game can be a bad thing, particularly if you're prone to playing short sessions while you're waiting for something else to happen and your mind isn't focused on the game. If you are able to focus on poker while your kids light the grill to cook dinner, that's fine, but if you really should be outside to make sure they don't use gasoline instead of lighter fluid on the charcoal, be honest with yourself and at least sit a few hands out until you can be sure everything is OK.

Speaking of which, do you remember your kids? The sometimes cute and often annoying tax deductions that run around your house and eat your food? I'm sure they'd love to see their parents from time to time, even though they'd be horrified if their secret ever got out. The same thing goes for significant others, such as girlfriends, boyfriends, spouses, and pets. They all require nourishment, attention, and tender loving care, so you need to make time to get away from the neat video game you've found and fan the flames of whatever romance, friendship, or outside interest that makes life worth living.

One of the advantages of online play, the speed of the game and the increased number of hands you get to play per hour, is also one of the biggest downfalls for new players. We both took some time to adjust to the pace of online play, just as we went through a bit of a transition when we realized how fast casino poker games were as compared to the kitchen table games we'd played throughout college. Increasing the number of hands you play magnifies losing streaks as well as winning streaks, so your *variance* (a statistical measure of how much data in a set, such as your hourly poker wins and losses, jumps around) is much, much higher.

Another serious disadvantage of playing online is the lack of human contact. Yes, if you're awkward around your fellow humans, it might seem like a dream come true to be able to play in the privacy of your own home, but the best way to overcome social awkwardness is to put yourself out there and learn. Another down side of not being able to see your competition is that there is no way to verify whether or not your opponents are sharing information. It's pretty easy to prevent players from exchanging information verbally in a live game, but there is absolutely no way you can detect a cell phone when you're in one country and your opponents are somewhere around the globe. Along the same lines, you can't see a player's hand shake when they place a bet. You still have to decide whether that shaking means they're nervous because they're bluffing or because they flopped a straight flush and are afraid you *won't* call, but at least the information is there for you.

Online Poker: Legal or Not?

Neither of your authors is a lawyer, and the discussion that follows is not legal advice. Every jurisdiction's laws are different, and court rulings can be superseded by later decisions. The information provided here may not apply to your circumstance. If you have any doubt as to whether online poker is legal where you live, seek competent legal advice from a licensed attorney.

Online Poker in the United States

Is it against the law to play online poker while in the United States? The United States federal government would like you to think it is, but the only relevant case was decided against it. The Federal District Court for the Eastern District of Louisiana found that the Federal Interstate Wire Act, which outlaws sending or receiving sports bets over a wire-based communication medium, didn't apply. Here's the part of the Wire Act the court considered most relevant:

The Wire Act, found at 18 U.S.C. §1084 provides in pertinent part as follows,

(a) Whoever being engaged in the business of betting or wagering knowingly uses a wire communication facility for the transmission in interstate or foreign commerce of bets or wagers or information assisting in the placing of bets or wagers on any sporting event or contest, or for the transmission of a wire communication which entitles the recipient to receive money or credit as a result of bets or wagers, or for information assisting in the placing of bets or wagers, shall be fined under his title or imprisoned.

The Department of Justice's argument boiled down to the assertion that the word *sporting* only modified the word *event* and not the word *contest*. Under their interpretation, betting of any sort over a phone line or telegraph service would be illegal. The court disagreed with the Department of Justice's semantic juggling, however,

The defendants argue that plaintiffs' failure to allege sports gambling is a fatal defect with respect to their Wire Act claims, while plaintiffs strenuously argue that the Wire Act does not require sporting events or contests to be the object of gambling. However, a plain reading of the statutory language clearly requires that the object of the gambling be a sporting event or contest. Both the role and the exception to the role expressly qualify the nature of the gambling activity as that related to a "sporting event or contest." A reading of the case law leads to the same conclusion.

As the plain language of the statute and case law interpreting the statute are clear, there is no need to look to the legislative history of the Act as argued by plaintiffs. However, even a summary glance at the recent legislative history of internet gambling legislation reinforces the Court's determination that internet gambling on a game of chance is not prohibited conduct under 18 U.S.C. §1084. Recent legislative attempts have sought to amend the Wire Act to encompass "contest[s] of chance or a future contingent event not under the control or influence of [the bettor]" while exempting from the reach of the statute data transmitted "for use in the news reporting of any activity, event or contest upon which bets or wagers are based.'" Similar legislation was introduced in the 106th Congress in the form of the "Internet Gambling Prohibition Act of 1999." That Act sought to amend Title 18 to prohibit the use of the internet to place a bet or wager upon "a contest of others, a sporting event, or a game of chance...". As to the legislative intent at the time the Wire Act was enacted, the House Judiciary Committee Chairman explained that "this particular bill involves the transmission of wagers or bets and layoffs on horse racing and other sporting events."

> *Comparing the face of the Wire Act and the history surrounding its enactment with the recently proposed legislation, it becomes more certain that the Wire Act's prohibition of gambling activities is restricted to the types of events enumerated in the statute, sporting events or contests. Plaintiffs' argument flies in the face of the clear wording of the Wire Act and is more appropriately directed to the legislative branch than this Court. [Internal citations and footnotes omitted.]*

The government appealed the ruling to the United States Court of Appeals for the Fifth Circuit, which also found against them. With specific regard to the Wire Act, the appeals court wrote:

> *The district court concluded that the Wire Act concerns gambling on sporting events or contests and that the Plaintiffs had failed to allege that they had engaged in internet sports gambling. We agree with the district court's statutory interpretation, its reading of the relevant case law, its summary of the relevant legislative history, and its conclusion.*

The appeals court further found that "[b]ecause the Wire Act does not prohibit non-sports internet gambling, any debts incurred in connection with such gambling are not illegal."

So don't think you can get out of your online poker debts by claiming the credit card companies have no right to collect a gambling debt. As the courts interpret the law, all you're doing with your credit card is taking out a cash advance. What you do with the money you receive is up to you.

Online Poker in Individual U.S. States

According to the Fifth Circuit Court of Appeals, there is no national law on the books that prohibits non-sports Internet gambling. However, each state has its own gambling laws. The laws are too numerous and varied to discuss here, but you can find both a summary and the full text of each state's gambling laws at www.gambling-law-us.com/. Chuck Humphrey, the lawyer who runs the site, specializes in gaming, business, securities and exchange, and venture capital law.

It's interesting to note that the laws are all constructed to prevent interstate gambling, but it's OK for state residents to place a bet on a game run by a legal gambling operation based in that state. For example, it's only legal for a Nevada resident to place a bet at an online casino that is hosted by a Nevada corporation. How convenient.

Laws of Countries Other than the United States

As with individual U.S. states, keeping track of the gaming laws in foreign lands is a full-time occupation. Even the U.S. government's General Accounting Office (GAO) had a hard time figuring out where online gambling was legal, as noted in a 2002 GAO report:

> *For example, gaming laws in many countries, like those in many U.S. states, apply to gaming in general rather than to Internet gambling. Although we were*

unable to determine the exact number, an interactive gaming industry services group reported that over 50 countries and foreign jurisdictions, mostly in Europe, the Caribbean, and the Australia/Pacific region, have legalized Internet gambling.

You can find the full GAO report online at www.gao.gov/new.items/d0389.pdf.

Conclusion

Our best guess is that online poker is probably legal in the United States unless your state or locality has a law that prohibits you from placing bets over the Internet. Other countries' laws depend on each nation's court and judicial system, so it is your responsibility to check your local laws and, if necessary, get legal advice to aid your decision on whether to play or not.

Getting Started

To get you playing online poker, the first step is to establish an account on one or several Web sites. This chapter will explain the process one goes through to set up an online account. By the end of this chapter, you will know how to

- ✦ Go to a poker Web site and download and then install the client software to run the program.
- ✦ Install the software and get it ready for use.
- ✦ Differentiate among the different sites as to the bonuses and other benefits they offer their players.
- ✦ Access options one may use in transferring funds to play with in "real money" games.
- ✦ Request that your winnings be sent to you.

Once through the minor drudgery of establishing the account is complete, you'll be able to move on the main part of the book—actually playing poker!

Basic System Requirements

Poker sites operate under the same constraints as other software applications developers in that they are motivated to provide the best, most functional, and most aesthetically pleasing sites for their players within the bounds of what their typical customer will have under their computer's hood. Because of this, the newest computers will have horsepower to spare, while the older ones will have the hamster or squirrel in the computer's guts, running flat out to handle the software client's demands. As of this book's writing, here is what UltimateBet.com recommended as its minimum hardware configuration:

✦ **Operating System**: Windows 95 or newer or Macintosh OS 9 with the Microsoft Virtual PC Windows emulator

✦ **Processor Speed**: Windows: Pentium 200MMX, Macintosh: 500MHz G3 or G4

✦ **Memory**: Windows: 32MB, Macintosh: 192MB

✦ **Free Hard Drive Space**: Windows: 20MB, Macintosh: 2GB (to accommodate the Microsoft Virtual PC)

✦ **Modem**: 28.8Kbps

As you can see, most computers are readily able to handle the software's required workload. If you don't have a computer that meets these specifications, it may be best to buy one first. It used to be that $1,500 or so was the minimum price for a decent computer. As of October 2004, computers for $500 and less are commonplace in the U.S.

Selecting a Site and Installing the Software

Armed with a sufficiently burly computer, you are now ready to head out on the Internet and find one or several poker rooms in which to play. The question now becomes, Where should I play? One way to decide is to follow the crowd and get on the most popular site.

May We Suggest. . .

Learn how to navigate the sites and play the games using "play money," as it won't cost you any actual money if you mistakenly fold when you have the best possible hand. Imagine, you're just about to win a big pot in a tournament that will guarantee you'll be "in the money," but through some silly mistake you hit the wrong button and fold! Another common rookie mistake comes in not knowing how to use the "slide bar" in games in which a bet may vary in amount. If what you just read looks like English, but you have no idea what the heck it's saying, you should *definitely* begin on the play money tables. We would never presume to tell you how to go about your business, but do realize that once you become comfortable with the mechanics of play over a short period of time, you'll have the rest of your life to play! Don't feel rushed; there's always a game. Don't think so? Log on at any time of day and see if a game in which you might want to play has a seat available in less than 20 minutes. We can't guarantee there will always be one, but gaps will be few and far between. We'll talk about the mechanics of play in Chapter 3.

A quick visit to www.pokerpulse.com established that the most popular online room at the moment these words were written was PartyPoker. But there are other well-established rooms: PokerStars, Paradise Poker, and UltimateBet make strong showings. We aren't sponsored by any poker rooms and don't recommend one over another, but for this example let's be followers and go to www.partypoker.com to download the software. Here's a screenshot of the main page (see Figure 2.1). Can you find something to click on to get the program on your computer?

Figure 2.1 PartyPoker main page

Pretty obvious, isn't it? The entire *raison d'être* of the Web page is to get you to download the software and start playing. Once you've done that, there's no reason to go back to the page if all you do is play cards. All, or nearly all, functionality is handled by the client software on your machine.

After clicking the Download link, follow the instructions to install the software. To conserve space for more actual poker play discussion in later chapters, we'll assume you know how to install software. If you haven't done it before, you should be able to simply follow the prompts until you get to the magic Finish button. Do be aware that at some point in the process you will be required to accept a user's agreement of some sort. Read it carefully if you are concerned about what, if any, spyware and/or marketing permissions you're granting the company. If you can live with the conditions, hit Accept and move on. If not, you won't be able to install the software, but you will have preserved your privacy. Call or e-mail the company with any questions you may have, and don't install the software until you're satisfied with the answers they give you.

When you establish your account, you will be required to provide your real name and other information, including a valid e-mail address and your current mailing address. This is used to send you your winnings. You will also be asked to establish a screen name. Some try to be funny (Hugh_Jass still makes us laugh), while others try to intimidate (Cap_It). What you do is up to you.

Other Ways Online Poker Rooms Compete for Your Business

With hundreds of entrants in the online poker market, the competition for your attention and deposits must go beyond simply offering a good place to play cards. Anyone can do that! All one needs to do is get enough money together to license the software from a solution provider to get over the technical hurdle. You need more, you need...

Branding

Beers proclaim themselves "king" or "president" of beers or imply that good-looking folks will like you if you consume their product. Or they can use celebrity spokespeople. Dearly departed Rodney Dangerfield was a spokesman for Miller Lite for years and was hilarious. Poker sites are following suit and are leveraging paid or coincidental associations with famous poker players. PokerStars, for example, is the site from which the 2003 and 2004 World Series of Poker Main Event ($10,000 buy-in No-Limit Hold 'em) champions emerged. Chris Moneymaker, the 2003 champion, was strictly an online player when he invested about $40 in a satellite (qualifying) tournament and parlayed it into $2.5 million. Greg Raymer, the 2004 winner, was a veteran semi-professional player when he won his place via an online tournament at PokerStars. Elite professional players are the key celebrity spokespeople for the card rooms. UltimateBet, for example, has enlisted several players such as recent $2 million WSOP Tournament of Champions winner Annie Duke and Phil Hellmuth, Jr., 1989 WSOP Main Event champion. PartyPoker has World Poker Tour expert commentator and poker pro Mike Sexton in its corner. These folks have their own tables and will at times be available to play with the poker proletariat at an affordable limit, such as $3–$6 Hold 'em.

Player Perks

These benefits are the bread and butter of how one site differentiates itself from the others. Check the rooms' sites for specific offers, but here are some general offerings:

- ✦ **Deposit bonuses**. New customers will often receive a fixed amount or percentage of their initial deposit, and existing players will get bonuses for deposits made during promotional periods. It's free money, so take advantage of it!

- ✦ **Refer-a-friend bonuses**. Existing customers are encouraged to bring new customers into the fold by granting bonuses and/or points toward other benefits to them for each new customer they refer. The new player fills out the form, indicating the site that referred them, and both receive their bonuses!

✦ **Points toward benefits**. An online poker room makes its money from taking a small percentage of the pot each hand (this is known as the "rake"). The more hands played, the more rake comes in to the site's coffers. Because of this, active players are able to garner additional perks such as entry into promotional tournaments. Just like in Vegas, the good customers get the good bennies!

Take a look at UltimateBet's player benefits page in Figure 2.2.

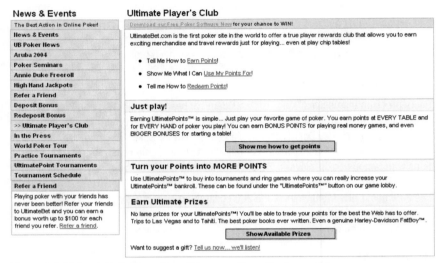

Figure 2.2 UltimateBet's Player Benefits page minus the fine print.

Depositing Money into an Account and Cashing Out

There are several options for transferring funds into an online poker account. The first is to transfer funds directly from your bank account to the site. Be aware: Transfers such as this are known to trigger security alerts in some banks. Two other good choices exist, in the form of online financial service companies. They may be found at www.firepay.com and at www.neteller.com. PayPal, a well-known financial service provider, supported transferring funds to poker sites in the past but was forced to abandon the practice through legal pressure. When you first use these sites, there may be a delay of a few days while the company makes a small deposit in your bank account and waits for you to respond with the amount from your e-mail in order to verify it was indeed you who set up the account.

To help quell problem gambling (and, perhaps, money laundering), sites may and do place limits on how much a player is allowed to deposit and withdraw within a given time period. $600 per day and $1,500 per week are representative sums.

Cashing out has several options, but read each room's policies carefully, as it will likely not be as simple as having a certified check mailed to you overnight. It could be that if you want to cash out $500, but your original deposit was $300 on a credit card, some sites have been known to pay the credit card the $300 and send the remaining $200 to you in the form of your choice. Read your room's policy statement carefully, and don't get caught short of money because you didn't know how you would be paid back!

CAUTION

Be very careful about entrusting your money to a poker room with which you are not familiar. We strongly suggest that you do "due diligence" research on each card room before you send your money to them. Go to the discussion forums we'll tell you about later and see what, if any, criticisms are out there. These companies are not subject to U.S. laws, so there is little recourse if a company decides it needs your money more than you do. Many sites also go out of business because they cannot make enough income to pay the bills, so be careful; the gambling should be on the turn of a card, not whether the room's good for what it owes you.

Summary

This chapter was what we needed to tell you so you could get set up for the next step: playing the game! Actually, this is a perfect opportunity to read the rest of the book while you're waiting for your real money account to be established. Or maybe you'd prefer to mix in some free money play to get used to how the sites work. As you wish!

The Mechanics of Online Poker

Now that your account is set up, you are able to start playing. Well, except for one small detail: the ranks of hands and the various actions a player is able to take while playing. If you know these things, then by all means skip this chapter. If not, read on! By the end of this chapter, you will know

✦ The ranking of poker hands.

✦ The purpose of antes and forced bets.

✦ The various actions available to you during the hand.

✦ The concept of "table stakes" and its application to poker.

Poker Hands' Rankings

The good news is that you'll be able to learn in the play money games until you have this and the other basics mastered to an appropriate comfort level. Please don't play for real money until you know this and, preferably, more about the relative strength of your hand at the various stages of the hand. It's not only about the strength of your starting cards; each new betting round brings a new opportunity to evaluate where you are relative to the remaining players and to decide which action is best (discussed later in this chapter). We'll get to the Kenny Rogers "know when to hold 'em, know when to fold 'em" analysis later! As for what beats what, here it is from high to low:

✦ **Straight Flush**. All cards are of the same suit and are in sequence. Another way to think of it is as a "suited straight." An Ace-high straight flush is the "Royal

Flush," and it beats all other hands. Example: T♠ J♠ Q♠ K♠ A♠. As a slightly bitter aside, Doug lost with a Queen-high straight flush at the Borgata poker room a few weeks before this chapter was written. The other guy had a Royal Flush. Ugh. Congratulations, by the way, as you may have just been subjected to your first "bad beat" story! A bad beat is when you have a winning hand but lose when someone gets very lucky or when your 400-lb. gorilla hand loses to an 800-lb. gorilla hand. The result: People get to hear about it for hours and hours and weeks and weeks and years and years. Doug's had his fair share of giving other players bad beats, though. If you're good, maybe later on we'll tell you about how he hit the longest odds possible to win a hand.

✦ **Four of a Kind**. Also known as "quads," this hand is another "monster" and will win the pot 99.9999 percent of the time. Example: A♠ A♥ A♦ A♣ K♠.

✦ **Full House**. This hand features three cards of one rank and two of another; it is also known as a "boat" or a "full boat." The proper way to describe the hand is to say the rank you have three of is "full of" the rank you have two of. Example: A♥ A♦ A♣ K♠ K♣ is read "Aces full of Kings." There will at times be two or more players with full houses. In this case, the first tiebreaker is the rank of the three-card "set." Thus, A♥ A♦ A♣ 2♥ 2♣ beats K♥ K♦ K♣ Q♦ Q♥. When both players have the same set of three cards, you look to see what the players are "full of." (OK, keep it clean!) For example, K♥ K♦ K♣ Q♦ Q♥ beats K♥ K♦ K♣ J♣ J♥. If you're noticing each player is using the same three Kings to make their hand, and you don't see how this is possible, be assured that it will be explained later. (Preview: It's possible in Hold 'em and Omaha, but not Stud).

✦ **Flush**. This is when all five cards comprising your hand are of the same suit but are not in sequence. Example: A♥ T♥ 9♥ 5♥ 3♥. A flush is properly read as a(n) "___-high flush." In this case, the example is an Ace-high flush. The person with the highest card wins. In case both have the same high flush card, one looks at the next-highest card in the players' hands until the tie is broken.

✦ **Straight**. To make a straight, the player must have five cards in sequence but not all of the same suit. Example: 5♥ 6♣ 7♦ 8♠ 9♥. A straight is properly described as being "_____-high." The example given is a Nine-high straight.

✦ **Three of a Kind**. Also known as "trips" or a "set." This is when a player has three cards of the same rank. Example: 2♦ 2♠ 2♥ K♥ 6♣ would be declared as "trip Deuces" or "a set of Deuces."

✦ **Two Pair**. For this hand, a player has two cards each of two different ranks. Example: A♥ A♦ K♥ K♣ Q♦. This hand would be read as "Aces up" or "Aces and Kings."

✦ **One Pair**. This hand is two cards of a single rank. Example: K♦ K♣ Q♦ T♥ 4♠. This hand may be read as "Kings" or "Kings with a Queen."

◆ **High Card**. This hand has no two cards of the same rank and not all are of the same suit. This is a very common hand, unfortunately. Two particularly annoying examples are A♠ K♠ Q♠ J♠ 2♦ and 5♥ 6♣ 7♦ 8♠ T♥. Get used to seeing these hands and others like them. The first hand is read "Ace high," and the second is "Ten high."

One final point to address is how ties are broken when the hands are otherwise identical. Say, for instance, that the following hand occurs:

Player 1: K♦ K♣ Q♦ T♥ 4♠

Player 2: K♠ K♥ T♠ 4♦ 3♦

In this case, Player 1 is the winner, as the next highest card she holds is higher than Player 2's next highest card (a Queen being of higher rank than a Ten). The next card after the "made hand" (the pair of Kings) is known as a "kicker" and comes into play in hands in which a "five-card hand" (a straight, a flush, a full house, or a straight flush) has not been made. Player 1's pair of Kings with a Queen kicker beats Player 2's pair of Kings with a Ten kicker. Table 3.1 provides a summary of the hand rankings.

Table 3.1 Poker Hand Rankings

Hand	Example
Straight Flush	T♠ J♠ Q♠ K♠ A♠
Four of a Kind	A♠ A♥ A♦ A♣ K♠
Full House	K♥ K♦ K♣ Q♦ Q♥
Flush	A♥ T♥ 9♥ 5♥ 3♥
Straight	5♥ 6♣ 7♦ 8♠ 9♥
Three of a Kind	2♦ 2♠ 2♥ K♥ 6♣
Two Pair	A♥ A♦ K♦ K♣ Q♦
Pair	K♦ K♣ Q♦ T♥ 4♠
High Card	A♠ K♠ Q♠ J♠ 2♦
Kicker	The hand's next-highest card

Mandatory Action

One of the ways a card room guarantees it will be able to generate revenue through the rake and ensures the game will not simply be one in which everyone folds every hand is by forcing some players to put some money in the pot each hand. For this action, there is no choice on the part of the affected player as to whether they'll put the money into the pot. There are four kinds of mandatory spending: antes, bring-ins, blinds, and time.

Antes are chips each player must put into the pot before the cards are dealt. The chips go into the center of the table and add to the amount of money that hand's winner will collect. Antes are typically found in Stud games, and most tournaments for any type of game, and typically range from 5¢ to $5 in real money games.

Bring-ins are found in Stud games. In seven-card Stud, as you'll see in Chapter 4, each player is given two cards face down and face up. The player with the lowest face up card is forced to make a bet called the *bring-in*. In a $5–$10 Stud game the bring-in is typically $2, and if the player decides to only "bring it in" each of the other players is only compelled to match the $2 to stay in the hand. The player may also choose to "complete the bet" and throw, well, click, in $5. In case two or more players have the lowest card showing, such as a 2, the lowest suit is responsible for the bring-in. The suit order, from low to high, is clubs, diamonds, hearts, and spades. As such, if one player has the 2♠ showing and another has the 2♦, the 2♦ is responsible for the bring-in. Play then continues clockwise around the table.

Blinds are forced bets for players in "board games" such as Hold 'em and Omaha. Because all betting is done with each player's cards unseen by the other players, there is no way to have a bring-in. The solution to this problem is to force two players in each hand to put money in the pot "blind," that is, before they see their cards. A plastic disk called the Dealer button rotates one seat clockwise around the table after each hand. The player immediately to the left of the button must put up half the small bet, and the next person must put up a full small bet. As an example, if the game is $2–$4 Hold 'em, in which the first two rounds of betting are in $2 increments and the second two are in $4 increments, the "little" or "small" blind must put $1 in front of himself before the cards are dealt, while the next person, the "big" blind, must put $2 at risk. To stay in, all other players must also put in at least the $2 the big blind posted. As opposed to an ante, which is "dead money" in the center, these blinds are "live" in that the blinds count toward their total obligation to stay in. If there is no raise to the big blind's $2, the little blind must only put in $1 more to stay in (or raise to $4 by putting in $3). If there is no raise, the big blind may choose to "let them live" and not raise or raise as they wish.

Time is an alternate means for the card room to generate its income. Rather than taking a percentage of each pot, each player is required to give the dealer a specified amount of money at a prescribed time interval. Paying time generally starts at the $10–$20 level and replaces the rake. We doubt you'll see this online, but if you ever sit down in a brick-and-mortar card room, don't be surprised.

Player Actions

Now that we've talked about what happens before a hand is dealt, we can now move on to what happens once you've got the cards in your hot little virtual hands.

- ✦ **Check**. When a player checks, it means they take no action, neither putting chips into the pot nor folding. It is not possible to check during the first round of betting because of the mandatory actions described in the previous section. There will always be some bet you'll need to match to stay in the hand. In the other rounds a player may decline to bet if no player acting before them has bet.

- ✦ **Bet**. This is when you like your hand to the point that you're willing to put some money behind it. Betting amounts may be fixed or may vary, depending on the game.

- ✦ **Call**. You like your hand enough to stay in and match the current bet. If the big blind is $2 and no one has raised to $4, for example, it will cost only $2 to stay in. If one or more raises have happened, you must match the total amount it is "to go."

- ✦ **Raise**. When you feel it is in your best interest to force your opponents to put more money in the pot, you may raise. Raising says to your opponents "I have a good hand! How good is your hand?" If someone "re-raises" you, they're saying "My hand's better than your hand!" Of course, that may not always be the case. Bluffing is a very common tactic, especially at the higher-dollar and no-limit games. Future chapters talk about when to bluff and how to go about deciding if your opponent is bluffing.

- ✦ **Fold**. Living to fight another day, you give up your hand and all the chips you've put into the pot to that point. Fresh cards, please...

- ✦ **Check-raising** is allowed. In this case, a player wanting to make the pot larger will decline to bet at their first opportunity, hoping another player will bet. When it comes to the player who originally checked, they raise! Traditionally, check-raising was frowned upon in "friendly" games. For some, this is still the case. In any brick-and-mortar or virtual card room, however, it is allowed and is seen as a legitimate tactic.

Table Stakes

A final important concept for this chapter is the concept of "table stakes." In short, *table stakes* means that the number of chips you have on the (virtual) table at the beginning of the hand is what you are eligible to wager on the hand. Two critical points arise from this rule:

- ✦ First, a player may not "go into their pocket" to bring out more money during the hand. One reason, obviously, is that it is unfair to the other players for one player to be able to decide how much they like their cards before deciding how much they'll put at risk. Many decisions as to whether to bet and (where applicable) how much to bet are made based upon how much money an opponent has left to risk. Playing table stakes means there is no money-related camouflage.

◆ Second, because a player isn't allowed to bring out additional money during the hand, they do not automatically lose if they run out of money during the hand. For example, if the bet is $10 and you only have $5 left, your hand is not folded. Instead, you may put your final $5 into the pot. If there is only one other player in the hand, the betting is over. The player takes back $5, and the hand is completed with the pot going to the winner. If another player decides to match the $10, your $5 and the other players' $5 are put into a "main pot," while the extra $5 from the other players are put into a "side pot," which you are not eligible to win. The players with money remaining play the hand out and "showdown" for the side pot. After the side pot is awarded, your hand is shown and compared with the side pot winner's hand, with the main pot going to the better hand.

An easy way to understand the idea behind the second point is that you may only win as much from other players as you had when the cards were dealt. If you have $20, the most you can win from any other player is $20. If you and nine other players put in $20 and you win, you have $200! Good work if you can get it, but don't count on it.

Conclusion

In this chapter, we have introduced you to the rankings of five-card poker hands, forced bets, the actions available to a poker player during a hand, and to the governing concept of table stakes. This information should be second nature before playing for real money. At this point, we feel it is important to make the following point:

When a person is new to an activity, they are often able to understand conceptually what they read the first time, but they sometimes lose that knowledge when a situation comes up where that knowledge must be applied. OK, maybe it only happens to us, but if it happens to you as well, don't feel badly about coming back to review this, and any other chapter, to brush up on the information. We read and re-read several poker authors all the time. As our games have improved, we've been able to review more and more complex material, but every now and then it helps to look at the basics. It's really amazing what a person can forget over time, and looking back helps a lot.

Games You Can Play

In this chapter, we'll show you the basics of flop games, such as Hold 'em, Omaha, and Pineapple, seven-card Stud, and the high-low split variations of those games. There are a number of rules these games have in common:

- ◆ Your goal is to create the best possible five-card hand.

- ◆ Remember, the rank of poker hands is as follows: straight flush, four of a kind, full house, flush, straight, three of a kind, two pair, one pair, high card. Do note that these rankings are reversed when the object of the game is to get the lowest hand possible.

- ◆ When two players have a hand of the same rank, such as a pair of Aces, the next highest card in the players' hands determines the winner. For example, if two players have a pair of Nines and a pair of Kings, but one player has an Ace as their fifth card and the other player has a Queen, the player with the Ace wins the hand. This extra card (or cards, if you need to use more than one to create the best possible five-card hand) is called a *kicker*.

- ◆ The suits have no value (i.e., they can't be used to break ties).

- ◆ If the hands are exactly the same, such as if both of the players above had an Ace as their fifth card, the pot would be split evenly between the players.

Playing Flop Games

A flop game's distinguishing characteristic is the set of shared cards displayed in the middle of the table after the first round of betting. Depending on which of the three games you're playing, the dealer distributes two, three, or four cards face down to each player (your *hole cards*), after which there is a round of betting. At that point, the dealer turns three cards up in the middle of the table, as shown in Figure 4.1.

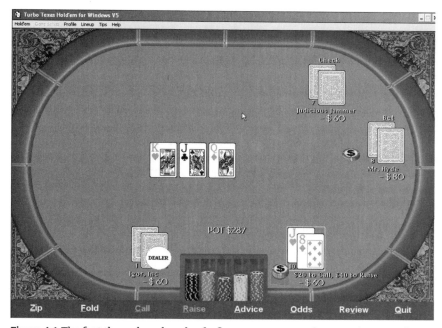

Figure 4.1 The first three shared cards of a flop game are turned over at the same time.

So what are the flop games you can play? They are, in order of descending popularity, Hold 'em, Omaha, and Pineapple.

Hold 'Em

Texas Hold 'em is currently the most popular game in online and brick-and-mortar card rooms. The game has received a lot of attention as a result of television programs, such as the World Poker Tour, the World Series of Poker, and Late Night Poker, but Hold 'em has a number of other factors going for it as well. First, Hold 'em is relatively simple to learn. Second, there's the opportunity for weaker players to go wrong from the very start of a hand and put money at risk with underdog hands. Third, there's a lot more to the game than meets the eye, which means skilled players can tear chunks out of their opponents' bankrolls through superior knowledge and tactics. Fourth, there's a fair amount of luck involved, so even if you do get trapped by a better player or a better hand, you will often have a shot to come out ahead.

In a brick-and-mortar card room, the dealer discards the card on top of the deck, deals three cards face down, and then turns the three cards face-up, spreading them out in one smooth motion. We can't decide whether the action is "flipping" or "flopping" (we each voted for one version, then changed our minds and went for the other), but pretty much everyone calls that first group of three cards *the flop*, so we'll call it that as well.

The three cards in the middle of the table, and the two cards that will appear later in the hand, are *common cards*, meaning they're in everyone's hand. If the flop contains three Aces, as is the case in Figure 4.1, then everyone still in the hand has, at a minimum, three Aces. If you have the A♥ as one of your hole cards, you have four Aces and an extremely good, though not yet unbeatable, hand.

After the flop, there is a round of betting. When the action in that round is done, the dealer adds a fourth common card to the middle of the table. This fourth card is called *the turn*, in the sense that horses come around the final turn before the home stretch in a race. There's another round of betting after the turn, and then the dealer adds a fifth common card to the middle of the table. This card is called *the river*, in the sense that horses need to cool off with a drink of water after a race. (No, we don't really know why the final card is called the river. It might be a Texas thing.)

The Hold 'Em Betting Structure

The most common way to play Hold 'em is as a fixed-limit game, which means that all bets and raises are of a fixed amount. A common limit new players play is $2–$4, where the first two betting rounds allow bets and raises of $2 (called a *small bet*), and the third and fourth betting rounds allow bets and raises of $4 (referred to as a *big bet*). Most online card rooms allow a bet and three raises per betting round, so the maximum you can risk on a single hand of $2–$4 Hold 'em is $48 ($8 + $8 + $16 + $16). When you play on a site that allows a bet and three raises, you can figure out your maximum exposure on a single hand by multiplying the big bet by 12. If you play on a site that allows a bet and four raises per round ($10 + $10 + $20 + $20), multiply the big bet by 15 to find your total exposure per hand ($60 per hand at $2–$4).

You should also be aware that there is usually no limit on raises any time a betting round starts with only two active players. If you have a Royal Flush and your opponent wants to keep raising, you can raise back until one of you runs out of money.

Playing the Game

Your goal in Hold 'em is to make the best five-card hand you can from the two cards you're dealt individually and the five common cards dealt in the middle of the table. You can use both, one, or none of your hole cards in building the hand. Hold 'em tables typically seat 10 players.

> ♠♥♣♦ **Note**
>
> We'll show you how to create the best possible hand from your hole cards and the common cards for each game mentioned in this section. Identifying the best possible hand, which poker players call *the nuts* or *a lock*, from a set of common cards is a critical skill. When you have the nuts, you can bet without fear; if you don't have the nuts, you need to be careful when throwing your money around.

A Hold 'em hand starts with one player being given the Dealer button, which is an indicator signifying the player who gets to act last in a betting round. (We explain in Chapter 8 why acting last in a Hold 'em hand is such an advantage.) If you're starting up a new game, the house deals a card to each player; the player receiving the highest card gets the Dealer button. If you're in an ongoing game, the button moves around the table clockwise, so the player one seat to the left of the button will have the button during the next hand.

Poker would be a boring game if there were no way to compel players to put money into the pot, so remember the first two players to the left of the button are forced to make a bet before they look at their cards. These bets are usually one-half of a small bet for the player to the left of the button and a full small bet for the player two seats to the left of the button. At $2–$4, the small blind is $1 and the big blind is $2. Online poker rooms don't let players enter a game for free, so you can either sit out until it's your turn to pay the big blind or post a big blind out of position and start playing immediately. If you're new to the game, or if you don't recognize most of the players at your table, we recommend watching a few hands to start to get a read on how your opponents play.

It's also common for a player who is taking up a seat in the game to sit out their blind hands so they can answer the phone, get something to eat, or take a bathroom break. To get back into the game, that player will need to make up the blinds by waiting for the big blind to come around or by posting both a small and big blinds ($3 in a $2–$4 game where the blinds are $1 and $2) on one hand. The big blind is considered a *live bet*, meaning that it is an automatic call, but the small blind is a *dead bet* and doesn't count as a raise.

When all of the blinds are posted, the house deals each player two cards. The results of the deal are shown in Figure 4.2.

The two players to the left of the button already have money in the pot, so the player to the left of the big blind has to decide whether to fold, call the big blind, or raise. Action continues around the table until it reaches the small blind, who can fold and forfeit the money already in the pot, call, or raise. The big blind can then check (if there has been no raise), call any raises, or raise. Action continues around the table until everyone has either called all bets or folded.

Figure 4.2 Everybody gets two cards to start a Texas Hold 'em hand.

When the first betting round is over, the dealer turns over the three-card flop, as shown in Figure 4.3.

As soon as the flop comes down, you know a lot about your hand. Most importantly, you now know five of the seven cards you can use to create your hand. If you have 6♠7♠ in your hand and the flop comes A♦K♦Q♥, you should fold your hand at the first opportunity. If the flop comes 6♥ 6♣ 6♦, you need to start thinking about how to extract the most money possible from your opponents.

When the dealer puts out the flop, the player to the left of the Dealer button (the player who posted the small blind at the beginning of the hand) can choose to check or bet. The action continues around the table until everyone has either called all bets and raises or folded. When that has happened, the dealer puts up the turn card. After the turn card, all bets and raises double. When you play $2–$4 Hold 'em, bets and raises are now $4. If there are two or more players left after the turn card, the dealer displays the river card, and a final round of betting occurs. At the end of that round of betting, any players remaining in the hand turn over their cards, and the program determines the winner.

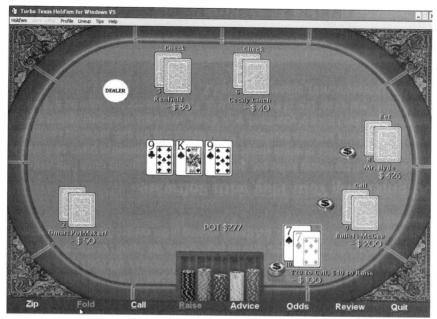

Figure 4.3 The flop is the first of many moments of truth in a Hold 'em hand.

♠♥♣♦ Note

Some sites have an Automatically Fold Losers button that lets you throw away your cards without exposing them when another player shows a hand that beats yours.

Determining the Best Hand in Hold 'Em

When you stay in a Hold 'em hand to the end, you need to show your cards to make a claim for the pot. When you display your cards, the dealing program reads your hand and makes the best five-card hand possible using both, one, or neither of your cards. For example, if the five cards on the board are the T♦ J♦ Q♦ 4♥ 5♠ and you hold the A♦ K♦, you have a Royal Flush. Similarly, if you hold the A♦ 5♠ and the board reads T♦ J♦ Q♦ 4♥ K♦, you would also have a Royal Flush because your A♦ completes the hand with the four shared diamond cards. If the five cards on board are T♦J♦Q♦K♦A♦, it doesn't matter what you hold because everyone who is still in the hand at the river has a Royal Flush. And, yes, we've seen a Royal Flush on the board, though neither of us was in the game. It happened at a high-only Omaha table at a Knights of Columbus–sponsored charity casino in Maryland in 1994. The odds against a Royal Flush appearing on a five-card board are 649,739 to 1, which is awfully darn impressive.

Hold 'Em Practice Hands

Work through the following three practice hands to form the best five-card hand from the board and the assigned hole cards. Once you've determined the best hand you can create using your hole cards, try to figure out the best possible hand you could create using any two hole cards. The first hand appears in Figure 4.4.

Until you read hands automatically, you might find it useful to determine whether you can create a straight flush or flush, then four of a kind, then a full house, and so on until you hit the highest-ranking hand possible with your hole cards. There are only two diamonds on the board, so you can't have a straight flush or, by definition, a flush. Also, because neither of your hole cards matches any of the cards on the board, you can't have four of a kind or a full house. However, you can form an

Figure 4.4 What is the best hand you can create with your hole cards? With any two hole cards?

Ace-high straight using the T♥J♦A♣. Is your Ace-high straight the best possible hand? Yes. There needs to be three cards of a suit for a straight flush (or flush) to be possible, so there can be neither a straight flush nor a flush. There are no pairs on the board, so no one can have four of a kind or a full house. You can be tied by anyone else who holds KQ, but in that case you'd split the pot. You also beat anyone with three of a kind or less, so you know you have a winner.

But don't stop thinking when you identify the best hand! We'll get into betting strategies in Chapters 8 through 11, but you should pay attention to what the second and third best hands are (and more if your opponents aren't skilled players). If one of your opponents has AA in the hole and the other has JJ, they each might be convinced that their three of a kind is best; the same could be true of a player who holds AJ, which is the highest possible two-pair hand given this board.

Figure 4.5 contains the second practice hand.

There are three cards of the same suit as your two hole cards on the board, but the board cards don't combine with your hole cards to create a straight flush; however, you do have a flush. In fact, you have a King-high flush, the second-best possible flush. There are no pairs on the board, so no one can have four of a kind or a

Figure 4.5 What is the best hand you can create with your hole cards? With any two hole cards?

full house. You've created the best possible hand from your hole cards and the board, so you can now think about what the other players might have. The suited board cards aren't close enough together to create a straight flush, so you don't have to worry about that. There are no pairs on board, so no one can have four of a kind or a full house. We know flushes are possible, but you're only beaten by one other flush: the Ace-high flush, which is the best possible hand. There are a number of possible straights out there (any Five with a Four or any Seven with a Nine), but you beat all of them. One or more players might also have three of a kind or less, but you beat them as well.

Figure 4.6 contains the third practice hand.

It's a good thing you're playing online so no one can see you jumping up and down. You flopped a Jack-high straight flush! It's not the best possible hand, though; if another player has the K♦Q♦ you had in the first two sample hands, you'll lose a big pot. Please also notice that there are all kinds of straights and flushes possible, not to mention the potential for four Tens or four Jacks. When you flop a huge hand,

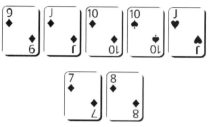

Figure 4.6 What is the best hand you can create with your hole cards? With any two hole cards?

you want to play it slow, allowing your opponents to make stabs at a pot that is rightfully yours. You run the risk of a player catching the Q♦ or K♦ to make a higher straight flush, but it's a risk you should be willing to take. Don't expect to see this type of hand very often. You'll go through plenty of paired and double-paired boards before you see a hand like the one we just described.

Omaha (High Only)

As a flop game, Omaha has a lot in common with Hold 'em. There are 10 players at a full table, and the two players to the left of the button post small and big blinds; you receive a set of hole cards (four, in this case), and there are four rounds of betting. Aside from the four hole cards, the big difference between Hold 'em and Omaha is that *in Omaha you must use exactly two of your hole cards to create your final hand*. That difference is important, and it often trips up players used to playing Hold 'em.

Playing the Game

As in Hold 'em, an Omaha hand starts with one player being given the Dealer button. If the game's just starting, the house will deal each player a card and assign the button to the player with the highest card. After each hand, the button moves around the table in a clockwise direction, so the player one seat to the left of the button will have the button during the next hand.

The two players to the left of button are forced to make a bet before they look at their cards. These bets are usually one-half of a small bet for the player to the left of the button and a full small bet for the player two seats to the left of the button. In a $2–$4 Omaha game, the small blind is $1, and the big blind is $2. Online poker rooms don't let players enter a game for free, so you'll either have to wait for the big blind to come around or, if you would prefer to start playing immediately, post a big blind out of position. If you're new to the game, or if you don't recognize most of the players at your table, we recommend watching a few hands to start to get a read on how your opponents play.

If you want to sit out a few hands without giving up your seat, you can do so (there's a button you can press in the casino software program that tells the dealer to skip over you). If you don't miss a hand where you owe the big blind, you can jump back in at any time. Once you've missed the big blind, you'll need to make up the blinds by waiting for the big blind to come around or by posting both small and big blinds in one hand ($3 in a $2–$4 game where the blinds are $1 and $2). In this case, the big blind is considered a *live bet*, meaning that it is an automatic call, but the small blind is a *dead bet* and doesn't count as a raise.

When all of the blinds are posted, the house deals each player four cards. The players who posted the small and big blinds are already in the pot, so it is up to the player to the left of the big blind to fold, call, or raise. Action continues around the table until everyone has called all bets or everyone except the big blind has folded (yes, it happens, but not that often). After that first round of action, it's time for the flop, so the dealer turns up three cards in the middle of the table, as shown in Figure 4.7.

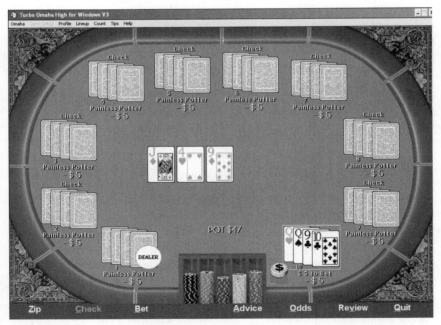

Figure 4.7 Getting four cards to start with doesn't always make the game easier to play.

At this point there is another round of betting at the lower increment ($2 in a $2–$4 game). If there are two or more players still in the hand after the flop, the dealer adds a fourth card (the turn) to the board. Now all bets and raises are at the higher increment ($4 in this example). After this round of action (or inaction if everyone checks), the dealer displays the river card, and there is a final round of betting. If there are two or more players left after this round, the players who are still in the hand show their hands to determine a winner.

Determining the Best Hand in Omaha High

It is vital to remember that you use *exactly* two of your four hole cards to build the best possible five-card hand in Omaha! For example, if you are dealt A♣A♥A♠A♦, you have a pair of Aces and precious few ways to improve your hand. Don't think a situation like this will ever come up? You're probably right, but it's not impossible. The odds of being dealt quads is only 20,824 to 1 against, after all. A friend of ours, who was very new to Omaha at the time, received 6♣6♥6♠6♦ as his hole cards, bet all the way to the end, turned over his hand, and announced that he had four Sixes. He was shocked to learn that he only had a full house (there were three Fours on the board to go with his pair of Sixes), but he was relieved when he won the pot anyway!

The odds of being dealt three of a kind in the hole is a much more reasonable 867 to 1 against, but that's the end of the good news. When you have three of a kind in the hole, your hand is almost as bad as if you had quads in the pocket.

!

CAUTION

i

The possibility of making mistakes like this one reinforces the need to play against a specialized poker program or in free online games before you risk money in a new game.

As an example, suppose you hold A♠K♦Q♠J♥ and the board reads T♠4♣J♣Q♦6♠. You hold two spades, but there are only two spades on the board, so you can't create a straight flush or flush. There are no pairs on the board, so you can't have four of a kind or a full house. The best hand you can create using exactly two of your hole cards and three of the board cards is an Ace-high straight, T♠J♣Q♦K♦A♠.

Omaha High Practice Hands

Work through the following three practice hands to form the best five-card Omaha hand from the board and the assigned hole cards. Once you've determined the best hand you can create using your hole cards, try to figure out the best possible hand you could create using any two hole cards. The first hand appears in Figure 4.8.

There are three spades on the board, but you only have one spade in the hole, so you can't make a straight flush or a flush. There is a pair of Tens on board, but you only have one Ten and can't make four of a kind. You can, however, combine your T♥9♣ with the T♦T♠9♠ to create a full house. Is your full house the best possible hand? You have the T♥, so three of the four Tens are accounted for, which means that no one can have TT in their hand to create four of a kind. There is no

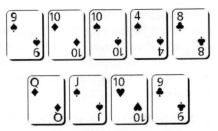

Figure 4.8 What is the best hand you can create with your hole cards? With any set of hole cards?

card higher than a Ten on the board, so no one can have a bigger full house than yours, but one other player could have the T♣ and either the 9♥ or the 9♦ and tie you. Anyone with 99, 88, or 44 can also create a full house, but you beat those hands as well as any straights made possible by the Eight, Nine, and Ten on the board.

The second practice hand appears in Figure 4.9.

If it weren't required to use exactly two of your hole cards, you would have a straight flush: A♣2♣3♣4♣5♣. You do, however, have an Ace-high flush with A♣K♣5♣4♣3♣. There is no pair on the board, so no one can have four of a kind or a full house. You have the best flush possible, so you can stop worrying about

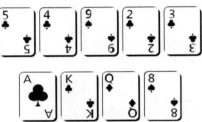

Figure 4.9 What is the best hand you can create with your hole cards? With any set of hole cards?

anyone who also has a flush, straight, or worse. What you do need to worry about is whether any of your opponents might have the 7♣6♣, which would give them a Seven-high straight flush (3♣4♣5♣6♣7♣). Given the impossibility of four of a kind or a full house, 7♣6♣ is the only hand that can beat you. You may need to show some restraint if an opponent raises or re-raises after the last card comes out, but overall you're in very good shape.

The third practice hand appears in Figure 4.10.

There aren't three cards of one suit on board, so you can't create a straight flush or flush. You don't have the pair of Eights you would need to make four of a kind, but you do have the 4♦4♥, which you can use to create a full house, 4♦4♥4♣8♥8♦. That's the best hand you can create, but is

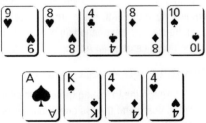

Figure 4.10 What is the best hand you can create with your hole cards? With any set of hole cards?

it the best hand overall? Nope. In fact, there are quite a few hole card combinations that beat yours. Any player with the 8♠8♣ will have four of a kind. In addition, any player with a pair of Tens, a pair of Nines, T8, 98, or 84 has a bigger full house than yours. You have to hone your judgment to perform well in hands such as this one. It's no exaggeration to say that knowing when to lay down your small full houses is a key to playing winning Omaha high.

Pineapple (High Only)

The third member of the flop game family, Pineapple (a.k.a. Crazy Pineapple), has nothing close to the following of Hold 'em and Omaha. We found only a few sites out of the top 15, as ranked by PokerPulse.com, to offer the game. That said, Pineapple is an interesting game that offers players some difficult choices. Here are the basics.

In Pineapple, you are dealt three hole cards, but you throw one of the cards away after the second betting round is completed. As in Hold 'em, the goal is to make the best five-card hand you can using any combination of your two remaining hole cards and the five cards on the board. The player to the left of the Dealer button posts a small blind equal to one-half of a small bet (e.g., $1 at a $2–$4 table), the player to the left of the small blind posts a big blind ($2 at a $2–$4 table), and each player receives three cards face down. There's a round of betting, during which all bets and raises are $2, and the dealer flops three cards in the middle of the table. At this point there is another round of betting and, when it's done, each player still in the hand discards one of their hole cards. From this point on, the hand is played exactly as if it were a Hold 'em hand. After the dealer displays a fourth card in the middle, the turn, there is a round of betting where all bets and raises are double the amount in the first two betting rounds ($4 in a $2–$4 game). The dealer then flips over the river card, there is a final round of betting, and any players left display their cards to determine the winner.

♠♥♣♦ Note

For practice creating five-card hands from any combination of your two remaining hole cards and the five board cards, see the "Hold 'Em Practice Hands" section earlier in this chapter.

Seven-Card Stud

Flop games such as Hold 'em and Omaha are the most popular games in online and brick-and-mortar poker rooms, but the old favorite seven-card Stud still has a solid following. Some players insist that seven-card Stud is a simpler game than Hold 'em, but we don't believe them. Yes, you can determine each player's possible hands from the cards they have showing, but you can do the same thing in Hold 'em. One skill you need in seven-card

Stud that you don't need in Hold 'em is remembering which cards have been thrown away and are no longer available to improve anyone's hand. When you play online, you can use a spreadsheet or other tool to keep track of these *dead cards*, so the burden isn't quite as onerous. If you plan to play seven-card Stud in a brick-and-mortar casino, where you can't use such aids, you should play online using only your memory, at least part of the time.

Playing the Game

In seven-card Stud, each player throws in an ante before the cards are dealt. If you play $2–$4 seven-card Stud, the ante is typically 25¢. Online you play seven-card Stud eight-handed, so at a full table the eight antes add up to $2, a small bet. After the antes are taken, each player receives three cards: two face-down and one face-up, as shown in Figure 4.11. We'll indicate hidden cards by putting them in parentheses, so a hand with A♠A♦ underneath and the K♦ showing would be written as (A♠A♦)K♦.

Figure 4.11 The player with the 4♥ showing must make the bring-in bet.

You will recall that the player with the lowest card showing may not fold, but must instead make a forced bet, called the *bring-in*, which is usually of an amount less than the small bet in the game. For example, the bring-in might be $1 in a $2–$4 game. And, yes, this is an occasion where card suits might matter. If two players are tied for the lowest valued card, you break the tie based on suit ranks. The suits are ranked, from lowest to highest:

clubs, diamonds, hearts, and spades. If two players have Fours showing, but one of them is the 4♥ and the other is the 4♠, the player showing the 4♥ must make the bring-in bet.

The player who makes the bring-in bet can choose to "bring it in" for a full bet ($2 in a $2–$4 game) instead of the smaller bring-in amount. If you have the aforementioned (A♠A♦)K♦, you might consider bringing it in for a full bet to try to win as much money as you can.

When a player posts the bring-in, the player to that player's left may fold, call the bring-in, or *complete the bet* to the full amount for this first round. In a $2–$4 game, calling the bring-in would only cost $1, and the first raise would be to $2. Once it is $2 to go, players may raise two more times in $2 increments. After every player has either called all bets or folded, the dealer deals another face-up card to each of the remaining players, as shown in Figure 4.12.

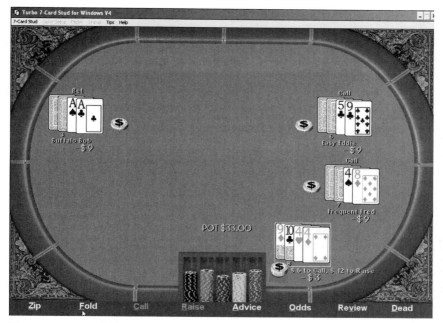

Figure 4.12 Every player receives a second face-up card, but now the player with the highest hand showing gets to act first.

This betting round is called *fourth street* because each player has four cards. On this betting round, and all subsequent rounds, the player with the best cards showing is first to act. Again, if there is a tie between the hands showing, such as if two players show an Ace and a King, the suit of the highest card determines who acts first.

On fourth street, all bets and raises are (again assuming a $2–$4 game) in $2 increments unless a player has a pair showing. If a player's two upcards are paired, that player may choose to check, make a small bet of $2, or make a big bet of $4. Whichever amount that player chooses is the increment for the round. If the player with the pair checks, all bets and raises are of the smaller amount ($2 in this case).

After the action on fourth street is completed, the dealer gives each remaining player a fifth face-up card. On this round, *fifth street*, all bets and raises are of the larger amount. The same pattern holds true for *sixth street*. The seventh card, which is usually called the river and very occasionally *seventh street*, is dealt face down so that each player has four cards face up and three cards face down. After a last betting round, the players turn over their cards and make the best five-card hand possible out of their seven cards to determine a winner. In the case of a tie, the pot is split between the players with the best hands—suits don't come into play.

High-Low Split Games

In the games described earlier in this chapter, the goal is to create the best possible five-card hand. Poker players are, by turns, both optimistic and pessimistic, so somewhere along the line some would-be clever individual thought it would be neat to play games where you went for the lowest hand possible, with straights and flushes not counting against you. After that, a would-be even cleverer person no doubt thought it would be neater to create games where players could go for the lowest *and* the highest possible hands, with the pot split evenly between the two winners. Thus high-low split poker was born.

What If We Run Out of Cards?

You might have done some quick math and determined that if all eight players stay in for the entire hand, thus requiring seven cards each, you'd need a 56-card deck. You can't add cards to the game, but there is a procedure in place in case this unlikely event occurs. If there are fewer cards in the deck than are required to give all remaining players a final face-down card, the dealer instead turns up a common card in the middle of the table. Like the board cards in flop games, such as Hold 'em, this common card is assumed to be in every player's hand.

Qualifying and Evaluating Low Hands

Unlike games played for low only, which allow any hand to be considered a low hand, high-low split games require that a low hand consist of five unpaired cards where every card is an Eight or lower. Thus 8432A qualifies as a low hand, but 9432A does not. You also need to know that low hands are counted from the highest card down, not from the lowest card up. For example, if one player has 86543 and another player has 8732A, the player with the Six as the second highest card beats the player with the Seven as the second highest card.

> ♠♥♣♦ **Note**
>
> You can play low-only games online if you like. Razz is seven-card Stud played for low, and triple-draw Lowball is five-card Draw played for low. There are two variations of Lowball: A-5 Lowball (also called *California Lowball*) and 2-7 (*Deuce to Seven* or *Kansas City Lowball*). In California Lowball, straights and flushes don't count against you and the Ace is considered a low card, so the best hand is A2345. In 2-7 Lowball, the Ace is considered a high card and straights and flushes count against you, so the best hand is 23457 of mixed suits. These games aren't that popular, and neither of us has played them, so we won't cover them in this book.

To practice creating the lowest possible hand, consider the seven-card Stud hands in Figures 4.13, 4.14, and 4.15 to determine if a low is possible, and, if so, what the best low hand is that you can make.

You can make a low hand from the cards in Figure 4.13. The lowest hand you can make is 7♥5♣4♦2♣A♣.

You cannot make a low hand from the cards in Figure 4.14. The lowest hand you can make is 9♥8♠4♦3♦A♠, which doesn't qualify.

You can make a low hand from the cards in Figure 4.15. The lowest hand you can make is 8♠5♣ 4♠3♠2♣.

Figure 4.13 Is it possible to make a low hand from these cards? If so, what is the best possible low hand you can make?

Figure 4.14 Is it possible to make a low hand from these cards? If so, what is the best possible low hand you can make?

Figure 4.15 Is it possible to make a low hand from these cards? If so, what is the best possible low hand you can make?

High-Low Split Games

There are three high-low split games you can play online: Omaha, seven-card Stud, and Crazy Pineapple. Each game's betting rounds proceed exactly as if the game were being played for high only, but at the end of the hand, each player makes the best five-card high hand and lowest five-card hand they can based on the rules of the game.

- ◆ In Crazy Pineapple, you create your high and low hands using any combination of your two remaining hole cards and the five board cards.

- ◆ In Omaha, you create your high hand using exactly two of your hole cards and any three cards from the board; then you create your low hand using exactly two of your hole cards and any three cards from the board.

- ◆ In seven-card Stud, you create your high and low hands from the seven cards dealt to you (and a community card, if applicable).

Omaha High-Low Practice Hands

Work through the following three practice hands to form the highest and (if possible) lowest five-card Omaha hand from the board and the assigned hole cards. Once you've determined the best hands you can create using your hole cards, try to figure out the best possible hands you could create using any set of hole cards. The first hand appears in Figure 4.16.

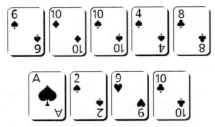

Figure 4.16 What are the best high and (if possible) low hands you can create with your hole cards? With any set of hole cards?

The best possible hand you can create using exactly two your hole cards and three board cards is an Ace-high flush, A♠2♠4♠6♠T♠. It's not the nuts, though, because the pair of Tens on the board makes full houses possible (quad Tens is not possible because you have one in your hand).

With regard to possible low hands, there are three cards ranked Eight or below on the board, and you have two hole cards (the A♠2♠) you can use to create a five-card hand where every card is unpaired and ranked Eight or below. That hand, 8♣6♠4♠2♠A♠, is the lowest possible hand given the three board cards, so you have the nuts on the low side.

The second practice hand appears in Figure 4.17.

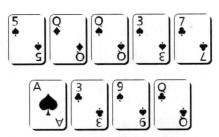

Figure 4.17 What are the best high and (if possible) low hands you can create with your hole cards? With any set of hole cards?

♠♥♣♦ **Note**

We gave you some seven-card Stud practice hands in the "Qualifying and Evaluating Low Hands" section earlier in this chapter. The answers for the best possible low hand follow Figures 4.13, 4.14, and 4.15, but go through and determine the highest possible hand you can make from the seven cards in each hand.

The best possible hand you can create using exactly two of your hole cards and three board cards is a full house, Q♣Q♦Q♠3♠7♣. There is no possible straight flush on board. Your full house has the highest possible trips, but you can lose to a player who has the Q♥ and the 7♦, the 7♠, or the Queen and another Five.

Unfortunately, you can't make a low hand using two of your hole cards and three board cards. Your 3♣ pairs the 3♠, and the 9♠ isn't an Eight or lower, so you can't make a five-card hand where every card is unpaired and ranked Eight or below.

The third practice hand appears in Figure 4.18.

You've got the absolute nuts on the high side of this hand: a Five-high straight flush in spades (A♠2♠3♠4♠5♠). No one can touch you on the low side, either, though that fact may not be obvious at first. Your A♣, 3♥, and 5♠ all pair cards on the board, but remember that the object is to make the best five-card hand using two of your hole cards and three of the board cards. Your Five-high straight flush is also the best possible low hand. Figure 4.19 shows a similar situation, where all of your hole cards pair board cards, but you can still create the nut low hand.

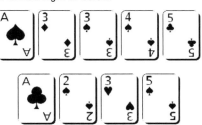

Figure 4.18 What are the best high and (if possible) low hands you can create with your hole cards? With any set of hole cards?

To create the nut low hand, take the A♣2♠ from your hole cards and combine them with the 3♠4♠5♣, or take your A♣3♥ and combine them with the 2♦4♠5♣, and so on. Of course, anyone with two unpaired hole cards ranked Five or below will also have the nut low hand, but beginning

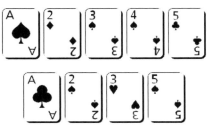

Figure 4.19 Yes, you can create a low hand even though each of your hole cards pairs a board card.

players may think that their paired cards can't be used to make a low and throw away their hands on the turn. How do we know beginners can make that mistake? Because Curt made that mistake when he started playing Omaha high-low.

Crazy Pineapple High-Low Practice Hands

Because you can use both, one, or neither of your remaining hole cards to create your high and low hands, Crazy Pineapple is a bit more of a guessing contest than are games where you don't have to discard a card after the flop.

Work through the following three practice hands to form the highest and (if possible) lowest five-card Omaha hand from the board and the assigned hole cards. Once you've determined the best hands you can create using your hole cards, try to figure out the best possible hands you could create using any set of hole cards. The first hand appears in Figure 4.20.

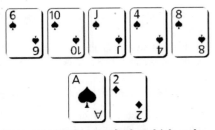

Figure 4.20 What are the best high and (if possible) low hands you can create with your hole cards? With any set of hole cards?

For this hand you have an Ace-high flush, but it's not the best possible high hand. The best possible high hand is a Queen-high straight flush, which could be made by a player holding Q♠9♠. Someone could also make a straight flush with 9♠7♠. There are no pairs on board, so there's no possibility someone could beat you with four of a kind or a full house. You also have the best possible low hand, 8♠6♠4♠2♣A♠.

The second practice hand appears in Figure 4.21.

The best possible hand you can create from the seven cards available to you is three of a kind, Q♣Q♦Q♠A♠6♣. Your hand isn't the best possible hand, however. It's not possible to create a straight flush given the board cards, and no one can have four of a kind because you hold one of the Queens, but there are plenty of other hands that can beat you. Anyone with the Q♥ and any remaining Three, Five, or Six has a full house, as

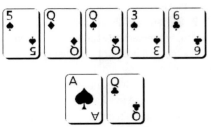

Figure 4.21 What are the best high and (if possible) low hands you can create with your hole cards? With any set of hole cards?

would anyone with a pair of Sixes, Fives, or Threes. There are also three spades on board, so any player with two spades in the hole would beat you with a flush.

It is possible to create a low hand given the three cards ranked Eight or lower on the board, but you only have one card ranked Eight or lower in the hole and can't make a low hand.

The third practice hand appears in Figure 4.22.

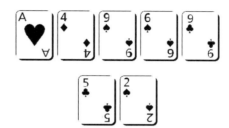

The best possible high hand you can create with your hole cards isn't all that hot: 9♠9♣A♥6♠5♣. Anyone with a card that matches any of the board cards beats you, so don't count on getting any money from the high side of this pot. You do, however, have the second-best low hand, with 6♠5♣4♦2♠A♥. Only a player with a Three and a Two in the hole beats you, so you should feel pretty good about your chances.

Figure 4.22 What are the best high and (if possible) low hands you can create with your hole cards? With any set of hole cards?

Dividing a Pot with Multiple Winners

In a high-low split game, a player could always win the entire pot, or *scoop*, by having both the highest and lowest hand, such as with a Five-high straight flush (remember, straights and flushes don't count against you when you're going for low). But what would happen if a player had the highest possible hand and two players tied for the lowest hand? Rather than split the pot into thirds, the high hand wins half of the pot, and the two players tied for the low would each win one quarter of the pot.

Cash Games versus Tournaments

Are you the sort of player who likes to sit in a game for a long time and grind out your wins, using your skills to keep your losses to a minimum while you wait for those big hands to come along? Or are you the sort of player who likes to sit down in a game and be willing to risk everything for a huge payoff, or perhaps nothing, after five hours of hard work? Perhaps a bit of both, depending on your mood? Online poker rooms cater to both tastes. For those of you who prefer to play for long periods of time at set limits, you can play cash games. If you're a fan of big action, strong bluffs, and weak winning hands, you might be game for the tournaments online card rooms offer many times a day.

Playing in Cash Games

When you log on to a poker site and take a seat in a cash game, you can keep playing until you run out of money in your account or you decide to leave. How long you stay is up to you, but there are some aspects of cash games you should keep in mind before you take up residence at a table.

Analyzing Cash Games

It always pays to know whom you're going up against. After you've been playing for a while and have notes on some of the players who play in your games, you should look for soft spots. Take the time to examine the lineups in each game at the limits you're willing to play and take a seat or get on the waiting list in games where you recognize players you think you can beat. Players leak money in all sorts of interesting ways: calling too much early in hands, chasing any flush draw, not recognizing when they're beat, and habitually calling on the end to see what you have when they have a weak hand. When you play $2–$4 or $3–$6, those extra few small and big bets may not seem like a lot of money individually, but if only one player per hand makes a $2 call they shouldn't, there will be an extra $90 or so in circulation every hour. It's your job to take advantage of their slips while minimizing your own.

When you log on to a site, you should take a look at the information provided in the lobby so you can choose a game based on something other than a cool table name. PartyPoker, for example, displays the number of players in a game and the average pot size in their game list (shown in Figure 5.1). You're looking for a game that has a fairly large average pot, but an average pot size that is significantly larger than in other games could mark the presence of a maniac or two who raise at will, making the game that much more expensive to play and increasing the swings you'll go through. If you're fine playing at a table with wild action, especially if you're usually a $5–$10 player and have the bankroll to absorb some short-term setbacks, feel free to snap up that seat. If, on the other hand, you're uncomfortable playing in pots that are raised on every hand, get on the list for another game and bide your time on the play money and lower limit tables.

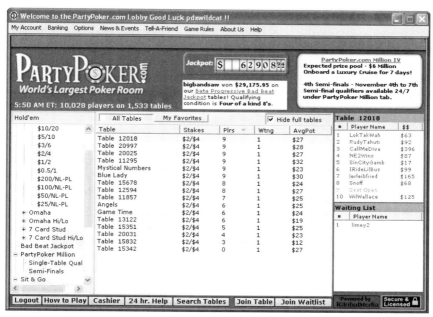

Figure 5.1 The lobby information helps you choose the best games at a site.

If you get on the waiting list for a game, make sure the game is still good before you take the seat! If the player or players you wanted to play against have moved on, you might want to wait for a better game to play in.

Finally, remember that there is more than one good poker site out there. If you can't find the game you want on one site, try another.

Going to Your Pocket

How many times have you been in a game, online or in a brick-and-mortar card room, where a player had a few dollars on the table, went all-in with an unbeatable hand, and ended up winning a tiny pot when they could have won three or four times as much money? Has it happened to you? WHY???!!! If you have money left in your account, and you're willing to risk it during the current session, for goodness sake put that money in play! We're always disgusted when we play in Las Vegas or Atlantic City and see someone pull out a one hundred dollar bill for the hand *after* they go all-in to call the first two raises. Don't get us wrong—it's a mistake of such epic proportions (it'll often save us five or six big bets, which is a lot of money at $10–$20 and higher) that we're happy our opponents make it occasionally, but do not ever allow yourself to make that mistake. Either buy in for your entire bankroll or buy in for the amount you want to risk and be done with it.

Formulating Cash Game Strategies

Aside from having enough money on the table to call all bets and raises for the next betting round, what can you do to get ahead in online cash games? Aside from the play of the hands, which we cover in Chapters 8 through 11, and creating an environment where you're comfortable, there are a number of things you can do to approach online cash games sensibly.

Playing a Number of Hours Makes Sense

Winning players, especially those winning players whose average profit is more than one big bet an hour, are coming around to the idea that they aren't playing with a particular monetary target in mind. Instead, these players put in a set number of hours every day and accept the outcome when they're done. Because they've established themselves as a favorite regardless of when or where they play, they aren't afraid to leave a good game. After all, the game they play in tomorrow, or when they get back from their round of golf this afternoon, will be almost as good.

Even if you don't quite play at that level (and very, very few players do), you should consider playing a set number of hours per day. Knowing when you will start and stop playing takes a bit of pressure off of you and helps you maintain a healthy attitude toward gambling. Playing poker online may be some players' job, but if you have to do something else to keep food on the table, then you should limit when and for how long you play.

Limiting Losses Makes Sense

Determining how much money you want to risk during any playing session is one of the fundamental decisions you must make whenever you log on to a poker account. Even if you're a player with a lot of money in the bank, you still need to figure how much of your money you're willing to risk in general and on a particular day. One handy guideline to use is that if you lose two buy-ins in a session, it's either time to pack it in for the day or to move to a lower limit table for the remainder of your play. If you're playing $5–$10, buy in for $250, and lose a total of $500, it's just not your day. If your bankroll can stand the loss and you believe you can beat the game, don't hesitate to plop another couple of hundred dollars on the table. If you're at all suspicious of the game, you're tired, or you're playing at a higher limit than you would normally, then you should strongly consider moving down in limit or calling it quits. One of the nice things about online poker is that you can find games at limits as low as $0.05–$0.10 if you want, though games in the $0.50–$1.00 range are routinely available if you're on a losing streak or you're waiting for a deposit to go through.

Limiting Wins Does Not Make Sense

Not many players subscribe to the theory that you should put a cap on the amount of money you win in a session, but we hear enough talk about limiting one's wins, or stopping play after you give back 50 percent or more of a win, to make us wonder what folks have been smoking. If the game you're in is good, why in the world would you want to leave your seat and let someone else come in and make money that is rightfully yours? If your opponents are helpless and can't defend themselves, as mad genius Mike Caro likes to say, then the only reasons you should sit out a hand during your allotted play period are to put out fires, use the bathroom, get something to eat, and refill your drink. Gotta stay hydrated, after all. If you limit your wins you are, in essence, saying, "You know, I could win $300 off of these rubes, but I'll stop at $100 today."

The second half of the theory, that you should stop playing after you've given back half of a win, isn't quite as ludicrous. Your attitude probably won't be very positive after you've given back $100 or $200, so it's not unreasonable for you to cash out and be happy with the money you did win for the day. On the other hand, if you think you're a strong favorite in the game, you're playing well, and your opponents have been catching miracle cards for the past two hours, don't leave the game. You're still a favorite!

Don't believe us? Think of it this way. Suppose you're playing Hold 'em and your opponents have improved their two-pair hands to a full house five times in a row, overcoming 5:1

odds against each time. Given that your opponents have improved five times in a row, what are the odds that an opponent will improve their two-pair hand to a full house on the next hand? It's still 5:1 against; what's happened in the past has no bearing on the current hand.

CAUTION

Poker hands are *independent trials*, which means that the distribution of cards on a previous hand has no effect on the distribution of cards on any future hands. When you rely on reasoning like "He's gotten his miracle card five times in a row, so I'll fold and break the streak," you're committing the *gambler's fallacy*. It's like betting on red at the roulette wheel because the last seven numbers have been black. The wheel has no memory of past events, so it doesn't know that a red number is "due." Repeat after us: "Streaks only exist in the past."

Playing in Tournaments

If you are willing to wait until you find a good game and exhibit good discipline, playing in cash games is a steady way to make a few bucks online. When you limit your risk by playing in small games, such as $3–$6 and below, you can compete against players who lack either the bankroll or experience to move up to the higher levels. Sure, there are some sharks at the lower levels, such as players who are waiting for seats in bigger games, but if you know what you're about, you can gain a pretty safe edge over the lower-limit games and learn to avoid the skilled players.

What you don't find in cash games is the huge payoff for a day's work. In a cash game, three hours of solid play against lesser opponents can net you $20 an hour or so, but $60 isn't exactly life-changing money. No, to get the big money you have to play in tournaments, where anywhere from 20 to 2,000 players sit down together and see who comes out on top. Chris Moneymaker, the Tennessee accountant who turned a $39 PokerStars online tournament buy-in into the $2 million 2003 World Series of Poker (WSOP) main event first prize, is the poster boy for online poker. The 2004 World Series winner, Greg Raymer, is also a PokerStars player, though he had competed in several previous WSOP main events and plays a lot of high-limit Stud at Foxwoods casino in Connecticut.

The remainder of this chapter discusses tournament strategies you can follow to maximize your chances of finishing in the money. For further reading, be sure to pick up a copy of *Championship Tournament Poker* by Tom McEvoy (Cardoza, 2004). Tom is a WSOP veteran and an exceptional tournament player, so you should listen to what he says when it comes to tournaments.

Buying In to a Tournament

Buying an entry into a tournament seems like a straightforward affair: You put down your money and pick up your chips. That's true for smaller tournaments, but you can also try to qualify for tournaments with large entry fees, typically $200 or more, by winning a smaller tournament where the prize is an entry into the larger tournament. These qualifying tournaments, called *satellites*, often charge you either one-tenth of the larger tournament's entry fee and give away one seat, or charge you one-fifth of the larger tournament's entry fee and give away two seats. You can also put up a smaller amount of money and play in a *super satellite*, where you compete against a bigger field for the same number of seats. If the satellite you're in gives out multiple seats, you play until you get down to the number of players as there are seats on offer; there is rarely any additional money on offer for winning a satellite.

If you choose to go the satellite entry route, T.J. Cloutier advocates buying into three satellites to give yourself a shot at getting in for less than the full entry fee. There's a lot more to think about when playing in satellites than we can cover here, so we recommend you buy *Championship Satellite Strategy* by Brad Daugherty and Tom McEvoy (Cardsmith Publishing, 2003). They cover all the angles and then some.

Achieving Goal One: Surviving

Regardless of the type tournament you enter, you'll have to have at least one chip, and preferably a lot more, in front of you to keep playing. In a tournament, you must base every decision on the impact a win or loss will have on your chances to remain in the tournament. You must be especially vigilant when you play in a pot limit or no limit tournament, where you can be knocked out of action in a single hand.

Consider a sample hand in a no limit Hold 'em tournament where you're up against three other opponents, each of whom has gone all-in in front of you. It's early in the tournament, and you're still near your original chip count. You will have to go all-in to call, so if you lose the hand, you'll be out of action. You hold Q♠Q♣. What do you do?

You should fold. We know it's hard to throw away a pair of Queens before the flop, but you've got three opponents all-in in front of you, and at least one of them is bound to have either a pair of Kings or a pair of Aces. Not to mention the fact that even if you do have the best hand, there's a real chance you'll be unlucky and lose the hand anyway. Take a look at two scenarios: one where your opponents have premium hands and the other where you have the best hand of the four before the flop.

In the first case, assume that one of your opponents has a pair of Aces, another has an unsuited Ace and King, you have Queens, and your final opponent has a pair of Jacks. Table 5.1 displays the percentages for each hand to win, lose, or tie.

As you can see, the pocket Aces are a huge favorite to win the pot despite the fact that

Table 5.1 A Pair of Queens Is Not Good Enough to Take On Three All-In Opponents

Hand	Win	Lose	Tie
A♠ A♣	59.35	39.45	1.20
K♣ A♦	3.68	95.12	1.20
Q♦ Q♥	19.48	80.14	0.38
J♠ J♣	16.30	83.32	0.38

there is an Ace in another player's hand. What's worse, you will only get a share of the pot around 20 percent of the time, which means that the odds are 4:1 in favor of this hand being your last hand of the tournament. Even the pocket Aces, which are the best possible starting hand, are only 3:2 favorites over the rest of the field when you consider those three hands as a group.

In the second case, let's assume that you have Queens, another player has a suited Ace and King, another opponent has a pair of Jacks, and the fourth opponent has a suited Nine and Ten. Table 5.2 displays the percentages for each hand to win, lose, or tie.

Table 5.2 Even with the Best Hand, You May Not Choose to Confront Three All-In Opponents

Hand	Win	Lose	Tie
Q♦ Q♥	34.32	65.46	0.21
A♣ K♣	33.01	66.78	0.21
J♠ J♣	16.13	83.66	0.21
T♥ 9♥	16.32	83.47	0.21

When you don't have players competing against each other for the same cards, as was the case in the first sample hand, the race between hands is much tighter. The odds against you winning the hand are 2:1 in this scenario, so the prudent action would be to curse your luck, toss in the Queens, and let the other players fight it out.

Doyle Brunson, two-time winner of the World Series of Poker main event and author of *Super System* (Cardoza, 1979), argues that the only hand you should be willing to go broke on before the flop is a pair of Aces. The previous analyses support his view.

Achieving Goal Two: Increasing Your Chip Stack

You'll eventually need to get all of the chips into your stack if you want to win a tournament, but you can't get them all in the first 10 minutes unless it's a really small field. But, because tournaments increase the limits you play at as time goes by, you need to win money to stay ahead of the blinds and antes. How do you do that? By winning pots, of course, but you may not always have the best cards to work with. You should be patient at first, playing a solid game and waiting for opportunities to win as much money from your opponents as you can. Your tactics for extracting the most chips from other players depend on the structure of the tournament (limit, pot limit, or no limit), how you have played against that particular opponent in the past, and whether you think they have a hand that can beat you.

Achieving Goal Three: Making It into the Money

When you survive in a tournament long enough to be in a prize-paying position, you are *in the money*. The most critical time in any tournament is often when you are a few positions away from getting paid. There's nothing more nerve-wracking than seeing a player who was all-in win a hand without knocking someone else out when you're low on chips and have to pay the blinds for the next two hands. When there only need to be a few players eliminated before the remaining players win money, all remaining tournament tables will go *hand for hand*, meaning each table starts a hand at the same time and waits for the other tables to complete the hand they're on before beginning a new hand. Going hand for hand prevents a table from playing more slowly than other tables, resulting in fewer hands and less risk of a player being eliminated from that table. If the tables didn't go hand for hand, eventually no one would make any moves and the tournament would not progress.

When only a few more players need to be eliminated before all remaining players are in the money, and you have more chips than some of your opponents, you can often pick up pots from them by raising. Raising opponents with short stacks forces them to decide whether they want to risk being eliminated out of the money. Many opponents will want to guarantee that they get some money out of the tournament, especially when they're so close to getting paid, so they will often fold and let you pick up a relatively small pot. If you have a short stack and another player raises enough to put you all-in, you need to make the same decision. In most cases it's just fine to fold, based on the premise that you should secure a guaranteed prize and fight to improve your position afterward.

Achieving Goal Four: Making It to the Top Three Positions

Winning any money in a tournament is an exhilarating experience, but you find the real money in the top three positions. As an example, consider the data in Table 5.3, which shows the standard payout structure for a $40 PokerStars tournament with 500 players.

> ♠♥♣♦ **Note**
>
> You can find the full standard payout schedule for PokerStars tournaments at www.pokerstars.com/tourney_prize_pool.html.

Table 5.3   The Standard PokerStars Payout Structure for a $40 Entry Fee Tournament with 500 Players

Place	Percent	Payout for $40 Buy-In
1st	25%	$5,000.00
2nd	15.4%	$3,080.00
3rd	10.5%	$2,100.00
4th	7%	$1,400.00
5th	5.5%	$1,100.00
6th	4.5%	$900.00
7th	3.5%	$700.00
8th	2.6%	$520.00
9th	1.7%	$340.00
10th to 18th	1.1%	$220.00
19th to 27th	0.7%	$140.00
28th to 36th	0.5%	$100.00
37th to 45th	0.4%	$80.00

As the payout figures show, it doesn't matter financially if you finish in 36th or 28th place. It does, however, make quite a bit of difference if you finish third instead of fourth. The difference between fifth place and fourth place is only $300, but the difference between fourth and third place is $700, between third and second it's another $980, and between second and first it's a whopping $1,920. That's a significant difference when your tournament investment was a $40 buy-in and $4 entry fee.

What's the lesson? When you survive to the next payout level, such as making it to 36th place in the tournament described in Table 5.3, and it's a long way to the next payout increase, try to make a move to build your chips if your stack is below average. When your opponents can put pressure on you because you don't have that many bullets to fire back at 'em, you should be more willing to find a good hand and take a stand. If you're only one or two places from the next increment, however, hang on for dear life.

Playing in Rebuy Tournaments

Some tournaments, called *freezeouts*, only allow you to buy in once. The chips you get at the start of the day are all you can buy for that tournament. Many tournaments, particularly those with buy-ins of $100 or less, let you rebuy one or more times during the first hour of the tournament. As the name implies, a rebuy gets you another set of chips to play with. Most of the time you receive the same number of chips that you got at the start of the tournament, but some tournaments offer higher chip amounts for successive rebuys. For example, if the field started with $5,000 in tournament chips, a second rebuy might get you $6,000, and the third rebuy $8,000.

Players in rebuy tournaments who have set aside money for rebuys will often be much more aggressive than players who intend to buy in only once. For that reason, you'll often find players going all-in very early in the tournament with marginal hands in an attempt to double up and gain leverage against their opponents. Set aside whatever money you want to play for in the tournament, including any rebuys, and buckle your seat belt. You'll be in for a wild ride until the rebuy period ends.

Practicing Tournament Play

The best way to gain experience in playing tournaments is to jump right in and buy in to some tournaments on your online poker sites of choice. UltimateBet has no-limit Hold 'em tournaments for buy-ins as low as $5, plus a $0.50 entry fee. Two nice things about those $5 tournaments are that they run several a day, and they don't allow rebuys. The low cost means players won't be too upset about blowing off their chips early in the tournament, but at least the really reckless ones are likely to go out early. Watch out for the ones that catch cards, though!

If you'd rather practice against the computer, you can invest in Tournament Texas Hold 'em from Wilson Software. As shown in Figure 5.2, you can choose between limit, pot-limit, and no-limit betting; play against average, above average, or tough competition; choose the number of players; allow or disallow rebuys; and choose the starting chip count and blind structure.

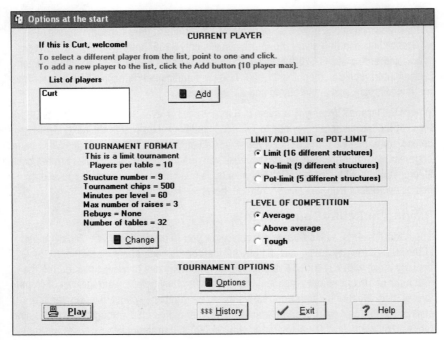

Figure 5.2 Set up the tournament you'd like to play today.

Each type of tournament offers a number of blind structures and progressions you can follow. Many tournaments in online card rooms raise the betting limits very quickly to eliminate players and get the tournament over with, while the larger tournaments raise the betting limits more slowly so that better players can choose the hands with which they want to take on the competition. Figure 5.3 shows you the screen you can use to choose the blind structure and progression for no-limit tournaments.

Recommended Reading

Some legendary tournament players have written books that share their tournament and poker experiences. You would do very well to have these books in your library:

Championship Tournament Poker, by Tom McEvoy, is the best general poker tournament book available. McEvoy covers all of the major game types (Hold 'em, Omaha high, Omaha high-low, Stud, and Razz) and offers valuable insights into the life of the tournament professional.

Championship No-Limit & Pot-Limit Hold 'Em by T.J. Cloutier and Tom McEvoy (Cardoza, 2004). This book covers a fair amount of tournament strategy in addition to the core cash game skills.

Super System by Doyle Brunson. This book is the first great book on no-limit Hold 'em, but the coverage of seven-card Stud, Lowball, Razz, and other games is also first-rate.

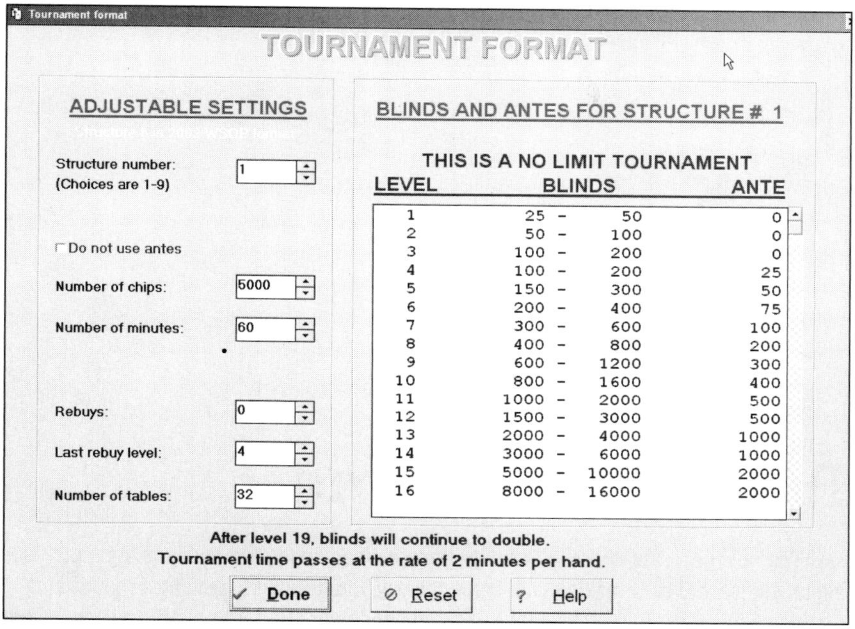

Tournament format		

TOURNAMENT FORMAT

ADJUSTABLE SETTINGS

BLINDS AND ANTES FOR STRUCTURE # 1

Structure number: `1` ⬍
(Choices are 1-9)

THIS IS A NO LIMIT TOURNAMENT

LEVEL	BLINDS		ANTE
1	25 –	50	0
2	50 –	100	0
3	100 –	200	0
4	100 –	200	25
5	150 –	300	50
6	200 –	400	75
7	300 –	600	100
8	400 –	800	200
9	600 –	1200	300
10	800 –	1600	400
11	1000 –	2000	500
12	1500 –	3000	500
13	2000 –	4000	1000
14	3000 –	6000	1000
15	5000 –	10000	2000
16	8000 –	16000	2000

☐ Do not use antes

Number of chips: `5000` ⬍

Number of minutes: `60` ⬍

Rebuys: `0` ⬍

Last rebuy level: `4` ⬍

Number of tables: `32` ⬍

After level 19, blinds will continue to double.
Tournament time passes at the rate of 2 minutes per hand.

✓ **Done**   ⊘ **Reset**   ? Help

Figure 5.3 With these controls, you can better approximate the type of tournament you'll play online.

Playing the Game

OK! You now understand exactly how the games work, and you're ready to log on to your site of choice and start making people rue the day you decided to pick up a mouse and do this online poker thing. The online poker environment requires a player to know where and when to click, so we've dedicated the first part of this chapter to showing you the screens you'll be seeing and to describing briefly the functions the various tabs, buttons, and check boxes serve. Then we'll talk about other online-unique aspects of the game. After reading this chapter, you will know

+ What an online poker "lobby" is, what it contains, and what information it gives you.

+ What to do to select a table and "buy in."

+ What options will appear on your screen as you play and what they mean.

+ What happens if you don't act in time.

+ What playing multiple tables simultaneously involves.

+ What is and is not allowed when "chatting" with other players.

The Lobby

To log on to your card room, double-click its icon on your desktop (which will have been created when you installed the host software) and let your and their computer do the connection-establishing thingy they do. Enter your user name and password in the appropriate places, and you will see something similar to Figure 6.1.

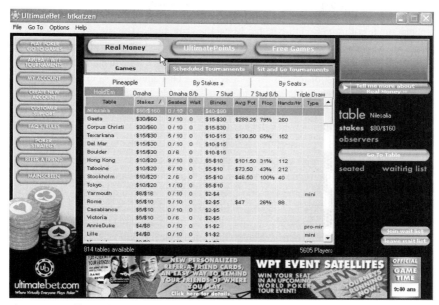

Figure 6.1 Online poker room lobby

The first thing you notice is that the screen has several different sections from which to choose. The top line, with Real Money, UltimatePoints, and Free Games, allows you to see the different games and tables available to you at that time in each of those three categories. (Note: UltimatePoints is an UltimateBet-unique promotion; other sites have their own customer rewards programs.) In this example, you are looking at UltimateBet's real money Hold 'em page. Notice that the table listing the available games is divided by type of game (Hold 'em , then Omaha, Omaha 8/b, etc.), and then in descending order by stakes ($80–$160 to $4–$8 are pictured, but notice there is ample room to scroll down for smaller stakes and some likely no- and pot-limit games). Beside the Games tab, you see there are also tabs for Scheduled Tournaments and Sit and Go Tournaments. A scheduled tournament is exactly that: At 7 PM, for example, as long as a minimum number of players pay the entry fee, the tournament will begin, with prize money being determined by the total number of players entered. A sit and go tournament, on the other hand, begins as soon as 10 (or however many) players buy in.

Figuring Out Which Tournament or Table to Join

For best results, a poker player aspiring to make a profit over time should be strong at as many games as possible and should also be a strong ring game and tournament player. Over time, you will be able to use the lobby as a tool to put yourself in situations in which you are most likely to succeed. There's an old saying we're sure you've heard before: "It's no good being the tenth-best poker player in the world if you always play against the first-through-ninth-best players at the same time." This simply means that there will be games in which you are the weakest player or at least an underdog. Because it's easy to tell a poker player "OK, so just don't play" when conditions are unfavorable but almost impossible for them to resist playing, the best alternative is to be a strong player in several games and to be able to identify the table with the weakest field against which you would be competing. We'll tell you in this chapter and elsewhere about what you can do to scout out the best games.

The first thing you want to decide is which games you do or don't want to play during the session. A friend of mine who plays higher-limit games is cognizant of when he's not as alert as he should be. He doesn't play Stud at those times because he's not able to "follow the cards" as well as he should (in Stud, it is very important to remember which cards your opponents have had face-up in their hands but have folded, so you have a lot of information as to how many cards will help your and your opponents' hands). When he's tired, he sticks to Hold 'em , which still requires a player to be alert but doesn't tax the memory as badly as Stud. After deciding on games from which to choose, you should then decide how "high" you want to play. As you will see when perusing the lobby, there are Hold 'em games for relatively high limits ($15–$30 and $20–$40 are commonly available) all the way down to what are known as "micro-limits" (25¢–50¢, for example).

After you decide on the range of limits you want to play, check out the information on each table from the lobby. In Figure 6.1, there are several bits of information available to you. First, you will see a listing of the players currently playing and at least some of the players waiting for a seat. Additionally, you will see that the average pot size, the percentage of hands in which there is a flop (i.e., there are at least two players who remain after the first round of betting), and the number of hands per hour. This data will tell you how desirable this table is for you; because you will see if there are a lot of flops and big pots with players who you know are not as good as you are, this is a prime opportunity for you to increase your bankroll! You will be able to join either the table or the waiting list. When you sit down, you will be asked how much you would like to "buy in" for, meaning how much money you would like to put at risk. There is a minimum buy in, typically five times the big bet, and for certain games there is a maximum buy in. Maximums are for the pot- and no-limit games, and they protect a table from a person deciding to sit down with $2,000 and push everyone out of the pot.

The Cards Are Out! Now What Do I Do?

When the cards come out (what you do with them we'll discuss in Chapter 7), you will be presented with some check boxes to automate your actions. In a typical card room there will be two types of check boxes. The first type allows you to automate actions for all hands; the second type is what you want to do for your next action.

To set your preferences for actions that occur routinely, you will have the opportunity to select some or all of the following:

✦ **Autopost blinds**. You'll remember from our earlier discussion that there are forced bets in flop games known as *blinds*. Because you'll need to post these bets before the hand can proceed (the game will actually stop until you have done so), the best thing to do is to go ahead and post your blinds automatically. It is very annoying when a player does not do this because it slows down the game, but it is entirely up to you. A reason against doing this is, when you're playing at more than one table simultaneously, you might not be able to keep up with which ones and how many players are at the table, and you might not be interested in continuing to play.

✦ **Show winners**. At the end of a winning hand, if you have checked this box, your cards will be shown to the other players. If you don't, you will get the option to "show cards" or "muck without showing." We suggest against showing all your winning hands. Why give the other players information they didn't pay for? If you are interested in advertising to the table the hand you won with, such as a bluff, two ridiculous cards, or the absolute best hand ("the nuts"), you will have the option to click a button that says something like "show cards" as opposed to "win, don't show."

✦ **Automatically muck losing hands**. This is when you've gone all the way to the "showdown" but have come in second or worse. The general rule we suggest is to simply allow the cards to be taken without showing them. If, however, you want to show how you were very unlucky to lose (such as your opponent hitting one of two or the only card that beat you), then go ahead and click "show cards." We advise strongly against showing your cards any time you either don't have to or you feel there is an advantage to be gained in doing so. Don't let a fit of pique make you tell your opponents how you play your cards.

The following are what you'll see during a hand in which you are waiting your turn to act.

✦ **Fold**. Since this is what you should be doing a good percentage of the time, we'll go ahead and get it out of the way first. You don't want to play any more, so check the box and see how the hand plays out, and/or shift your attention to another table. Fresh cards are often less than a minute away.

✦ **Check.** After the first round, and when no one has bet, you will have the opportunity to also not bet. If no one else bets, it's free poker for that round!

✦ **Check/Fold.** After the first round, you will have this option. Once a bet has been made "in front of" you, the box will change to show Fold only.

✦ **Call.** As explained earlier, to call is to simply match the amount already bet. Other players behind you may raise, which would mean that to stay in the hand you would need to match any additional amount. If another player before you raises before it's your turn, this box will be de-selected automatically. There may also be a box allowing you to Call Any bets, which means you will match whatever it is "to go" (one bet, two bets, etc.). This box will stay checked unless you uncheck it yourself.

◆ **Raise.** You like your hand so much, you know before any betting occurs that you'll be wanting to "pump it up," and this box will allow you to raise if no one else raises after you check it. Should someone raise before it's your turn, you'll need to re-select it. There will also often be a Raise Any box, which means you'll be raising as long as you have enough money and the maximum number of raises (three, in most cases) has not been reached. When playing in a pot- or no-limit game, you will have the opportunity to raise an amount of your choice. Rather than have you type in the amount, which is what Wilson Software's Tournament Hold 'em application has you do, online programs give you a "slide bar" to move. The farther you move it to the right, the more you're betting. A box above the bar will let you know the amount as you move the bar. Some people move the slide bar all the way to the right so often they might wear a groove in their mouse pads!

There are some other check boxes you should know about.

◆ **Sit Out.** Checking this box will allow you to miss hands until you are ready to resume playing. You will not be responsible for posting blinds or bring-ins during this time. There is a limit to how long you are allowed to sit out before you will be removed from the table (known as being "picked up"). Once a player has missed three big blinds, he will typically be removed, and the first player from the waiting list will be given the opportunity to join the table.

◆ **I'm Back!** Checking this box or clicking on the button tells the card room's computer you're ready to resume playing. In Hold 'em , if you come in when it is your big blind, you may post it only. If you come in from any other position (you aren't allowed to come in as the small blind, typically), you will be obligated to post both the big blind and the small blind. The big blind is "live" in that when the betting comes to you, you will be allowed to raise if you wish. The little blind will be "dead" money in the pot, not counting toward what you owe to stay in.

◆ **Leave Table**. You've completed your conquest, have collected as many riches as you care to for the session, and you decide to get some sleep or to do something else productive, such as eating or showering. You'll get a response requesting that you confirm you departure, something to the tune of "Are you sure you want to leave your seat?" Click Yes, and you're gone. One technique that protects your bankroll is to leave a table when you're up a significant amount (especially in pot- and no-limit games). Get back in line, go to another table or site, or even give yourself the rest of the day off! These are the good times. If you go to another table or site, you will only be risking the maximum buy-in for pot- and no-limit games, while going to a limit game will also limit short-term losses because you won't be able to blow your entire stack on one hand.

Other Stuff You Need to Know About Game Play

There are a few other topics we'll need to cover to get you fully up to speed for the online poker environment, and here they are!

The Rake

As we've mentioned previously, a card room makes its money by taking a percentage of each pot for itself. Remember, unlike traditional casino games such as slot machines and blackjack, a player is not competing against the house for the money. In poker, we're playing against the other folks at our table. The house has no interest whatsoever in who wins and loses, so it uses the rake as its source of income. Rake schedules vary, so search around your favorite card room's lobby to find how much they take and at what intervals. As a general rule, online rakes are less than those in brick-and-mortar rooms.

The Dealer's Rack

We've addressed requesting hand histories elsewhere, so simply use this as reinforce-ment. Get those hand histories! You can usually do it by clicking on the rack of chips where the "dealer" sits. You can also select the Rebuy option on the rare occasion when you have lost to the point where you need to reload. You will be required to put yourself back up to at least the table minimum and, for pot- and no-limit games, not more than the maximum buy-in.

Note Boxes

This is another powerful tool we'll talk about in our discussions on the "data" part of online poker in Chapters 12 through 14. If you do a certain "click trick" (right-clicking or perhaps double-clicking) on the player's icon/circle/oval, you'll be able to enter comments such as "plays any two suited cards" or "tight, aggressive player." You'll be able to com-bine these notes with the hand histories to develop a profile of your adversaries, and then be able to seek out the weaklings as you prowl for the best hunting!

Playing Multiple Games

In a brick-and-mortar poker room, a player is not allowed to be in more than one game at a time. The beauty of the online poker world is that playing multiple games at once is permitted! When playing Hold 'em, a player will usually see at least 100 hands per hour per table. Two hundred, 300, 400, or more hands per hour are possible with the multiple table option. But how do you make this work? The normal way to do it is for the player to toggle back and forth between tables, because at the monitor's default resolution a table takes up the entire screen. The problem is that it is very easy to lose track as to which table is in the active window! More than once we've acted on the wrong game, folding strong hands or calling with junk. It's a truly disgusting feeling, believe us.

A good way to avoid this is to increase the resolution of your screen to the maximum, which you can do by clicking on Start, Control Panel, Display, and finally clicking the appropriate tab for the resolution. Move the slide bar all the way to the right for maximum resolution. The effect will be to make the image smaller, allowing you to fit two or more games on the screen without them overlapping. Another trick is to set up your system so you can use two monitors from the same computer. The games will be full screen, and you'll be able to play them using a single mouse. Be aware that there are limits on how many games you may play at any one site at the same time. The way around this is to log on to a second card room and play there as well.

When playing multiple games, be certain you're acting on the correct game! Don't accidentally fold your winners and call or raise with your losers because you lost track of which game was "active." Be aware: When it is your turn to act on a game, that window will automatically become your active window. You could be just about to click your action on one game, only to have the screen switch on you in mid-click! We recommend strongly that you increase your screen resolution in order to keep your games obviously distinct.

All-Ins and Disconnections

Sometimes we all come to a point where we run out of money partway through a hand, where we get disconnected because the leprechaun in the computer temporarily runs out of magic Internet dust, or maybe the power goes out. In this case, an "all-in" situation arises. If you have been able to meet any of the action in the hand, you are eligible to win that much from each of your opponents, as we mentioned in our earlier discussion of "table stakes."

For example, you are playing $2–$4 Hold 'em and have $10 at the start of the hand. You have A♠A♥ and raise the bet to $4 before the flop. Three other players call. The flop is A♣A♦7♠. Bingo! You're a winner, unless something truly traumatic happens (FYI: the only way you could lose this hand is if someone hits "perfect perfect" to make a Royal Flush of clubs or diamonds or a straight flush using the 7♠). Let's say that for some reason two other players are feeling extraordinarily lucky. One bets $2, one player folds, and the other calls. You call as well. On the turn, the 7♦ shows up! The first player bets $4, and the second player raises (meaning both likely have a 7, which is a moronic play because all you need is a single Ace to have a better full house, but just play along for a minute). You want to raise but, guess what, you can't. Of your $10, you committed $4 of it before the flop and $2 on the flop, which means that on the turn you have only $4 left. All you can do is click the Call–All In button that will appear. You will then need to wait for the other two players to fight it out for the remainder of the hand. You are not eligible to win any additional bets, and that money is used to make a "side pot." When the showdown occurs, the two players in the side pot will see who wins that money, and then the winning hand (or hands, in the case of a tie) will be compared to yours. You have four Aces, so you'll get the "main pot." Not bad, but with the way the betting was going it could have been more. Lesson: Keep enough on the table to maximize winning hands! Minimize losing hands through knowing when to fold, etc. Another way to become all-in is through your connection to the site server going down. The site server will notice you've become disconnected and will wait until you have run out of time to act. At that point, you will be treated as all-in and will only be eligible to win as much as you've already put in the pot from each of the other players, as in the previous example. Be forewarned: There is a limit per day (usually two) of how many times you may become all-in as a result of becoming disconnected. After that, your hand is FOLDED. This is to ensure an enjoyable playing environment for the other players by removing the frustration of having a player with a bad connection constantly being all-in. In the past, players would simply let their time to act expire and the site would put them all-in. What would happen is, players would use the rule to their advantage by staying in the hand without needing to risk additional money. To correct this loophole, the sites have instituted a rule that if your computer is connected to the site when you time out, your hand will be folded. We believe they can also tell when you intentionally disconnect your machine, so be aware of that as well.

Assuming you have used all of your allotted all-ins, you will need to click on the dealer's chip tray and request an all-in reset, which is usually granted. Should you miss three big blinds while you are disconnected, you will be "picked up" from the table. Your chips will be placed back into your account for your use the next time you enter the site.

Chat

Many people enjoy poker as a social event, and online poker gives you the chance to communicate with other players through a chat function. The chat bar is found near the bottom of the screen and may be turned off if you wish. Chatting at an online table has many of the same characteristics as at a physical table: Most players carry on small talk, or talk about the hand (nh= nice hand, ty= thank you, gl= good luck, for example). Others like to try to put other players *on tilt* by making fun of the rest of the table when they win a hand. Some solid players can't stand it when someone makes a low-percentage play and gets lucky, winning the pot. Instead of just letting the player happily contemplate their win, they feel compelled to *tap the glass* and tell them what a bad player they are. This is a terrible idea because many bad players are playing for fun, and if they are berated, they'll take their "dead money" to another table. You WANT these players at your table; you NEED these players at your table. Just grit your teeth and give 'em an insincere "nice hand."

There are two big No-Nos regarding the chat bar. First, all chat must be in English. This is somewhat unfair to folks from non–English-speaking countries, but it is a rule. So those of us for whom English is our first language benefit greatly. Of course, it also becomes obvious that a lot of folks speak (type) some pretty darn good English. Good thing we don't have to chat in German or French! Second, while some witty banter is allowed on the chat bar, you can get in trouble for being outright abusive. Calling someone a moron or cursing may be grounds for a complaint and for revocation of chatting privileges. Remember, everything that happens on the site is recorded, so it's not like being in a physical card room where you may be able to say something without anyone hearing you. If you type it, it can be retrieved from the server. So if you're an a**hole, be assured you'll get nailed eventually.

Summary

This chapter has gone over the mechanics of play as far as the different options with which you will be presented as you get in the game. After a couple of sessions, they will be familiar; after a couple of weeks, they will be second nature. Playing multiple tables is a great way to leverage an advantage, but be sure you're on the correct table when you act. Pay attention to how many all-ins you have left if your connection has been spotty or if the power keeps blinking. When chatting, please use common courtesy!

Cheating

When the World Wide Web was first becoming commercialized in the mid-to-late 1990s, many surfers were wary of shopping online and entrusting their credit card numbers to someone they didn't know in a location that was hundreds, if not thousands, of miles away. Many surfers were even less willing to provide checking account or credit card information to a gambling site hosted outside the United States, particularly because there was no way for the players to verify that sites ran honest games or that they weren't a scam. Many online poker rooms are licensed by the Mohawk Council of Kahnawake, a Native Canadian territory, so there is the potential for a licensee to lose its permit for cause.

Assuming the games are on the square, which seems a pretty safe assumption in light of the money an online poker room can make legitimately, there is still the potential for systemic problems, such as predictable card orders or players teaming up against you, that give other players an unfair advantage. In this chapter, we'll show you how players have attempted to hack the system and what you can do to protect yourself.

Predicting the Order of a Shuffled Deck

Wouldn't it be cool if you knew the exact order of the deck after the dealer shuffled it? You could use that information to construct each player's hand, the board cards to come in a flop game, and (most importantly) determine whether you would be the eventual winner. You might have heard that it's possible to predict the cards that will come out of the deck in an online poker game. In 1999, a team of researchers from Reliable Software Technologies (www.citigal.com/) created a software tool that let them determine the exact order of the deck in play for a particular Hold 'em hand. Here's the story of how they did it and how the online casinos fixed the problem.

One of the fundamental principles of data security is that you should be able to publish the set of steps (or *algorithm*) you follow to deal cards, pick lottery numbers, encrypt data, or whatever, without compromising the process' integrity. In the physical world, anyone can find out that lottery drawings use a clear, circular tumbler partially filled with marked Ping-Pong balls and blown air to pick the winning numbers. The on-site security, equipment verification regime, and physical randomness of the tumbler mean that even if there is some way to hack the system, such as by modifying a few balls to increase the chance of particular winning combinations, the security system makes it very difficult to implement the attack effectively.

The same philosophy applies in the digital world. In January 1997, the United States federal government began a competition to select a data encryption algorithm to be used for the Advanced Encryption Standard (AES). One of the competition requirements was that each algorithm submitted would be published in full so anyone could analyze it. After three-and-a-half years of public and private analysis, the U.S. government selected the winner: Rijndael, an algorithm submitted by two Belgian cryptographers.

Why did the government take so long to pick the winner? Because digital security processes are extremely hard to implement flawlessly. Subtle mistakes a dozen tenured professors miss could seem obvious to a first-year graduate student, and even one such mistake might be enough to render an otherwise secure algorithm, or a specific implementation of that algorithm, worthless. When you're dealing with a security specification as important as the AES, it's only prudent to review the candidate algorithms thoroughly.

It was in that spirit of openness that ASF Software published the details of its shuffling algorithm, used at the time by sites such as PlanetPoker, PurePoker, and DeltaCasino, for public scrutiny. The result of that analysis was shocking: Because the Hold 'em games' shuffling algorithm used an easily guessed random number to begin selecting the cards to be dealt, it was possible to predict the entire deck's order after seeing only five cards. Yep, if you stayed through the first round of betting, you could determine whether you would be the eventual winner without putting another dollar into the pot unless you wanted to. Figure 7.1 shows the graphical user interface the security researchers put on their prediction program. The numbers just above the hole cards show each player's rank at the end of the hand.

> ### ♠♥♣♦ Note
>
> You can find the full story of the Reliable Software Technologies team's exploit on the Web at www.cigital.com/news/index.php?pg=art&artid=20.

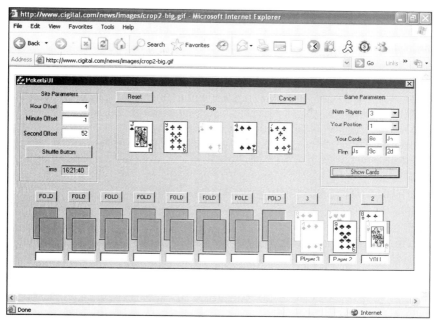

Figure 7.1 You didn't need this program to know that another player would beat you with a miracle draw on the river.

PlanetPoker, the most popular site using the ASF Software shuffling algorithm, changed its procedures in very short order. Now when you go to online poker sites and sift through their frequently asked questions (FAQs), you see some geekily entertaining detail on how they randomly determine which card appears next. Here's a part of the UltimateBet explanation, which you can find on the Web in its entirety at www.ultimatebet.com/about-ub/rng.html.

> Our approach is to forgo pseudo-random number generation wherever
> possible and instead use true random number generation from proven random
> physical devices. Our system utilizes thermal noise on a zener diode—shielded
> to prevent any environmental interference. The characteristics of this device are
> governed by the laws of quantum physics and are provably non-deterministic.
> Through the use of true random numbers and our shuffling algorithm
> (see below), we ensure first that it is impossible to predict the next card
> coming off the deck, and second that every possible shuffle combination
> is equally likely, all $8.06581751709439 \times 10^{67}$ of them or
> 80,658,175,170,943,900,000,000,000,000,000,000,000,000,000,000,000,000,000,000,000,000,000,000.

What's nice about the explanation is that it's true. The zener diode's state is physically unpredictable when it's isolated from close-in heat sources and the like, so it generates a string of truly random numbers. And if this complex procedure seems like overkill, just consider the good will PlanetPoker had to recapture after its debacle with the ASF Software algorithm.

The bottom line is that the major online poker rooms appear to be much better about ensuring the randomness and fairness of their dealing procedures. We don't know for sure that the sites' shuffling algorithms have no weaknesses. We haven't verified the systems ourselves (as if we'd know how), but there's nothing in the current literature indicating any weaknesses.

Augmenting Your Play with Software

Keeping track of the money in the pot, determining which remaining cards help your hand, and keeping track of which visible cards have been discarded in seven-card Stud is a lot of work. Some software developers have stepped into the gap, providing computer programs that keep track of your hand, your draws, your odds of winning against certain other hands, and so on. One of those programs, PokerInspector (available for $79 from www.pokerinspector.net/), appears in Figure 7.2.

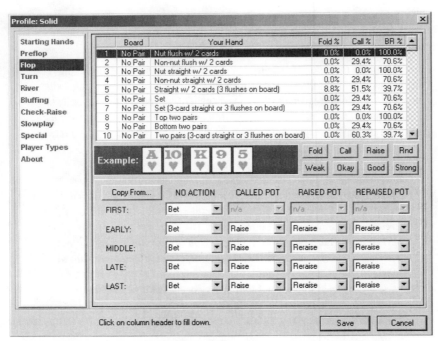

Figure 7.2 Here's some more in-flight information to help you make your Hold 'em decisions.

Programs such as PokerInspector or Texas Calculatem (available for $39.99 from www.calculatem.com/) can give players a significant advantage. We wrote Lee Jones, the Poker Room Manager at PokerStars.com and author of *Winning Low Limit Hold'Em* (Conjelco, 2nd edition, 2000), to ask about PokerStars' policy regarding such programs. Here's his response:

> *PokerStars' position on such programs is that as long as the program*
>
> 1. *Does not automate the playing of the hand in any way, and*
>
> 2. *Does not participate in any collusion or other cheating methods, and*
>
> 3. *Uses only information available to the player,*
>
> *it is acceptable. There are some "assistance" programs which follow these rules and some that do not. The ones that do not we detect and defeat.*

Lee didn't name any specific programs that did or did not fall within their guidelines, which is fine, but it appears that PokerStars would have no problem if you chose to use PokerInspector to help your game. We're interested in knowing how (and whether) they can tell the difference between a program that derives its information from upcards only and one that lets you enter your partners' cards in as well, but it wouldn't be in their best interest to tell us, and we didn't press the matter.

> ♠♥♣♦ **Note**
>
> For more information on using poker-specific software to analyze your play based on hand histories, rather than to provide advice while the hand is in progress, see Chapters 12 and 13.

Collusion Between Two or More Players

If you can't hack the machine, you have to hack the players. To do that, you need to team up so you can share information about which cards are available for draws, who has the best possible hand, and how to get the most money from the unsuspecting players. With the advent of cheap or even free long distance phone calls, cheaters can phone a friend and get a lifeline on which cards are out there and how to approach the hand. Players who want to form teams of three or more need to go through instant messaging (IM) services to avoid conference call charges, but there's always the danger that someone will type "8s 9d" in the poker software's chat box instead of the IM client software. Oops!

Surrounding the Sucker

When does a team really get a sucker in their sights? When one of the cheaters has the nuts, or close to it, and the other cheater has a hand they can claim they were either playing aggressively or bluffing with. For example, consider the following $10–$20 Hold 'em hand, shown in Figure 7.3, where the cheaters have a made flush and top pair, respectively, and the victim has top pair and the nut flush draw. There is $60 in the pot after the flop, and the dealer just put up the turn card.

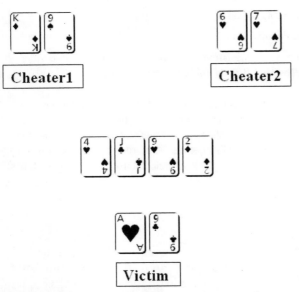

Cheater1   **Cheater2**

Victim

Figure 7.3 Teams can make suckers pay way more than they should to draw to their hand.

Normal play in this case might have Cheater1 bet, the victim call, and Cheater2 raise, after which both Cheater1 and the victim call. However, if the cheaters both raise, the victim must now call an additional $20 ($40 total) to draw to the nut flush. Here's how the action breaks down.

Without collusion:

> Status: $60 in the pot after the flop
>
> NonCheater1: $20 bet
>
> NonVictim: $20 call
>
> NonCheater2: $40 raise
>
> NonCheater1: $20 call = $160 ($20 for the victim to call)

With collusion:

> Status: $60 in the pot after the flop
>
> Cheater1: $20 bet
>
> Victim: $20 call
>
> Cheater2: $40 raise
>
> Cheater1: $40 raise = $180 ($40 for the victim to call)

The victim will probably realize in both cases that the player who raised on the turn already has a flush, which means there are at least two additional cards of the flush suit gone from the deck. With that knowledge, the victim can determine that there are only seven outs in the deck, instead of the regular nine (knowing the suit of two unseen cards is sufficient to discount them in this case). By that reasoning, there are 44 unknown cards, seven of which make the victim's nut flush. The odds of drawing one of those cards is 37 to 7, or about 5.3 to 1 against. If the cheater without the made flush has another card of the flush suit, then the odds are 38 to 6, or 6.33 to 1 against.

Now look at the pot odds with and without collusion. Without collusion, the victim must call $20 with $160 in the pot: 8 to 1 odds. With collusion, the victim must call $40 to have a shot at the $180 in the pot: 4.5 to 1 odds. Because the odds of making the flush draw are greater than the ratio of the cost of the call to the money in the pot (5.3 versus 4.5), it is not mathematically correct for the victim to call.

To avoid attracting any more attention, Cheater2 should only call the second raise (perhaps claiming to be in fear of a higher flush), but even that added $20 only makes the odds 5 to 1, which is still short of the 5.3 to 1 odds required to make the call mathematically correct.

A far simpler scenario, of course, is where the cheaters raise and re-raise to drive the other players out and capture a small or medium-sized pot. Smart cheaters will play most of their hands straight and only put the squeeze on their victims when they have a near lock on the hand and a reasonable second-best hand with which to push the action, so be on the lookout. Of course, if you suspect you're caught in the middle of two cheaters and you have the nuts, call all bets and take your share of the pot. There's very little that's better in life than letting two miscreants buy you and your sweetie a nice dinner.

Correcting Odds on Draws

Knowing when there is enough money in the pot to make a draw worthwhile is one of the most important skills in limit poker. Of course, you have to figure the number of cards that help you and do a little quick math, but cheaters' jobs are made easier when they know that one or more of the cards they need are out of play because their partner folded them before the flop. As an example, consider the hand shown in Figure 7.4.

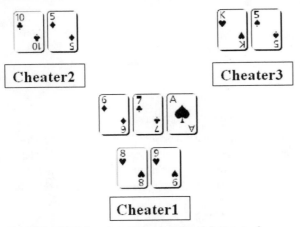

Figure 7.4 8♥9♥ is a decent enough hand, but not when two of the Tens and one of the Fives you need for a straight are out of play.

In this case, there are three colluding players at the same table, but two of them folded before the flop after the remaining cheater called with 8♥ 9♥. The flop of 6♦ 7♣ A♠ is pretty good, giving the cheater an open-ended straight draw, but when a non-teammate raises after another player bets, the cheater must figure they are either up against a set, two pair, or an Ace with a good kicker. Four players each put $20 into the pot before the flop, for a total of $80. The first player bet $10 and the second player put in $20, for a total of $110. The cheater at this point can draw to his possible straight or fold. Under normal circumstances, the player would be drawing at eight cards: all of the Fives and all of the Tens. In this case, however, one of the other colluding players folded T♣5♦ before the flop, and the other threw away K♥5♠. That means three of the cards the remaining cheater needs for his straight, which he figures he needs to win, are out of play.

If the cheater thought he was drawing to eight out of 47 unseen cards, the odds of completing his straight on the next card would be 39 to 8 against, or just under 5 to 1. He will have to call $20 to win the $140 in the pot, which is 7 to 1 odds on his money. If he misses, he gets another shot on the river. Assuming there is $200 in the pot after the turn and the board has not paired, the cheater will be getting 10 to 1 odds on what is essentially a 5 to 1 draw. Calling on the flop is correct, and calling on the turn would also be correct so long as the board didn't pair.

If the cheater knows he is only drawing to five out of 47 unseen cards, though, the math changes. It will cost him $20 to call after the flop, which means the $140 in the pot gives him 7 to 1 odds on the money. Because the odds against him completing his straight are 42 to 5, or 8.4 to 1, against, he knows he should fold.

Detecting Cheating

So how do you know when you're being cheated? It's hard to tell because players, particularly those at the lower limits, play so much more loosely than players at higher limits. You may not be able to tell whether you've been cheated in one instance, but the house can help you out.

Relying on the House to Police the Players

The big advantage that online card rooms have in relation to brick-and-mortar rooms is that the poker server records every hand on the site, which means that the site's administrators have access to everyone's hand histories, know when players were at tables with other players, and can tell whether players log on from related Internet addresses. Armed with that information, the sites can use data mining techniques to determine whether a player's actions are sufficiently out of the ordinary to suspect them of collusion.

The PokerStars policy statement on two or more players colluding is typical of the industry's stand on the issue:

> Collusion is a form of cheating in which two or more players signal their holdings or otherwise form a cheating partnership to the detriment of the other players at the same table.

> While on one hand it is easier to pass information between colluding players in online poker than it is in brick & mortar rooms, it is much more difficult to avoid eventual detection as the cards for all players can be examined after the play.

> No matter how sophisticated the collusion is, it must involve a play of a hand that would not be played that way without collusion. Our detection methods will catch unusual play patterns and warn the security personnel, who will then make a thorough manual investigation. We will also investigate all players' reports about suspected collusion.

> If any player is found to be participating in any form of collusion, his or her account may be permanently closed.

The key phrase in the second paragraph is, of course, "eventual detection." You can't tell anything from isolated incidents because a single occurrence of a phenomenon doesn't create a machine- or human-detectable pattern. If a team consists of 10 or more players who always play the same limits, only sit at tables with one other team member, and don't repeat who they sit with for a few days, the patterns are far harder to detect.

And just in case you were thinking about cheating, remember that if you get caught your account can be permanently closed. As in all the money stays with the online casino in Costa Rica. Or Antigua. Or the Dominican Republic.

Detecting Cheating on Your Own

After you've played at a site for a while, you'll probably start running into the same players, particularly if you consistently play at the same time of day. Here are a few characteristics you can watch out for:

◆ Same players always at the same table

◆ Same players always in the hand together

◆ Extremely aggressive two-way betting followed by a fold at the end

◆ Always/never chatting

◆ Chatting seems overly formulaic

If in doubt, report the hand to the site's administrators along with the names of the players you think might have been colluding. The sites take this sort of thing very seriously and will examine everyone's down cards and betting patterns to see if anything is amiss.

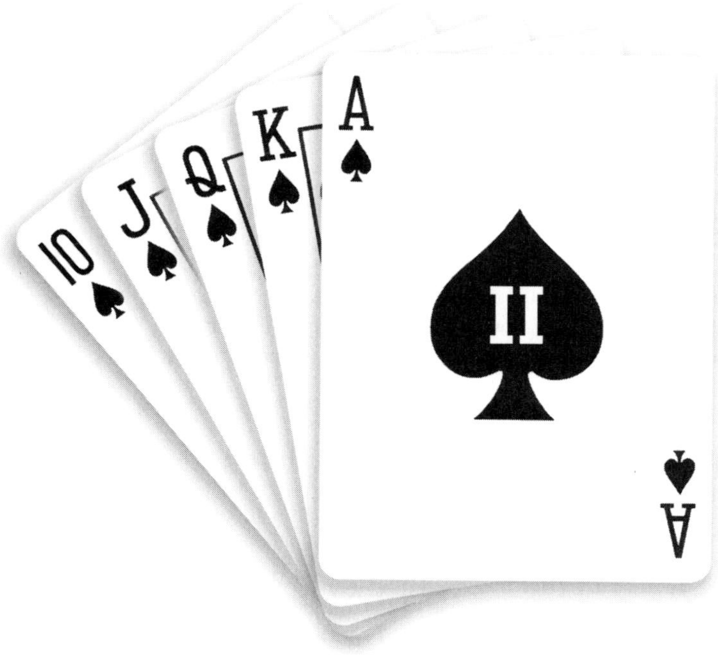
10
J
Q
K
A
II

Starting Hands

Many authors have researched the fundamental question of all poker games: Should I play this hand? In this chapter, we'll tell you how to answer that straightforward yet troubling question for Hold 'em, Omaha, Omaha high-low, Pineapple, Pineapple high-low, seven-card Stud, seven-card Stud high-low, and Razz.

Choosing Starting Hands in Flop Games

You don't have a lot of information when you start a hand in a flop game. In fact, because cards don't accidentally flip over in online card rooms, you will only know the two, three, or four cards you've been dealt. So, yes, in a way, you're feeling around in the dark, but there are ways to separate the good hands from the bad hands. But before we present our guidelines, you need to know why our advice changes, based on when you act in a hand.

Understanding Why Position Makes a Difference

Hold 'em, Omaha, and Pineapple may seem like games where any set of hole cards can win. That argument is true in that it's *possible* for any two, three, or four cards to win, but there are some hands that are much more likely to take down the pot than others. In Hold 'em, the best two-card hand you can have before the flop is a pair of Aces. You have the best possible pair going in, and the other players will have to make two pair or better to beat you. Of course, if one of your opponents does make two pair, you still have a chance to beat them with a higher two pair. The worst Hold 'em hand you can have before the flop is 72o, where you have extremely low cards, you need four cards to make a straight, you have no decent flush draw, and if you do make a pair, your opponents will almost certainly have a better kicker. Take the extreme case as an example. If two players are playing heads-up, and you give one player AA and the other 72o, the player with the Aces will win 90 percent of the hands. Yes, only 90 percent. Hey, if there were no luck, there would be no gambling.

Now that we've established that some hands are playable and some hands aren't, we need to analyze when certain hands are playable. In a flop game, the position of the Dealer button determines the order in which the players will act during the hand. Some players will probably fold during the course of the hand, which means that the player who acts first during a particular betting round might change, but the players who choose to stay in the hand will act in a known order until the next deal. Why is this consideration important? Because for every seat to the left you are of the big blind, there will be one fewer player left to act after you make your decision to play or not. And why is that important? Because when there are fewer players to act, it is less likely that someone behind you will raise and cost you more money than you wanted to put in to see the flop. After all, if you're playing $10–$20 and you wanted to play the first round for $20, you would have raised yourself.

For a practical example of why position makes a difference, imagine for a moment that you are *under the gun* (one seat to the left of the big blind) and are dealt an unsuited KT. KTo is a fair hand, but it's not a hand you want to invest a lot of money in before the flop. Yes, you've got two big cards, but there's plenty of bad news: You have to act first, you need four cards of one of your suits to make a flush (one of which will be pretty weak at Ten-high), you need both a Jack and a Queen to make a straight, and you only have a Ten kicker if you pair your King. Kind of puts a damper on the fun, eh? If you're still not convinced that playing KTo under the gun is a bad idea, take a look at the 100,000-hand Turbo Texas Hold 'em simulation results shown in Figure 8.1. In this simulation, seat 7 has the button, and Elsworth Tooey, representing you in seat 10, has K♥T♦ and always calls the first $10. We've created an average game with all sorts of players, many of whom are quite loose, but you can see the results aren't that promising.

Again, there's good news and bad news. The good news is that you won a lot of pots, but the bad news is that you're losing over $4 per hand on average. Now take a look at the results in Figure 8.2. You've still got Elsworth playing your money, but this time he has a choice of whether to call a raise or not.

In this simulation Elsworth still lost your money, but only to the tune of about $0.53 per hand. That's still a lot of money when you play 100,000 hands, but it's a lot less than the $400,000 loss he posted when playing KTo under the gun. The difference between the two positions? Elsworth won't play KTo if he has to call a raise. You probably play a lot better than Elsworth after the flop and can win more money than you lose by playing KTo on the button when no one has raised in front of you, but you're still facing an uphill battle when you play KTo with seven players yet to act. The same principle translates to all other hands in flop games: Many of the hands you can play when you're last to act are hands you should toss without a second thought when you pick them up under the gun.

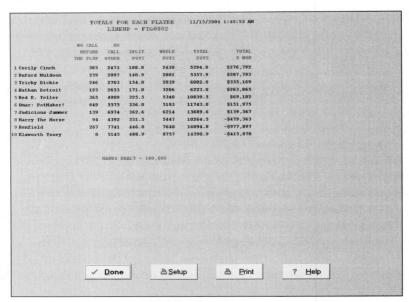

```
              TOTALS FOR EACH PLAYER     11/15/2004 1:40:53 AM
                    LINEUP = FIG0802

              NO CALL    NO
              BEFORE    CALL    SPLIT    WHOLE    TOTAL        TOTAL
              THE FLOP  OTHER   POTS     POTS     POTS         $ WON

 1 Cecily Cinch    303   2473   108.8    2430    5394.0      $276,792
 2 Buford Muldoon  239   2097   140.9    2081    5357.9      $207,793
 3 Tricky Dickie   246   2763   154.0    2839    6002.0      $335,169
 4 Nathan Detroit  193   2653   171.0    3206    6223.0      $263,065
 5 Red E. Teller   365   4809   325.5    5340    10839.5      $69,102
 6 Omar: PotMaker! 649   5575   336.0    5183    11743.0     $151,975
 7 Judicious Jammer 139  6974   362.6    6214    13689.6     $139,367
 8 Harry The Horse  94   4392   331.5    5447    10264.5    -$479,363
 9 Renfield        267   7741   446.8    7640    16094.8    -$977,897
10 Elsworth Tooey    0   5145   488.9    8757    14390.9    -$415,878


              HANDS DEALT = 100,000
```

Figure 8.1 Calling with an unsuited King and Ten when you're first to act is a surefire way to get rid of your money.

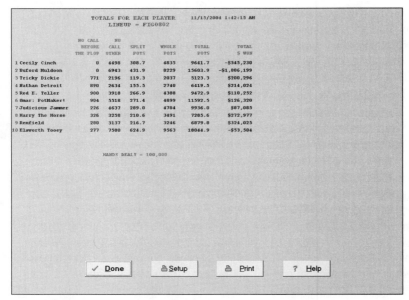

```
              TOTALS FOR EACH PLAYER     11/15/2004 1:42:15 AM
                    LINEUP = FIG0802

              NO CALL    NO
              BEFORE    CALL    SPLIT    WHOLE    TOTAL        TOTAL
              THE FLOP  OTHER   POTS     POTS     POTS         $ WON

 1 Cecily Cinch      0   4498   308.7    4835    9641.7     -$545,230
 2 Buford Muldoon    0   6943   431.9    8229    15603.9  -$1,006,199
 3 Tricky Dickie   771   2196   119.3    2037    5123.3     $200,296
 4 Nathan Detroit  890   2634   155.5    2740    6419.5     $214,024
 5 Red E. Teller   900   3918   266.9    4388    9472.9     $110,252
 6 Omar: PotMaker! 904   5518   271.4    4899    11592.5    $126,320
 7 Judicious Jammer 226  4637   209.0    4764    9936.0      $87,085
 8 Harry The Horse 326   3258   210.6    3491    7285.6     $272,977
 9 Renfield        280   3137   216.7    3246    6879.0     $324,025
10 Elsworth Tooey  277   7580   624.9    9563    18044.9    -$53,504


              HANDS DEALT = 100,000
```

Figure 8.2 When you're last to act, calling with an unsuited King and Ten isn't quite as wrong.

Choosing Starting Hands in Hold 'Em

Now that you've got a handle on how position affects the hands you can play in flop games, we can go ahead and recommend which hands you should play from what positions. We assume you're playing a fixed-limit cash game, not a tournament.

Playing Hands from Early Position

When you're one, two, or three seats to the left of the big blind, you're in *early position* and need to be very careful about the hands you decide to play. Again, you have to be cautious because there are so many players behind you who could pick up a monster and make you pay at least one more bet for the opportunity to draw to an inferior hand. Table 8.1 lists the hands we recommend playing from early position.

Table 8.1	Playable Early Position Hands If No Raise	
Pairs	**Suited Cards**	**Offsuit Cards**
AA	AK, AQ, AJ, AT	AK, AQ, AJ
KK	KQ, KJ, KT	KQ, KJ
QQ	QJ, QT	
JJ	JT	
TT		
99		

Yes, you will end up tossing a lot of hands into the muck when you're in early position, but it beats tossing a lot of money you'll never see again into the pot. If you can handle the extra stimulus and have a good read on how your opponents are playing, check your e-mail, visit a Web site, or read a book while you're waiting for the next hand. Never play a hand because you're bored!

Some other authors recommend playing pairs as far down as 77 in early position against average opposition, but we're not convinced that it's always a good idea to do so. Lou Krieger, the author of *Hold 'Em Excellence* (Conjelco, 2nd edition, 2000—a book we recommend highly), lists 77 as a playable early position hand, but he also notes that the starting hand requirements table at the back of his book is probably a bit liberal for a standard game. If you're in a loose, passive game where four or more players routinely see the flop and raises are few and far between, feel free to call in early position with pairs down to 77 and maybe, *maybe*, J9 suited and T9 suited. If you're in a wild game in which four or five players routinely call one or more raises before the flop, tighten up a bit, grit your teeth, and toss TT and 99, QTs and JTs, and KJo. Wait for the good hands to come, beat your opponents about the head and shoulders with them, and hope they don't catch a miracle card on the river.

Those are the hands you should call with, but which should you raise with? In early position, you should raise with any pair from JJ on up, but if you think you can force everyone to fold, you can raise with any pair down to 99. You should also raise with AKs, AQs, KQs, and AKo, but be careful with AKo. All you have is Ace high, after all. That's still a good hand, though, so you might consider raising only half the time. One hand to be very careful of is AQo. It looks so good sitting there in your hand, but the gap between the cards and their unsuited nature makes the hand harder to improve. The secret to playing AQo is that you want to limit the number of players in the hand so there are fewer opponents around to draw out on you. If you think you can knock some players out, go ahead and raise with AQo, but play carefully after the flop. The hand isn't as strong as it looks.

If there's a raise in front of you, re-raise with AA, KK, QQ, and (if you're up for some risk) AKs. You can call with JJ, AKo, AQs, and KQs, but don't waste your time or money on any other hands. Give your opponent credit for a hand, unless you know they're a maniac you don't mind taking on, and save your bullets for another battle. If you do want to limit the field so you can go after a player heads-up, go ahead and re-raise and take your chances. Use that last tactic with caution, though, because someone yet to act might have picked up AA or KK and will surely re-raise.

If there's a single raise behind you, we recommend calling with any of these hands. You already have some money in the pot, so it will only cost you another bet to call. If there are two or three raises behind you, you need to decide how likely it is that a player has AA, KK, or AK and give up your hand unless you are willing to take the risk that another hand *dominates* your hand. By "dominates," we mean that if you have KQ and another player has AK, you need to hit a Queen and only a Queen to improve your hand without improving your opponent's hand as well. Plus, if neither hand improves, your opponent has the better high card. The AK is only a 3 to 1 favorite over the KQ, but those aren't odds you'll want to tackle very often.

Playing Hands from Middle Position

You have to be conservative when you're close to the blinds, but when you're four, five, or six seats from the blinds, you can loosen up a bit and play more hands. Table 8.2 lists the additional hands we believe are playable in middle position if no one has raised in front of you.

In a loose game, you can play TT from early position, so it's no surprise you can play it in middle position. We cut of the playable middle-position pairs at 55, however, because a Five is the lowest card you can use to create the high end of a straight. In other words, if you have 5♥5♣ and the board is A♣2♦3♣4♥9♠, you don't have the best possible hand (a Six-high straight is the nuts) but you do have the high end of the straight.

Table 8.2 Playable Hands in Late Position

Pairs	Suited Cards	Offsuit Cards
TT	A9, A8, A7, A6	AT
99	K9	KT
88	Q9	QJ, QT
77	J9	JT
66	T9	
55		

You can play suited Aces with cards lower than a Ten in middle position because it's less likely that your opponents will raise and force you to pay an extra small bet for a hand that needs to flop a flush draw or two pair to be worth anything. The fact that you're on a draw from the start is also the reason why you don't raise: You want more players to call so there will be a lot of money in the pot in case you hit your hand. Be prepared to fold A6s a lot on the flop, though.

K9s is a hand with which you can build a good flush or a straight if you can catch the three cards (TJQ) to fill it in, but what do you do if you catch a King on the flop and another player bets into you? Your Nine is a lousy kicker, particularly against players who called the flop from early position. Whether you give up the hand when you flop top pair with a lousy kicker is one of the big decisions in poker, online and otherwise. You'll need to use your experience and observation of your opponents to make the best choice. Believe us, we'll have a lot more to say about that type of situation in Chapter 9. The other hands in this group suffer from the same defects, so be ready to make a straight or move on to the next hand.

If you're the first player in, you can raise with most of the suited or paired hands you'd play in early position, plus TT and 99. We probably wouldn't raise very often with KTs unless we thought we could get everyone to fold, but KQs is a very good raising hand when you open the betting from middle position.

Playing Hands from Late Position

As you have probably guessed, if no one has raised in front of you, you can play a lot of hands when you're last or next to last to act. You can also raise a lot with the goal of stealing the blinds, but you have to be on the watch for players who will defend their blinds aggressively. It's one thing to call $10 with 8♥7♥ when you're the first to come in, but it's another thing entirely to raise in an attempt to steal the blinds, only to have one of the blinds pop you back and make you decide if you want to put in a total of $30 on a marginal hand. When you get re-raised, you have to use your judgment to decide when to stand and fight and when to give it up without throwing any more gas on the fire.

Table 8.3 lists the hands we recommend playing from late position.

Table 8.3 Weaker Hands You Can Play in Late Position

Pairs	Suited Cards	Offsuit Cards
44	Ax	A9
33	Kx	K9
22	Q8	Q9
	J8	J9
	T8, 97, 87, 86, 76, 65, 54	T9, 98, 87

These are the speculatin' hands, folks. You want to flop a set, flush (draw), straight (draw), or two pair. If you don't flop something good, get out of the way and let the real hands take over.

If everyone passes to you, you should strongly consider raising with any pair of Eights or better, ATs or better, or KTs or better. Your raise will either push the blinds out of the pot or make them put in more money to defend. Your raise also camouflages your hand a bit. The remaining players will figure you have something, but they'll have no idea exactly what. Of course, you have no idea what they have, either, but you do have one big advantage: position. You get to act last during every betting round for this hand, so you can go after the pot aggressively.

Playing the Blinds

When you've put in money as either the small or big blind, you have a lot of leeway in deciding which hands to play. If you're the big blind and no one has raised, you get to play for free. You can raise, of course, and should with a big hand such as AA, KK, QQ, or AKs. We don't recommend raising with JJ, AKo, or AQs or lower because of the danger of overcards hitting on the flop (in the case of JJ) and because AKo and AQs and worse don't play well against a large number of opponents, unless you catch a good flop. It's not that AKo and AQs aren't good starting hands, because they are, but they're the sort of hand you want to play against two or three other players so there are fewer hands competing to draw out on you.

When you're the small blind, you have to determine whether to put in the rest of a full bet. If you're playing $15–$30 and the small blind is $10, calling that additional $5 is usually a no-brainer. Sure, you don't want to play hands such as 72o or 93o, but when you're in for most of a bet, hands such as Q7s, which you would normally never play if you had to put in a full bet, become playable. If the small blind is only $5 in a $15–$30 game, however, you're in a more difficult situation. Remember: You must act first in each subsequent betting round, so you should guard your extra two-thirds of a bet closely. We recommend calling with any hand you would normally play in late position, but to fold everything else.

If you're facing a raise in the blinds, you have to decide whether the player who raised is trying to steal the blinds with what is probably a weaker hand than someone would normally raise with or has a legitimate hand and wants a call to get more money in the pot. If you believe the raiser is bluffing and wants to steal the blinds, you can either call with any playable hand and try to catch a flop, or re-raise and try to pick up the pot right there. When you're in the big blind and the small blind has folded, we recommend re-raising with any hand you would play from early position and calling with any hand you would play from middle position. If you're in the small blind, we also recommend re-raising with TT or a higher pair, AQs or above, or KQs, but we only recommend calling if you could normally play the hand from middle position. Lower-ranked cards, suited cards with gaps between them, and small pairs need multiple opponents in the pot to make your draws lucrative enough to play, and when you're against one other player the money just isn't there to shoot at.

Ed Hutchison, someone you'll hear a lot about in the next two sections, has a system for evaluating Hold 'em starting hands that takes a lot of the memorization out of choosing which cards to play and which cards to toss. We think his system is a bit conservative, but it's a great bit of thinking and research. You can find his work online at http://erh2.homestead.com/hem.html.

Choosing Starting Hands in Omaha High

Omaha high is a devilish game. Because each player is given four hole cards, there are all sorts of ways to make trips, quads, straights, flushes, and full houses. There are so many cards in play, in fact, that every starting hand has what seems to be a decent shot at winning a given hand. As an example, consider the hands A♥A♦K♥K♦ and 2♥3♦7♣8♠. The first hand is the absolute best hand you can have in Omaha high: You have the two best possible pairs and two nut flush draws. The low-card hand is weak, lacking a pair or even a flush draw. Despite its obvious advantages, however, A♥A♦K♥K♦ only beats 2♥3♦7♣8♠ 70 percent of the time. Yes, we say "only," because the best Hold 'em hand, AA, will win 90 percent of the time against the worst hand, 72o. While having the worst hand win an additional 20 percent of the time might not seem like a big deal, it's a huge consideration when you play heads up. To state the problem in terms of odds instead of percentages, the best Hold 'em hand is just about a 9 to 1 favorite over the worst hand, but the best Omaha high hand is only a 2.3 to 1 favorite over the worst hand. When you play against more than one opponent, the edge a premium hand has over the field becomes quite small.

So why should you even consider playing a game where you can't get a big edge before the flop? Because good players can take advantage of their less-skilled opponents after the flop. Calling with marginal hands gives players opportunities to come up second best, and that's where good players make their money.

There are 270,725 possible Omaha starting hands, and even though many of them are equivalent to each other (A♣K♥Q♣J♦ is the same as A♠K♦Q♣J♥ before the flop), it's useless to try to enumerate which hands are playable and which hands aren't. Two authors, Mike Cappelletti and Ed Hutchison, have devised point count systems you can use to evaluate Omaha starting hands. You can find the Hutchison system online at http://erh.homestead.com/omaha.html. Ed was kind enough to give us permission to detail his system in our book, so we'll use it for our analysis.

Hutchison Point Count System

Hutchison used Mike Caro's Poker Probe software to find the winning percentage of selected four-card hands against nine opponents. After he finished running the simulations, he correlated the hand's winning percentage with characteristics of that hand, such as card rank, suitedness, pairs, and the distance between cards that could be used to make straights. His goal was to create a point count system that approximated the winning percentage for a given hand. He succeeded by assigning points for suited cards, pairs, and cards that can make a straight. Table 8.4 summarizes how to assign points for suited cards in the Hutchison system.

Table 8.4 Determine the Value of Your Suited Cards	
High Card	**Value**
A	4
K	3
Q	2.5
J	2
T, 9	1.5
8–3	1
Four cards of the same suit	−2

The second step is to assign points to your hand based on any pairs it contains. Table 8.5 lists those point values.

Table 8.5 Pairs Add Value to Omaha Hands

Pair	Value
A	9
K	8
Q	7
J, T	6
9	5
8–4	4
3–2	3
Three cards of the same rank	0 points for the hand

Finally, you need to take the possibility of making a straight into account. When your hand contains cards of four different ranks, you assign points based on the lowest card in your hand. Table 8.6 lists the values.

Table 8.6 Point Values for Potential Straights

Lowest Card	Value
J	14
T	13
9	12
8	11
7	10
6	9
5–4	8
3	7
2	5

If there's more than a two-rank gap between two of your cards, such as when you hold A♥K♦Q♠8♦, where the 9, T, and J fall between the Q♠ and 8♦, subtract one point from the total. For this hand, the total would be 10 points: 11 because the low card is an 8, minus 1 because of the gap of more than two cards.

There are two more cases you need to consider, though. The first case is when your hand contains a pair, which means it has cards of only three different ranks. If your hole cards contain exactly one pair, add six points if all cards are 8 or higher and four points for all other combinations. As before, you should subtract one point if there is more than a two-rank gap between any of your cards.

When you have two pairs in the hole, you only have two ranks and far fewer possibilities to make straights. As such, you should add four points when both of your pairs are 8 or higher; otherwise, add two points. Pairs more than one card apart are difficult to make the nut straight with, so subtract a point if there's a gap of more than one card. If one of your pairs is AA, subtract two points to reflect the Ace's limited ability to make straights.

Add and subtract points based on the contents of your hand to come up with a total. The total you come up with represents the hand's approximate winning percentage against nine opponents if everyone stayed through the river. Against nine opponents, you will win one out of every ten pots, or 10 percent of the time. Hutchison recommends playing only those hands with scores of 15 or higher and raising with hands of 20 or higher. In tight games, where only three or four players see the flop, you should strongly consider folding hands with scores of 15–17 when you're in early position. In loose games, you might relax your requirements a bit and play hands with scores of 13–14 in middle or late position, but those hands are only slightly above average and could cost you a lot of money if the cards don't fall your way.

Testing Hutchison's Point Count System

Because the Hutchison system determines a hand's approximate winning percentage if every player stayed through the river, we can test its accuracy in Wilson Software's Turbo Omaha High. We decided to start at the top, with A♠A♣K♠K♣ ("Ace, King double-suited"). The Hutchison system assigns this hand points in the following manner:

>   4 points for the Ace-high flush draw in spades
>
>   4 points for the Ace-high flush draw in clubs
>
>   9 points for the pair of Aces
>
>   8 points for the pair of Kings
>
>   4 points for the two pairs within two ranks of each other
>
>   −2 points for the Aces

The total is 27 points. How does the predicted worth correlate to the actual performance of the hand against nine opponents who never fold? Figure 8.3 shows the results of a 100,000 hand simulation in Wilson Software's Turbo Omaha High.

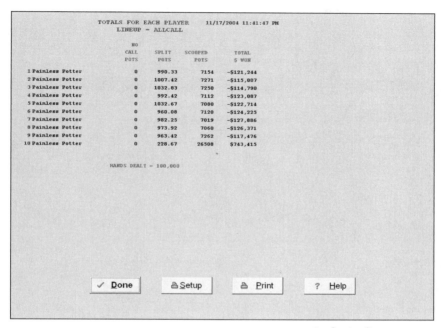

```
                    TOTALS FOR EACH PLAYER      11/17/2004 11:41:47 PM
                       LINEUP = ALLCALL

                        NO
                        CALL      SPLIT      SCOOPED      TOTAL
                        POTS      POTS        POTS        $ WON

     1 Painless Potter    0       990.33      7154      -$121,244
     2 Painless Potter    0      1007.42      7271      -$115,007
     3 Painless Potter    0      1032.83      7250      -$114,790
     4 Painless Potter    0       992.42      7112      -$123,087
     5 Painless Potter    0      1032.67      7080      -$122,714
     6 Painless Potter    0       960.08      7120      -$124,225
     7 Painless Potter    0       982.25      7019      -$127,886
     8 Painless Potter    0       973.92      7060      -$126,371
     9 Painless Potter    0       963.42      7262      -$117,476
    10 Painless Potter    0       228.67     26508       $743,415


                    HANDS DEALT = 100,000
```

✓ **Done**   🖳 Setup   🖶 Print   ? Help

Figure 8.3 When you add the split pots to the scooped pots, A♠A♣K♠K♣ wins at the predicted rate.

To interpret the results of this simulation, you need to know that the player with the test hand is in seat 10 (though you probably guessed that from the big positive number in the money column). The next step is to add all of the split and scooped pots for the nine players with random hands and compare it to the total split and scooped pots won by our hero with A♠A♣K♠K♣. The result? Our test hand won 26,736.67 out of 100,000 pots, which is near enough to the predicted 27 percent win rate.

Let's try another decent hand to test the Hutchison system: K♦K♥Q♣J♠. The system assigns points as follows:

> 0 points for flush draws
>
> 8 points for the pair of Kings
>
> 6 points for all cards Eight or higher in a one-pair hand

The total is 14 points. Figure 8.4 shows the results of a 100,000 hand simulation in Turbo Omaha High.

This simulation shows that K♦K♥Q♣J♠ will win 14,255.33 pots out of 100,000, which is right at the predicted 14 percent win rate.

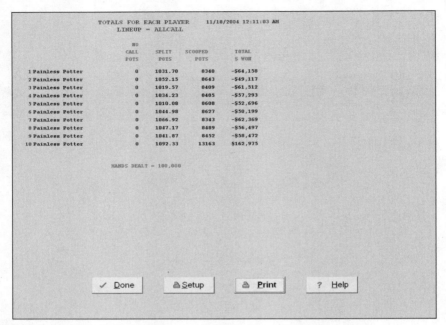

```
                TOTALS FOR EACH PLAYER     11/10/2004 12:11:03 AM
                LINEUP = ALLCALL

                     NO
                    CALL     SPLIT    SCOOPED       TOTAL
                    POTS      POTS      POTS        $ WON
  1 Painless Potter    0    1031.70     8340      -$64,158
  2 Painless Potter    0    1052.15     8643      -$49,117
  3 Painless Potter    0    1019.57     8409      -$61,512
  4 Painless Potter    0    1034.23     8405      -$57,293
  5 Painless Potter    0    1010.08     8608      -$52,696
  6 Painless Potter    0    1044.98     8627      -$50,199
  7 Painless Potter    0    1066.92     8343      -$62,369
  8 Painless Potter    0    1047.17     8489      -$56,497
  9 Painless Potter    0    1041.87     8452      -$58,472
 10 Painless Potter    0    1092.33    13163      $162,975


                HANDS DEALT = 100,000
```

[✓ Done]   [🖫 Setup]   [🖨 Print]   [? Help]

Figure 8.4 The Hutchison system accurately predicts another win rate.

Finally, let's see how the system handles a mediocre starting hand such as 8♠7♣4♥4♦. After all, the system wouldn't be of much use if the point counts in the middle of the pack and below weren't accurate. The Hutchison system assigns points to this hand as follows:

> 1 point for Eight-high flush draw in spades
>
> 4 points for the pair of Fours
>
> 4 points for the straight possibility in a one-pair hand where some of the cards are ranked Eight or lower

The total is nine points. Figure 8.5 shows the results of the Turbo Omaha High simulation.

In this simulation, 8♠7♣4♥4♦ won 8,436.42 pots out of 100,000, which is very much in line with the 9 percent predicted win rate.

♠♥♣♦ Note

The Hutchison system will occasionally be off by a percentage point or two in its predictions, but it's very accurate for such a simple system.

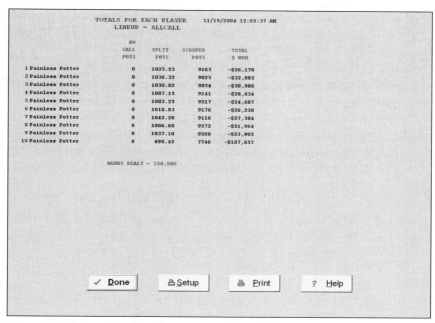

Figure 8.5 This hand is a dog. The system predicted it, and the simulation proved it.

Scoring Practice for Omaha High Hands

Here are five Omaha hands for you to score using the Hutchison system. You'll find the answers below the final hand.

> A♠A♦J♠4♣
>
> K♥Q♥J♠8♦
>
> T♣T♠7♥7♠
>
> 9♥8♦7♠6♣
>
> 5♥5♠4♥4♠

You should assign the following scores to the sample hands:

> A♠A♦J♠4♣ receives 4 points for the Ace-high flush draw in spades, 9 points for the pair of Aces, and 4 points for the straight cards (not all cards are an Eight or above), for a total of 17 points. There is only a two-rank gap between an Ace and a Four, so you don't subtract a point.

> K♥Q♥J♠8♦ receives 3 points for the King-high flush draw in hearts, no points for pairs, and 11 points for an Eight-low hand with four cards of different ranks, for a total of 14 points.

T♣T♠7♥7♠ receives 1.5 points for the Ten-high flush draw in spades, 6 points for the pair of Tens, 4 points for the pair of Sevens, and 2 points for the straight possibilities, but −2 points because there is a gap of more than one rank between the pairs, for a total of 11.5 points.

9♥8♦7♣6♣ receives no points for flush draws or pairs, but it does receive 9 points for the Six-low hand with four cards of different ranks, for a total of 9 points.

5♥5♠4♥4♠ receives 1 point for the Five-high flush draw in hearts, 1 point for the Five-high flush draw in spades, 4 points for the pair of Fives, 4 points for the pair of Fours, and 2 points for the straight possibilities, for a total of 12 points.

Choosing Starting Hands in Omaha High-Low

Picking good starting hands in Omaha high-low is even more difficult than picking hands in Omaha high, but once again Ed Hutchison spent the time to develop a hand scoring system (available online at http://ehutchison.homestead.com/omahasystem.html and used by his kind permission) that you can use to determine whether a four-card hand is playable in Omaha high-low.

The first step is to figure out whether you can play the hand for high only. You can play a hand with no chance of a low (remember, there need to be three cards ranked Eight or lower on the board for a low to be possible) if your all four cards are ranked Ten or higher, does not contain three of a kind or quads, and meets one of these criteria:

◆ The hand contains two pairs.
◆ The hand contains one pair and two suited cards.
◆ The hand contains two sets of suited cards.

If one of your hole cards is below a Ten, you can't play the hand for high only. Instead, you need to evaluate whether your hand has a reasonable chance at winning the low part of the pot. The second step in the process is to score the lowest two cards in your hand. Table 8.7 lists the values for the relevant card combinations.

Next, look at the other two cards in your hand (your *kickers*) and add points as shown in Table 8.8. Add no points for a card that was already counted in the first step. If your kickers are paired, only add points once for that rank. (You'll count points for pairs in the next step.)

If your hand contains a pair, you should add points as described in Table 8.9.

But you're not done with the pairs step! If you have three of a kind, subtract half the points you added for the pair. For example, if you hold A♥2♥2♠2♣, you would add 1.5 points instead of 3.

Table 8.7 Point Assignments for the Lowest Two-Card Combination in an Omaha High-Low Hand

Lowest Cards	Value
A 2	20
A 3	17
A 4	13
A 5	10
2 3	15
2 4	12
3 4	11
4 5	8
Other	0

Table 8.8 Point Assignments for Kickers in an Omaha High-Low Hand

Kicker	Value
3	9
4	6
5	4
J, Q, K	2
6, T	1

Table 8.9 Point Assignments for Pairs in an Omaha High-Low Hand

Pair Rank	Value
A	8
K	6
Q	5
J	2
2	3
3, 4, T	1

Finally, you need to account for the value of possible flushes you can make. Table 8.10 lists the values you should assign for the higher of your flush cards.

Table 8.10   Point Assignments for Flush Possibilities in an Omaha High-Low Hand

Higher Flush Card	Value
A	4
K	3
Q, J	2
T, 9, 8	1

Holding three cards of the same suit decreases the likelihood you can make a flush, so subtract half of the points you added if you have three cards of the same suit. If you hold four cards of the same suit, award no points for flush possibilities. It's just too tough to make a flush when there are only nine other cards to help you do it.

The Hutchison system for Omaha high-low generates values from 0 to 45. Ed recommends playing any hand that scores a 20 or higher and to consider raising with any hand that scores 30 or higher.

As an example, try scoring the hand A♠K♦Q♦2♠. Here's how it breaks down:

◆ All four cards are not a T or above, so you can't consider playing the hand for high only.

◆ The hand contains an A2 combination, which is worth 20 points.

◆ There are K and Q kickers, which are worth 4 points total (2 points each).

◆ There are no pairs in the hand, so you assign 0 points for that step.

◆ The hand has an Ace-high flush combination for 4 points and a King-high flush combination for 3 points, for a total of 7 points.

The Hutchison system score for A♠K♦Q♦2♠ is 31 points, so you should strongly consider raising.

Testing the Hutchison Omaha High-Low System

As with his Omaha high scoring system, Hutchison notes that the high-low scoring system's results closely approximate a hand's winning chances against nine opponents if no one folds. Figure 8.6 shows the results of a 100,000 hand simulation using Wilson Software's Turbo Omaha High-Low program.

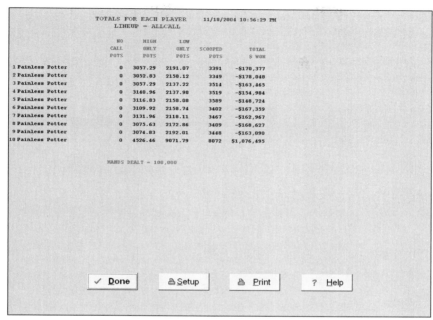

```
                TOTALS FOR EACH PLAYER      11/18/2004 10:56:29 PM
                   LINEUP - ALLCALL

                    NO      HIGH      LOW
                   CALL     ONLY      ONLY    SCOOPED      TOTAL
                   POTS     POTS      POTS     POTS       $ WON

 1 Painless Potter     0    3057.29   2191.07   3391    -$170,377
 2 Painless Potter     0    3052.83   2158.12   3349    -$178,048
 3 Painless Potter     0    3057.29   2137.22   3514    -$163,465
 4 Painless Potter     0    3140.96   2137.98   3519    -$154,984
 5 Painless Potter     0    3116.83   2158.08   3589    -$148,724
 6 Painless Potter     0    3109.92   2158.74   3402    -$167,359
 7 Painless Potter     0    3131.96   2118.11   3467    -$162,967
 8 Painless Potter     0    3075.63   2172.86   3409    -$168,627
 9 Painless Potter     0    3074.83   2192.01   3448    -$163,090
10 Painless Potter     0    4526.46   9071.79   8072   $1,076,495


          HANDS DEALT = 100,000
```

  ✓ **Done**   🖫 Setup   🖶 Print   ? Help

Figure 8.6 The Hutchison Omaha high-low system scores this hand differently than the win rate.

You've probably noticed that there's a discrepancy between the Hutchison system's score of 31 and the hand's actual winning percentage of 21.67 percent. Let's try another hand, such as A♣J♥J♦3♠, to see if there's a pattern. Figure 8.7 shows the simulation results.

The Hutchison system assigns this hand a score of 25, as shown by the following criteria:

◆ The two lowest cards are A 3, for a total of 17 points.

◆ There is a Jack kicker, which nets 2 points.

◆ There is a pair of Jacks, which nets 2 points.

◆ There is an Ace-high flush draw, which nets 4 points.

As before, the simulated winning percentage of 17.96 percent differs from the system point total. Not to worry, though, because there is a consistent relationship between the Hutchison scores and the winning percentages. As it turns out, a hand's winning percentage is approximately 70 percent of the Hutchison point total, so when Ed says you should call in Omaha high-low with hands of 20 points or more, he's actually saying you should call when you have a 14 percent or higher chance of winning. That recommendation is very much in line with his argument: You should call when you have a 15 percent or higher chance of winning in Omaha high.

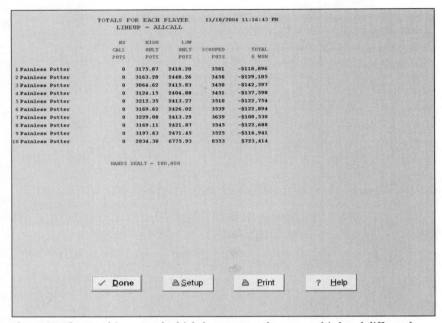

```
                TOTALS FOR EACH PLAYER      11/10/2004 11:16:43 PM
                  LINEUP = ALLCALL

                  NO       HIGH      LOW
                  CALL     ONLY      ONLY    SCOOPED      TOTAL
                  POTS     POTS      POTS     POTS        $ WON
 1 Painless Potter   0    3175.87   2418.20    3581     -$118,896
 2 Painless Potter   0    3163.20   2448.26    3458     -$129,105
 3 Painless Potter   0    3064.62   2415.83    3450     -$142,397
 4 Painless Potter   0    3124.15   2404.80    3451     -$137,598
 5 Painless Potter   0    3212.35   2413.27    3510     -$122,754
 6 Painless Potter   0    3169.62   2426.02    3539     -$122,894
 7 Painless Potter   0    3229.08   2413.29    3639     -$108,530
 8 Painless Potter   0    3169.11   2421.87    3545     -$122,688
 9 Painless Potter   0    3197.63   2471.45    3525     -$116,941
10 Painless Potter   0    2834.30   6775.93    8353      $723,414


            HANDS DEALT = 100,000
```

| ✓ Done | 🖨 Setup | 🖨 Print | ? Help |

Figure 8.7 The Hutchison Omaha high-low system also scores this hand differently than the win rate.

Scoring Practice for Omaha High-Low Hands

Here are five Omaha high-low hands for you to score using the Hutchison system. You'll find the answers below the final hand.

> A♣A♦2♠3♦
>
> A♠K♠J♦J♥
>
> 2♣3♥4♦5♦
>
> A♥J♦T♣4♥
>
> 8♣8♦9♣9♦

You should assign the following points to the sample hands:

> A♣A♦2♠3♦ has a lowest two-card combination of A2 for 20 points, a Three kicker, which gets 9 points, a pair of Aces nets 8 points, and two Ace-high flush draws for 4 points apiece (8 total), for a total of 45 points. That's the maximum score possible, which means that you're a big favorite before the flop. If you get this hand, raise until they make you stop.
>
> A♠K♠J♦J♥ is playable as a high-only hand. All of the cards are a Ten or higher, and the hand contains a pair plus a flush draw.

2♣3♥4♦5♦ has a lowest two-card combination of 23 for 15 points, a Four kicker for 6 points, a Five kicker for 4 points, and no points for a pair or a flush draw (there is one, but it isn't high enough to score points), for a total of 25 points.

A♥J♦T♣4♥ has a lowest two-card combination of A4 for 13 points, a Jack kicker for 2 points, no points for a pair, and 4 points for an Ace-high flush draw, for a total of 19 points.

8♣8♦9♠9♥ has no low possibility, no cards that gain points as kickers, no pairs that earn points, and no flush draws, for a total of 0 points. If you get this hand, throw it away as quickly as you can.

Choosing Starting Hands in Pineapple

Pineapple, also known as Crazy Pineapple, is a relatively new flop game that you don't see played a lot in brick-and-mortar casinos. In fact, the only time we've seen it played live was in a firehouse game in Maryland back in the early 1990s. You can find the game online at UltimateBet and ParadisePoker, but other than that, you'll have to deal it at home on your kitchen table.

Pineapple is like Hold 'em in that you can use both, one, or neither of your hole cards remaining at the river to make your hand. However, because you start with three cards in Pineapple and discard one after the flop, it's very difficult to simulate results based on your hole cards. So how do you play before the flop? We recommend the following strategy:

♦ Discard a hand with three of a kind, even Aces or Kings.

♦ In early position, play any pair of Tens or higher, and consider raising if your third card shares a suit with one of the paired cards and is also higher than a Ten. You should also play any three cards that are ranked Ten or higher, and three cards to a straight where the bottom card is Eight or higher.

♦ In middle position, play any pair of Sevens or higher where you have a suited card higher than a Ten as your third card, any hand with two flush cards that are Ten or higher that come with another card within two ranks of the bottom suited card, and three cards to a straight where the bottom card is Six or higher. When everyone has folded to you, consider raising with any hand you would call with in early position. If someone has raised in front of you, only play hands you would play in early position.

♦ In late position and the blinds, play any pair of Fours or higher where you have a suited card higher than a Ten as your third card and any three cards to a straight where the total gaps between the cards is no more than one. In other words, you would play 8♠7♠5♥ but not 8♠7♠4♥. If someone has raised in front of you, only play hands you would play in early position, unless you are in the blinds, in which case you may also play hands that you would play in middle position.

These guidelines take into account the fact that three-card hands are, in general, stronger than two-card hands, so you need to be a bit more cautious in deciding which hands to pursue.

Choosing Starting Hands in Pineapple High-Low

Playing Pineapple high-low seems to be a lot like playing Omaha high-low, but the similarities are deceptive when you remember that you need only use one (or none) of your remaining hole cards to form your low hand after the river has been dealt. Here is the strategy we recommend for deciding which hole card sets to play in Pineapple high-low:

- ✦ Always throw away three of a kind.
- ✦ In early position, raise any three card set that contains an Ace and two other cards ranked Five or below, where one of the cards shares a suit with the Ace. You should also play any A2 (regardless of kicker), any A3, where either the Three is suited with the Ace, or you have a kicker ranked Ten or higher that is suited with the Ace, any pair of Jacks or higher, and three cards ranked above a Ten, where two of the cards are suited.
- ✦ In middle position, you may also call with any A2 or A3, any A4, where either the Four or your kicker is suited with the Ace, any A5, where either the Five or a kicker that is a Ten or higher is suited with the Ace, any three cards ranked Five or below with an Ace, any pair of Eights or higher, and any three cards ranked above a Ten. If someone raises in front of you, you should only play hands you would play in early position.
- ✦ In late position or in the blinds, you may also call with any pair of Fives or higher and any Ace-high flush draw. If someone raises in front of you, only play hands you would play in early position, unless you are one of the blinds, in which case you may also play hands that you would play in middle position.

Choosing Starting Hands in Stud Games

Unlike flop games, when you play seven-card Stud you are on your own. The cards you get are the cards you're stuck with throughout the hand, except in the unlikely event that everyone stays to the last card and the dealing program needs to turn up a common card in the middle of the table. Seven-card Stud also differs from Hold 'em and other flop games in that you have a lot more information about which cards are available and which cards aren't. As an example, consider the hand in Figure 8.8.

In this eight-handed game, you know the identities of 10 cards that are no longer available for you to draw: the three cards in your hand and the upcards of each of your opponents. Unless you have the lowest upcard and post the bring-in, you have a very good sense of whether you should put any money into the pot. You have to keep track of dead cards in your head when you play in a brick-and-mortar casino, but you can use a software program to keep track of them when you play online. For example, you could use the Excel worksheet shown in Figure 8.9 to track which cards are out.

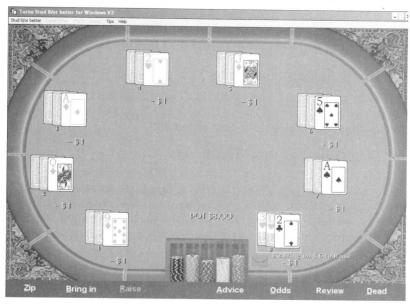

Figure 8.8 You get a lot of information early in the hand in seven-card Stud.

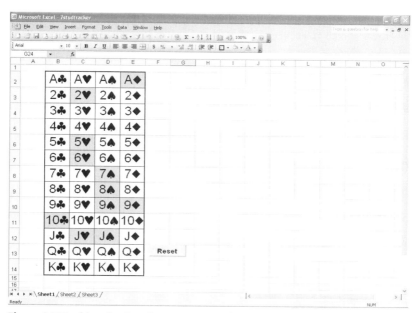

Figure 8.9 Tracking dead cards was never easier.

Clicking a cell with a card value shades the cell, indicating the card is out. When you click the Reset button, a macro removes the shading from the cells so you can track cards during the next hand. You can download the workbook from www.thatexcelguy.com/poker/.

Choosing Starting Hands in Seven-Card Stud

So which hands should you play in seven-card Stud? As opposed to breaking the analysis down by position as we did in Hold 'em, we'll break it down by type of hand and discuss how position affects your choices during each discussion.

Playing Three-of-a-Kind on Third Street

If you're dealt trips, you're *rolled up* and have a tremendous starting hand. In fact, according to a 100,000-hand simulation in Turbo Seven-Card Stud, trip Deuces wins 72 percent of the time, trip Eights wins 79 percent of the time, and trip Aces wins 84.5 percent of the time against seven random hands when everyone stays to the river. Trips are so strong that you don't have to worry if the fourth card of your rank is someone else's upcard. The winning percentage for trip Deuces, Eights, and Aces drops only by about 2 percent when the fourth card of that rank is in another player's hand. The bad news is that you won't be rolled up that often. But when you are, raise until they make you stop.

Playing Pairs on Third Street

Pairs from Tens to Aces are great hands, but they're a bit more vulnerable than trips, particularly when one or both of the other cards of your rank are dead, or you have a lousy kicker. For example, the hand in Figure 8.10 is pretty good if no one has an upcard larger than your pair, but it would be pretty dicey if there were a Queen and a King to follow you.

Figure 8.10 You can play unless you can't improve to trips, or there are bigger cards behind you.

You can play a pair of Aces in the hole regardless of your kicker and whether there are any Aces in other players' hands. The reason Aces are so good is that if you make two pairs, and there's a good chance you will, you will have Aces-up, very probably the best two-pair hand. Believe us, you will win a lot of hands with two pairs. In a 100,000-hand simulation in Turbo Seven-Card Stud, A♣A♠2♦2♥3♣4♥6♣ won right at 50 percent of the time when every other player stayed to the river.

With that information in mind, you can usually play any pair of Tens or higher as long as you have a good kicker and no one with a larger upcard has raised you. If a player with a bigger upcard has raised, you can still call if you have a good kicker (preferably one that duplicates the raiser's upcard) or re-raise if you have a larger pair than you figure them to have.

Pairs lower than Tens are still decent hands, provided your pair is live (there are no cards of that rank on other players' boards), your kicker is higher than any callers' door cards, and no more than one of your kicker's mates is gone. Be warned, though: When you play a small pair, you need to improve quickly or get out of the hand.

Playing Three to a Flush on Third Street

Flushes are powerful hands in seven-card Stud, but they're a lot harder to make than you'd think. When your first three cards are the same suit, the odds are 5 to 1 against you making your flush by the river, *assuming none of the cards you need are in other players' hands*. This guideline applies to any three cards of the same suit, but if the upcards behind you are high and unmatched (that is, there's an Ace, King, and Queen behind you), you might consider folding or just calling the bring-in.

If no one has raised before you, you can play if there are two cards of your suit out, but not if three or more are gone. If a player raises into you, and you have an Ace-high flush started, you need to determine whether the player is trying to steal or is raising on a good hand. If you have big cards and think your opponent may be trying to steal the antes, you can call if one of your flush cards is gone, or if you have three to a straight flush. If two flush cards are gone, and your cards aren't high enough to make a solid two-pair hand at the river, you should probably give the player credit for a better hand and fold.

Playing Three to a Straight on Third Street

It's easy to call when you have an Ace, King, and Queen as your first three cards, but calling with the hand in Figure 8.11 might give you pause if some of your opponents' upcards are Tens or higher.

Figure 8.11 Sure, you could improve to a straight, but will you?

When you have three cards with no gaps, and all of the cards you need are live, the odds are about 6 to 1 against you making a straight, so you can certainly call the bring-in or even a full bet if your lowest card is an Eight or higher. If there is a one-card gap in your potential straight, however, you need to think very seriously about folding if any of your straight cards are dead. In fact, you should fold to a full bet if any of the cards you need to fill the gap are in another player's hand.

You should also be careful of three-card straights that contain Aces, mainly because your outs are cut in half. For example, if you hold the hand in Figure 8.12, you must catch a Jack and a Ten to complete your straight. This hand contains three big cards, which is great, but it has a relatively low straight potential.

Figure 8.12 Big cards are good, but you have an inflexible straight draw.

Choosing Starting Hands in Seven-Card Stud High-Low

Omaha high-low is a game that takes the middle cards out of play, but Aces rule in seven-card Stud high-low. Because Aces play for both high and low, any hand with an Ace is definitively better than a similar hand without one. With that said, however, you do need to remember that both the high and low hand (if there is one) take half the pot, so you can still play for the high half of the pot if you have a good starting hand relative to how other players' hands develop.

You can always play three of a kind in the pocket, of course, because you have a very, very good shot at capturing the high half of the pot. The set of Eights we tested in the seven-card Stud high section won 26 percent of the money in a 100,000-hand Turbo Stud 8 simulation, 0.3 percent of which were from four consecutive low cards fulfilling the ultimate backdoor low draw. You're also a big favorite to win the money when you start with three consecutive suited cards ranked Five or below. With 5♣ 4♣ 3♣, for example, you would win 38 percent of all money put into the seven-card Stud high-low pot. Three consecutive but unsuited low cards are also a very good hand.

Other two-way hands you can play aggressively are a pair of Aces with another low card or three low cards (again, those cards ranked Five or lower) that include an Ace. On the high side, you're looking good when you start with three cards to a high straight flush or what appears to be the best high hand based on your opponents' cards. For example, if you have the hand in Figure 8.13, and the highest card on board is a Jack, you should figure to be in good shape to win half the pot.

Figure 8.13 This hand works in high-low, provided no one else has a competitive high draw.

Be very careful about playing three cards that are ranked Eight or lower, though. These hands are generally not strong enough to play against more than one other opponent going for low.

Choosing Starting Hands in Razz

Choosing starting hands in Razz, which is seven-card Stud played for low, can be fairly easy. If you want to take the simple way out, all you need to do is look at your cards and see if they're all unpaired and below an Eight. Because flushes and straights don't count, you can disregard many of the considerations that come into play in seven-card Stud and seven-card Stud high-low.

You do need to pay attention to the other cards on the board when you decide whether to play your hand or not. In Razz, you want to see cards on the board that duplicate the cards in your hand. Every card on the board that could have paired you is another breath of life to your bankroll. If you hold the A♠2♥6♣ and see two Fours, two Threes, and a Five on the board, for example, you should definitely fold the hand. In general, you should fold if you see more than three cards ranked Five or below that you need to make an Eight low or better.

Razz is a brutal game, with wild swings. Be prepared to weather a lot of storms if you take this game on.

The Flop and Fourth Street

So you're in the hand, off and running! Do you remember how many players are in the pot and for how many bets? This will help you figure out whether the odds will be correct for you to stay in the hand later on. When you see the flop or the remaining players' second upcards, you'll have a better idea of where you are in the hand relative to everyone else. It's not always the easiest thing to know, but you can go a long way toward figuring it out when you have paid attention to what your opponents have played and their betting patterns associated with those hands. With that information, you will have a good advantage over players who are not as diligent as you are. This, the second of four betting rounds (five in Stud), is important because it is your last chance to "get in cheap" before the bets double on the turn. By the end of this chapter, you will know

- ✦ How to evaluate how well you hit the flop.
- ✦ How to evaluate how much "work" you need to do to make certain hands.
- ✦ How to evaluate your hands relative to Sklansky, Malmuth, and Miller's pot-based odds.
- ✦ How to evaluate the amount of thinking you can do in the allotted time.

The Cards Come Out

In the board games, three community cards will be placed on the table, while in Stud games a second "upcard" will be added to each remaining player's hand, as shown in Figures 9.1 and 9.2.

As you'll remember from Chapter 4, the action in a board game will begin with the first active player to the left of the button. In Stud, of course, the highest hand showing begins the betting. But how did you do?

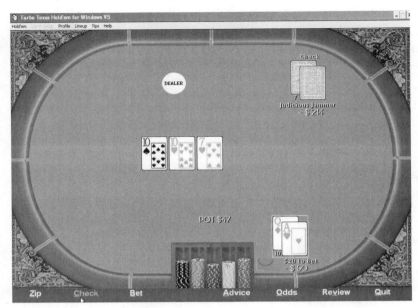

Figure 9.1 A sample Hold 'em flop

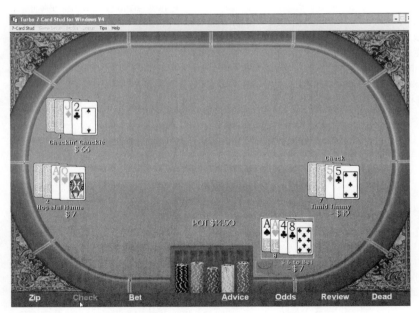

Figure 9.2 A sample Stud hand on fourth street

Hold 'Em Flops

As with any activity with an element of luck, there will be times when you feel you can do no wrong and times when, no matter what cards you start with, they won't win. You've put in your money, the flop comes out, and it's time to play the hand.

Bingo! Some Hands Play Themselves

The best-case scenario almost never happens, but it's great when it does. If you're holding 8♣9♣ and the flop comes 5♣6♣7♣, you're good to go! You have flopped the "absolute nuts," the absolutely unbeatable straight flush. That's great, but it can be very difficult to get paid for your trouble here. The best you can hope for is that someone also has a strong hand, such as A♣3♣, which gives your opponent what is normally a winning hand. They may be aware that they don't have the best hand possible, but a straight flush is so rare, they'll figure you will not have flopped the best hand and will bet into you. Another possibility is that someone will have a set, as can be made with a pocket pair of 5s, 6s or 7s. Even better would be if the board pairs, which would give them a full house or even four of a kind. No good! Don't count on this happening very often, if ever.

Another example comes when you flop quads, another extreme rarity. If you come in with a pair of 8s, for example, and the other two 8s come on the flop, you are also in great shape. Take a good look to see if there's a straight flush possible, simply to be sure you don't miss it if it comes. If somebody raises you, and there's an overcard on board, also be sure to notice if the last one shows up. Of course, most of the time you'll be playing against someone who has the top pair, most likely with a decent kicker. In this case, checking and calling from early position would be best, as any bets made will be coming your way. If you're playing against aggressive players, you can check again on the turn and then raise, because the times your quads won't win are so rare you should be sure to get as much money in the pot as possible. If someone beats your four of a kind, it's certainly disappointing but not the end of the world.

Another set of "bingo" hands is when you flop straights and flushes. These hands are quite strong, but are vulnerable in a loose game. You're in a hand with four other players with Q♥T♥ in the pocket. The flop comes as shown in Figure 9.3.

Figure 9.3 This flop meshes well with your hand.

This is a great flop, in that you have made a "nut" King-high straight. There are, however, some possibilities of which you should be aware as the hand progresses:

◆ You could be up against a spade (flush) draw. Any two spades, such as 5♠6♠, will often stay in the hand until the bitter end. 7♠8♠ would in fact be a straight flush draw.

◆ You could be up against a couple of different straight draws. Anyone with a Queen or a Ten will likely stick around for at least the turn because of the amount of money already in the pot. If one of those cards is a spade, they will also have three to a flush, known as a "back door" flush draw.

◆ It is also possible that you may be up against a "double draw," in which a player has to hit only one card to make either a straight or a flush. A♠T♠, in this case, is a powerful drawing hand in that any of the remaining Queens in the deck complete the best straight possible, and any spade completes the nut flush.

◆ Finally, you could be looking at either a set or two pair. If a conservative player raised before the flop, you could be up against a set of any of the cards on the board. In that case, you need to dodge a pair on board on the turn and on the river. If someone is playing K♥J♥, they will likely be in until the end. They will be shooting at one of the two remaining Kings and one of the two remaining Jacks to complete their full house.

> When you make an incredible hand on the flop, see if the hand will play itself via other players doing the betting for you. If you're in early position, either check or call and hope someone raises. Once you get to the turn, you'll be able to get many players to put more money in the pot, as they will be "pot committed." When you have a very strong but not unbeatable hand, it would help to vary your action. Jam (bet and raise) sometimes, check-raise, and limp in as you feel is appropriate.

Swing and a Miss—Oh Well

Everybody goes through this many times during any session lasting more than 20 minutes. For example, you are dealt A♥K♥ on the button, and five players have called the big blind. You happily raise and everybody calls. Nice! There are now 10 small bets in the pot (or 10.5 if the small blind folded). Assume the flop comes, as shown in Figure 9.4.

Figure 9.4 This flop looks nothing like your cards.

Ugh, no good. There are all sorts of problems with this hand. First, it's the wrong "flavor" in that you now have no chance at all of making a flush (at most there will be two hearts on board at the end of the hand for a total of four). If someone doesn't already have a flush, there is almost certainly at least one club in someone's hand. It's also very possible that someone has an Ace and an Eight, which means you would be drawing to the three remaining Kings in the deck to make a higher pair while under the mistaken impression that you would also be "good" if you hit an Ace on the turn or on the river. In fact, you would then be going against two pair with one or no cards to go. Another vulnerability is that it is very likely someone has a Nine in their hand, as in lower-limit games it is very common for someone to call two bets with a hand like

J♣9♦. In this situation, you would be vulnerable in two ways. First, this player has an open-ended straight draw, which means they will make a straight if either a Ten or a Five comes on the turn or on the river. In addition, they have a medium flush draw. Pop quiz! Why would J♣9♦ be a particularly strong hand here? Answer: Because if a Ten shows up, the hand will not just be a Ten-high straight but a Jack-high straight! And if the Ten is the T♣, the player will have an unbeatable straight flush! In the end, there's simply no way you can play this hand after the flop.

You are only as good as the flop! The perfect example comes when Doug slowplayed (limped in for one bet) a pair of Aces before the flop. The flop came two Sevens and a Deuce! Guess what the big blind had. Yep, Seven-Deuce! Imagine the embarrassment when the cards got turned over. Doug did have two shots at one of the two remaining Aces to make Aces full of Sevens, but still. Makes you sick....

Partial Success

This is the part where a player will have a hand requiring some skill, some knowledge of the players they're going against, and a solid grasp of the percentages involved to be a winning player.

Three of a Kind

Three of a kind ("trips" or a "set") is very often a winning hand in Hold 'em. To flop a set is mainly a great thing but is all too often a heartbreaker. When you have a pocket pair and a third one comes on the board, you're way ahead! Well, except for a few things.

Let's say you have 9♠9♣, and the flop shown in Figure 9.5 appears.

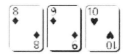

While you are obviously in a great position with your trips, this is a major *danger flop*, which means your strong hand is very vulnerable. Let us count the ways. First, you're vulnerable to any straight draw or made straight. QJ is a common hand in loose games, so that's a possibility. Unfortunately,

Figure 9.5 You're in good shape, but you aren't invulnerable.

any 7 or J now has an open-ended straight draw, giving them two shots at eight cards (any of the four 6s or Qs). In addition, anyone with two diamonds in the hole will now have two chances to catch another diamond and make a flush. Of course, you can solve this little problem by pairing the board with an 8, 9, T, or if the turn and river cards pair themselves—for example, if the turn and river are both 3s. Once in a great while, the T♦ and/or the 7♦ will come before the end of the hand and give someone a straight flush.

In that case, all you can do is raise a couple of times, either on the turn or the river, and have the sense to realize they're not going to stop raising and call. When you're on the Internet, no one will see you cry.

Two Pair (or Something's "Up")

This is another very good hand to get on the flop, but it also has vulnerabilities, similar to trips, in addition to being far behind someone else also holding trips. Doug actually met a good friend of his at a $10–$20 Hold 'em table when this scenario played out. He held T♥J♥ or something like it, and the flop in Figure 9.6 appeared.

Figure 9.6 You need to recognize when you're behind.

He of course bet and re-raised on the flop, oblivious to the fact that he was up against a set of Fives. Another Ten or Jack came at some point, and his full house was victorious over the *underset full house* over his opponent (Jacks or Tens full beat his Fives full). Doug didn't really understand how big of an underdog he was after the flop at that point in his poker career. In this case, he needed to hit one of the four remaining Jacks or Tens to win. Anyway, Doug was very pleased with himself and looked to the guy to his right, expecting some sort of positive feedback. What he got instead was a snort and "Wow, you were *way* behind!" Doug asked how that was, got it explained to him as just described, and learned from it.

Overpair

In this case, you have a hand higher than the highest hand on the board. To illustrate, let us tell you a brief story about Smitty, a good guy from a home game Doug used to play in. He likes to play what became known to the group as "Smitty Hands," which would be small suited or one-gap cards. Through an online promotional tournament, Smitty won a $5,000 seat in the initial Borgata World Poker Tour no-limit Hold 'em main event. He was going along well, until he got into a hand against top pro Layne Flack. Smitty held 3♥5♥, while Layne held a pair of Tens. The flop came, as shown in Figure 9.7.

Figure 9.7 It's better to have a made hand than a draw.

At this point Layne had the overpair of Tens and Smitty the top pair on board and a *straight flush draw* (any Ace, Six, Five, or heart would have won Smitty the pot, actually). Flack had more chips than Smitty and bet enough to put him all-in. Statistics demonstrate that Smitty held a 65 to 35 percent advantage after the flop because of his draws, but in this case he failed to improve and Layne busted him out. We'll talk more about the statistics surrounding such danger flops a little later in this chapter.

Overcards

To have *overcards* is when both of your hole cards are higher than the highest card on the board. A very common hand to have in this case is AK or AQ. To say you have overcards could mean you have a straight or a flush draw, but common usage is reserved for the times when you have neither. Instead, you're hoping to catch a pair higher than your opponents are holding. Of course, this could leave you in the position of having *false outs*, which are cards you believe will give you a winning hand but will actually put you even farther behind. Let's say, for example, that you have A♣K♦, and the flop comes, as shown in Figure 9.8.

Figure 9.8 This flop forces you to decide how good a hand your opponent has.

One of the most important skills a successful poker player must possess is the ability to *put someone on a hand*, meaning they are able to analyze the situation and figure out what hand their opponents are most likely to have. In low-limit poker, several players often see the flop, and it is not at all unusual for a player to play K9 suited or A9 either suited or unsuited. Should you be up against one of these hands, there are two implications. First, against A9 unsuited, you will only win around 13.2 percent of the total money over time. Against K9 unsuited, you will be for all intents and purposes just as large an underdog (winning only 14 percent of the money in our simulation) because in both cases you will be shooting for only three cards in the deck instead of six, as your hand is now *reverse dominated*. To be reverse dominated is to have an opponent who has made a pair on the flop who also holds one of your unpaired cards. In wrestling terms, they have "reversed" your hold in that your dominant hand is now the one dominated. So be aware of players who might have these hands, and look closely to see if you might have a drawing hand to get yourself back in.

Flush Draw

Any flush is consistently a winning hand when only three suited cards are on the board. Let's say you hold Q♦K♦, and you get the flop shown in Figure 9.9.

Figure 9.9 You have a good draw, but not the best draw.

This is a very good draw for you in one way, but it's also a vulnerable holding. Four ways in which your K♦Q♦ can be beaten come to mind immediately. First, someone could have A♦x♦, which means you're basically out of luck unless a King or Queen comes and you also dodge an Ace. Second, a player may have played small suited connectors such as 5♥6♥, which means you will now need to catch your flush to win the pot. It is impossible for you to make either a straight or a full house, so you're shooting for one of the nine remaining diamonds in the deck, which is a little bit more than a 5:1 disadvantage for you on each of the turn and the river.

A third way in which you are endangered is if someone plays what is known as "Ax." A, in this context, represents an Ace, and you'll recall that an "x" means any card under a Ten. In low-limit Hold 'em, it is very common for someone to play Ace-anything. It's what's known as *Aces and spaces* and puts the player at a huge disadvantage, but that doesn't stop them. A5 or A6 unsuited is particularly dangerous hands for you, as they give the holder a *double gut shot* straight draw. In this example, either a 2 or a 6 for the A5 and a 2 or a 5 for the A6 will give them a straight. In this case, they are not drawing to the nuts (neither are you, technically, since you don't have the Ace, but compared to them you are), but they do have six outs to beat you. Do you know why it's six and not eight outs? That's right, it's because one of each card is a diamond, which would make your flush, assuming your opponent is not holding a diamond.

Finally, someone could have a set. It's unlikely someone would have two pair because Threes, Fours, and Sevens don't play well. (One exception: Beware of someone who plays any two suited cards; they have an annoying habit of flopping two pair. It drives you crazy, it really does.) Low pairs, like Threes and Fours, are usually only good after the flop if they catch a set, but a pair of Sevens is a very different story. Phil Hellmuth, for example, puts pocket Sevens as one of his must-play hands for beginners, based on the success he's seen them have over his years of playing. If someone has a set, they can make quads by catching the *case* (sole remaining) card they made a set with, or the board can pair another board card on the turn or on the river, which is six, and then nine, chances for the three of a kind to *fill up*.

Straight Draw

Straights are strong hands and will often win in Hold 'em. Straight draws come in a few varieties. The best straight draw is one in which either of two cards will give you a straight. There are a few ways to get there. The first is an *open-ended straight draw*. Let's say you have T♣J♣, and you see the flop shown in Figure 9.10.

Figure 9.10 Open-ended straight draws are usually worth pursuing.

You will now complete your straight if an Ace or a Nine comes on the turn or on the river. This draw, also known as an *up and down straight draw*, is quite good in that anyone with two hearts, diamonds, or spades will need for them to come *runner-runner* on the turn and river. It will be very likely you will be behind in the hand because it's a safe bet someone's stuck around with a Queen or a King. Someone could also be playing Ace-2. If someone raised before the flop, it could be they've made a set, which should set alarms off in your head when that kind of flop comes out. If they have a pair of Aces, you have what is known as a *trap hand* in that if a third Ace comes before the end of the hand, they will have made trips and will often think they're in the lead, but you will have completed your straight. If there's no pair on the board, you have the nuts. If the board has paired, you will need to decide how aggressively you play the hand. It may do you well to check and call. If you don't think they have it, you could simply bet; but if the player is aggressive, they may be betting because they know the only way they're going to win is if you fold. The pot will almost always be big enough to call one bet on the end, so if you think you're probably beat, check and call. Do call, though, when the pot is in any way substantial.

A second way in which two ranks of cards will make your straight is when you have a *gut shot straight draw*. For example, if you have J♦Q♠, and the flop comes, as shown in Figure 9.11.

Figure 9.11 Drawing to inside straights will cost you money in the long run.

You will now finish your straight if you catch a King. As of now, you have only one way to make the straight, which could change on the turn. You are now hoping to catch one of the four Kings, which only gives you half as good a chance as an open-ended straight draw. At about 12.5:1 against, the pot must be quite large to justify staying in. If you were to have two suited cards, your hand would be slightly more playable, but don't count on making a living chasing gut shots.

Danger Flops

In previous discussions, we've described the various ways in which a hand has both strengths and weaknesses. We'll now specifically identify three scenarios you will commonly confront.

First, you could have a straight draw with two suited cards on the board. For example, you hold Q♠T♠, are against an opponent holding A♦4♦, and the flop in Figure 9.12 appears.

Figure 9.12 Be careful of potential flushes.

In this specific case the flush draw will win 70.5 percent of the money, as it is more likely a flush will come by the end of the hand with nine remaining diamonds out versus the six non-diamond straight cards. The news is much better if you are against A♦4♦ and the flop in Figure 9.13 appears.

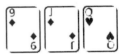

Figure 9.13 Making a hand on the flop improves your winning chances significantly.

In this case you would still have a straight draw but also a pair of Queens, the percentages change to 56.3:43.7 percent in your favor. We can work with that!

The second kind of seemingly vulnerable hand is when you flop a straight or a flush draw, but there is a pair on board. Let's say you have Q♠T♠, and the flop in Figure 9.14 appears.

Figure 9.14 This hand is dangerous for straight draws.

Against three random hands you will win 32 percent of the money, which isn't so bad. Check and call one bet here if you want to play conservatively. If you want to be a little cheeky, you can go for a check-raise, as flush draws will be afraid of a third Nine, and a Nine will be afraid of a flush draw as well as a Nine with a higher kicker. Danger hands for you here are of the JT or J9 variety, as they give the opponent a second pair, trips, or even a full house. These are both commonly played hands, so watch the betting pattern.

Straightforward play would be to check a Nine on the flop and bet it on the turn because of its strength, while a Jack will likely be bet out to get rid of straight draws. If someone does have a third Nine, such as A♥9♥, you are a major underdog, winning only 26.5 percent of the money. Against AJ, you are on the wrong end of the equation, but not as badly at 61:39

percent against. At this point, you need to decide whether the pot is large enough to stay in. More about that in a bit.

A flush draw with a paired board puts you in no better shape. Let's say you hold Q♠T♠, and you get the flop in Figure 9.15.

Figure 9.15 Potential flushes rarely beat made trips.

Against A♥6♥ you are a 25.2:74.8 percent loser going to the turn. Hey, the player holding the Six has made their hand and is more than happy to let you come a-chasing. Your one saving grace is that a player holding the Six will often check the flop, so you will perhaps get a free shot at one of the nine spades in the deck. It's even worth calling one bet if the pot's big enough. If you call two bets, turn off your computer and go to bed—you're too tired to play any more tonight.

Finally, we'd like to talk about when you flop two pair, but there is both a straight draw and a flush draw on the flop. Admittedly, this is not as common of an occurrence as the other two situations, but it will happen. Let's say you're in the big blind with 9♣7♥. Ick. Yuck. Never play these two cards, unless no one raises. If, by some miracle, you get to click Check and see the flop, you might see the miracle shown in Figure 9.16.

Yippee! You've hit the Big Blind Special. But have you? This hand is good, but there are a lot of ways it can lose. First, any-one playing JT will have a straight, leaving you with four cards (the remaining Nines and Sevens and, OK, two running Eights, whatever…) to win the pot. You are officially an 82:18 percent underdog as of now. Against a Ten or a Six, giving one op-ponent an open-ended straight draw, however, you are a solid favorite at 69.4:30.6 percent. Aggressive players will push

Figure 9.16 Sometimes trash turns to gold, then back to trash.

their straight draws, so it may behoove you to *bet* or *raise for information*. If a re-raise comes, it will be best to slow down, unless the turn gives you your miracle. If it looks like the turn completed someone's straight, and there are a few players left, it may just be time to cut your losses. Look at the pot, though, and think hard before mucking two pair. Just how crazy are these folks? One more big bet in limit poker rarely kills anyone, especially against only one other player. If someone has a *double draw* with A♦T♦, you are virtually 50:50 percent to win the pot.

A Final Hold 'Em Scenario: Love Those Aces

A lot of money is lost when a player *falls in love* with a great starting hand that doesn't end up so well when all the cards have come out. Some folks just can't stand losing with pocket Aces. Tragically, it happens all the time. Against three other random hands before the flop, pocket Aces won 63.8 percent of the money in our simulation. With the all-too-common seven players seeing the flop, however, it only wins 43.3 percent of the money. Even though this is true, give us Aces anytime! Remember, we're only as good as the flop. For example, you look down and see A♠A♣, so you raise and get three callers. You are against two pretty good hands: J♣9♣ and 6♥6♦and a random hand. The flop comes, as shown in Figure 9.17.

Figure 9.17 Your Aces are probably still the best hand.

With the hands as described, your pair of Aces is a heavy favorite, as J♣9♣ must either complete a straight, catch two running clubs, both a Jack and a Nine, or two of either by the end of the hand. In this scenario, your Aces will win 49.7 percent of the money, according to our simulation. J♣9♣ will win 34.6 percent, and the pair of Sixes will win 6.3 percent with the random fourth hand winning 8.9 percent, which tells you how strong the Sixes are in this situation. If, however, the flop is just a little different, as in T♦Q♣3♣, the statistics change dramatically as to the relative strength of the Aces versus the other hands. Because of the double draw J♣9♣ now enjoys, it is projected to win 49 percent of the money, while the pocket Aces will only win 39.7 percent. Those are still pretty strong odds for the *pocket rockets*, but when two draws are out there things change dramatically.

A brief note on Pineapple: Because you must discard one of your three cards before the turn, you will obviously need to decide your best two-card combination. If you have A♠A♥5♥, what are the chances you'll be mucking an Ace, do you figure? Pretty good, if the flop shown in Figure 9.18 appears.

Figure 9.18 Sometimes choosing which card to get rid of is easy.

The Ace of spades will be in the muck in the blink of an eye, its services no longer required. Obviously, a pair of Aces is a very strong starting hand, so chances are you'll be discarding the non-Ace more often than not. It all depends on how the flop fits your hand.

Omaha High and High-Low Flops

In both varieties of Omaha, some key questions to answer are these: How close am I to the nut hand and how far do I need to go to get there? If I have the nut hand on the flop, do I have a *redraw* that can make me even better? How many players am I against? What do I know about how they play? Finally, a key question:

What are the chances I'm playing for half or less of the pot?

Omaha High Flops

Of all the things you need to consider in Omaha games, how close you are to the nut hand and how you could only be in contention for less than the entire pot have everything to do with whether or not you should still be in the hand and how much money you should be investing. If you're way out in front, it is your duty as a profit-maximizing poker player to get your money in. In Hold 'em, it's possible you'll lose all your action if you push too hard on the flop, but in Omaha the possibilities are almost endless. This does mean you'll sometimes end up snatching defeat from the jaws of victory, but knowing where you are relative to other likely hands is paramount in Omaha. Let's look at some basic situations in which it appears your hand is strong but is in fact weak. Suppose you hold Q♥K♥T♠J♣, and you get the flop shown in Figure 9.19.

Figure 9.19 In Omaha, the nuts don't often stay nutty.

You have flopped the nut straight! As Andy Garcia's character said to Brad Pitt's character on the phone in *Ocean's Eleven*, "Congratulations, you're a dead man." The problem you are facing is that you have no redraw to speak of. The only way you could improve your hand is by making a full house, which would mean another King and one of your other cards would have to come runner-runner or two Queens, Tens, or Jacks would need to come runner-runner. Two Kings runner-runner would give you quads, but that's not terribly likely. The odds of exactly two cards coming on the turn are about 1,000 to 1. It's called *perfect-perfect* by the player who hits it and *@#%*$%! perfect-perfect* by the victim. But wait! You may say, "I thought I flopped the nuts. Doesn't that mean I have the best hand?" Yes, it does, but the problem is, the nuts can usually change when the next card comes. If the J♦ comes, for example, the nut hand has changed from an Ace-high straight to a Royal Flush, completed by Q♦T♦. Let's see how your straight on the flop holds up against three other likely hands, as seen in Figure 9.20.

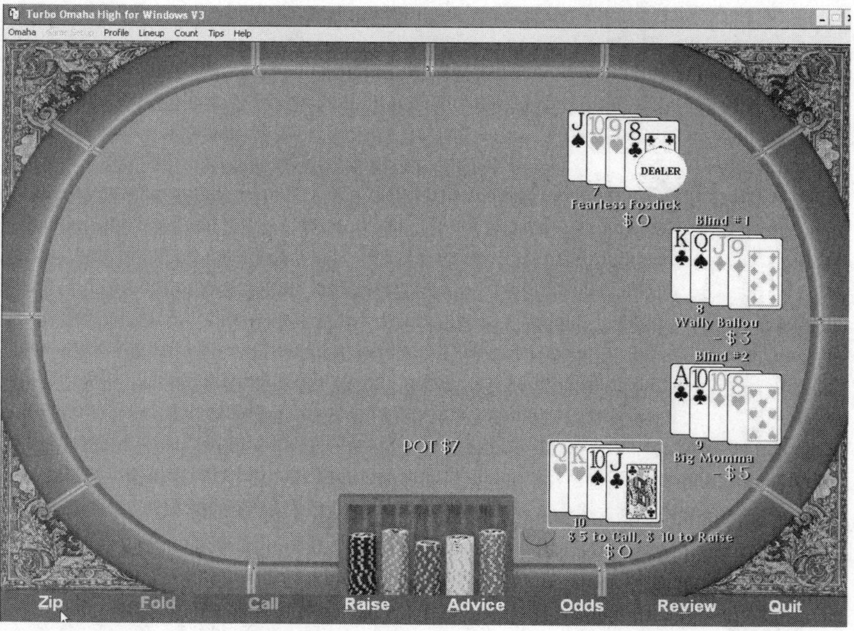

Figure 9.20 Nut straight but no good!

As amazing as it may seem, the nut straight hand with no redraw is close to dead against these hands. See Table 9.1 for how the simulation results break down.

Table 9.1   Omaha High Hand Results

Hand	Percentage of Money Won (Flop = A♦K♦T♥)
Q♥K♥T♠J♣	27.8%
A♣T♣T♦8♥	18.7%
K♣Q♠J♦9♦	53.5%
J♠9♣9♥8♣	0.0%

The important thing to consider here is that the dominant hand is behind after the flop, in that the player has two pair and a flush draw to go against the made straight. But how in the world will this translate into 53.5 percent of the money? Let's walk through it.

First and foremost is the fact that the big hand has the straight along with you and a flush redraw. This hand is the only one with two diamonds in it, which means it can *only* make a flush. It wins even if four diamonds end up on the board; remember that in Omaha, exactly two cards from your hand must be used. No singleton flushes, full houses, or straights work in this game. One card is good to make quads when three of a kind end up on the board, though, as any other card from your hand will be used as the fifth one. But anyway, the straight is made, and the flush redraw is also there. What's interesting is that the set of Tens held by the second player isn't all that strong, winning a little less than one-fifth of all money. Most of this player's money will be won when the board pairs, giving them a full house without giving someone a higher full house. It's difficult for an underset full house (in this case the set is of lower rank than the pair) to win in Omaha, but obviously it does happen regularly. Be wary if the board has high cards with one of them paired up, as someone who likes to play *wrap hands* (hands with lots of straight and flush possibilities) might just have caught a better full house. A good friend calls Omaha high the place where you "peddle the nuts." She makes sense when she says these things.

You can likely see how the lowly J998 is hopeless. First, it has no flush draw. Second, it has no chance to *counterfeit* the Ace-high straight because the highest straight it can complete is King high. Remember, two cards must be used. A straight starting at Nine only makes it up to the King. In addition, any full house will lose because the Nines will lose to the set of Tens, or any other set will necessarily win out over this hand. Finally, it is impossible for the poor slob to catch four of a kind, as another player has a Nine in their hand. Check and fold—oh well.

The second hand we'll look at is a key example of how a positively raggedy hand turns into a *monster* in the blink of an eye. As an example, look at the following four hands before the flop:

Table 9.2   Omaha High Hand Percentages before The Flop

Hand	Percentage of Money Won
A♦A♣8♦T♠	36.6%
J♣9♣T♥4♠	19.7%
6♥6♦K♣J♥	22.3%
K♠Q♠7♦7♣	21.4%

As you can see, the pair of Aces has a diamond flush draw and two ways to make a nut straight (Ace-high with a board of King-Queen-Jack and Jack-high with a board of Jack-Nine-Seven) as well as full house possibilities with the best set possible (Aces). Note that the rest of the hands will also do well less often but still with regularity. The second hand has one almost useless card in the 4♠, but it does enjoy the only club flush draw and a three-card wrap straight opportunity. The third hand has a high-straight opportunity with the K♣J♥ combination and a pair of Sixes as well as a bad but sole heart flush draw. Finally, the fourth hand has a high spade draw with the King and Queen, the nut straight possibility, and a pair of Sevens. It all depends on the flop, then! Say it is the flop you see in Figure 9.21.

Figure 9.21 Once again, the flop determines your hand's value.

Everything changes with this flop. The new percentages are in Table 9.3.

Table 9.3   Omaha High Hand Percentages after the Flop

Hand	Percentage of Money Won (Flop = 6♠8♣K♦)
A♦A♣8♦T♠	16.0%
J♣9♣T♥4♠	15.2%
6♥6♦K♣J♥	62.2%
K♠Q♠7♦7♣	6.5%

As you see, the hand with the pocket Sixes is now dominant. Even without a flush draw, as no hearts are on board, the set of Sixes after the flop approaches the two-thirds mark in total money won. Not only is it the only hand that will make a full house if the board pairs on the turn, but it will also make *Kings full of Sixes* if the *case* (only remaining) King comes before the end of the hand. The hand with the pair of Aces is drawing to another Ace to give it *top set*. Luckily for it, a third Ace on the turn will not give anyone a straight. It will also not complete a flush as the flop *came rainbow* (three different suits). It also has a *backdoor flush draw*, as runner-runner diamonds on the turn and river will win the pot. In fact, in this example, it is impossible for the board to pair if two diamonds do in fact show up. Can you see how that is? Notice the flop has one diamond, the King. Now see that the other two ranks, Six and Eight, already have the diamond accounted for in the third and first hands, respectively.

In pure matter of fact, this is a false dilemma, because in a board game like Omaha it is impossible to know specific cards are *dead* (out of play or in play in another hand) unless you yourself hold them (in brick-and-mortar games, cards may be exposed accidentally or people may not protect their hand well enough). But the ability to answer the question we posed to you demonstrates a skill that a poker player needs to succeed: Know what can beat you. In brick-and-mortar Stud, the ability to follow dead cards is critical.

Let's talk about the fourth hand, and incorporate the second into the discussion. The fourth hand has very limited possibilities and only wins 6.5 percent of the money over time. The only way it wins is if the turn and river cards both help it. The best way for it to win is for the two remaining Sevens to come *perfect-perfect*. A slightly more plausible way for it to win is for a King and a Queen to come, giving the player the best full house possible in that situation. A King and a third Seven would also give it a winning full house. But what if a Seven comes on the turn? Wouldn't that mean this hand is now crushing the set of Sixes? Yes, but that's not relevant because the second hand has just completed a Jack-high straight. So many possibilities? Yep. Welcome to Omaha. The player holding the straight would then hope something like the 3♥ comes on the river, as it would not pair the board, complete a flush, nor enable a higher straight. The second hand has several ways to make a straight, but it's a big underdog because there are a lot of ways for a higher straight, a flush, and a full house to *make* by the end of the hand.

Omaha High-Low Flops

If you thought the Omaha high-only discussion fills your brain to capacity, you're right, it does. When you add the ability of a low hand or hands to take half the pot, the complexity of the situation simply explodes. That being said, Omaha high-low is Doug's favorite game. It's a fickle lover, though. When luck is on your side, this game is the sweetest, but when it's not, it's the most bitter. Not for the faint of heart...

With that pleasant thought in your head, let's see what we can do with some good cards. We'll start with the mother of all Omaha high-low hands, *Ace-Ace-Deuce-Three Double-Suited*. This is strong in several ways. First, the holder has two *nut flush* draws. Second, they have a pair of Aces; and while it is common for a third and (less often) all four Aces to be accounted for, it does in fact mean that if an Ace does appear, it makes a possibility for the best full house (Aces full of Deuces or Threes). Playing four-handed against three random hands AA23 double-suited will win 43.3 percent of the money. So it's a little more than twice as likely to win money. But how could the best starting hand only be a 2:1 favorite over three *random* hands, you may ask?

First, a low hand will only be possible around 50 percent of the time. Remember, in order for a low hand to qualify, there must be at least three different cards ranked Eight or lower on the board, and a player must be able to use two cards ranked Eight or lower from their hand to complete a five-card low.

A qualifying low hand only shows up about half the time in Omaha high-low.

Second, flushes don't come regularly. True, you'll have twice the chance with a double-suited hand, but it's still not something you can count on. In addition, there is no way for this hand to make the nut straight unless it is *the wheel* (a Five-high straight). This is often good for a *scoop* (winning the entire pot), but it's vulnerable to redraws. For example, if someone's in the big blind and no one raises, they get to play 6♥7♣8♠9♦ for time served, er, what they've already put in the pot. Assume you see the flop shown in Figure 9.22.

Figure 9.22 Even this flop can produce unexpected winners.

An Ace-Deuce now gives you both the best low hand and what is known as the *ignorant straight*, or a straight made with two cards from your hand connecting on the low end of the cards on the board. You may also have a backdoor flush draw if you have clubs, spades, or diamonds. If you have no flush possibilities, though, the only way you can win the high part of the pot is if you catch a combination of Aces, Deuces, and Threes to make a full house. In addition, as we'll talk about in the next chapter, it is very possible that you may need to split the low portion of the pot with at least one other player. You will learn to hate the thought of getting *quartered*, which happens when you split the high or the low part of the pot with another player (a half of a half is a quarter). Twenty-five percent of the pot is certainly better than nothing, but it stinks relative to what you're hoping for.

With the flop we just described, you know you'll at least be getting some of the money back at the end of the hand that you initially put in the pot. A much more dicey situation comes if you have A♣2♣A♦3♦, and you get the flop in Figure 9.23.

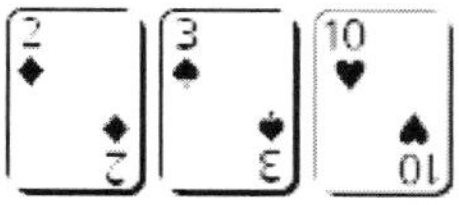

Figure 9.23 It's sad when a good hand goes bad.

Quite frankly, this flop is an unmitigated disaster. Your low draw is *counterfeited*, in that the Two and Three in your hand are now repeated on the board. The new *nut low draw* is Ace-Four, as it would make the Four-Three-Two-Ace countdown. The only way you can make a low is if two more low cards come, and then they would need to be a Four and a Five to make the nut low. We'll talk more about the low draws on the turn, but rest assured, if you get this flop with that hand, you'll be talking to yourself. In looking at the high part of the hand, you're in even more trouble, as you have *bottom two pair*. Anyone with a Ten and other cards will almost certainly make a better two pair, and chances are a straight draw will make. A pair of Tens is especially deadly with this flop. Our simulation established that the AA23 hand will only win 8.4 percent of the money against a player with a pocket pair of Tens and two random cards and two players with completely random hands. The set of Tens wins 49.4 percent of the money, which accounts for when its set of Tens holds up as well as when some sort of straight or random low holds up. The AA23 hand is basically hoping an Ace and another Two or Three comes or that it makes a low no one else can beat. As we mentioned in the Omaha high–only discussion, it's all about how you fit the flop. This situation is a great time to fold and curse your luck.

A much more common occurrence is for a flop to hit you pretty well but not perfectly. For instance, assume you have A♥2♥K♠5♠ and you see the flop in Figure 9.24.

Figure 9.24 This flop probably helped your opponents more than it helped you.

The possibilities are so numerous as to border on the absurd. The only thing you do know is that you will not be making a straight flush, four of a kind, or a full house. Remember, without a pair or three to a straight flush on the flop, it is impossible to make these hands. What you do have is bottom pair, an easily beaten low, and two possibilities to make a runner-runner flush (hearts and spades). Unless there is a lot of money in the pot, this may be a good hand to minimize your losses. First, any of several commonly played low combinations beat you. Any Ace-Three, Ace-Four, and Three-Four beats you as of this moment. If there are four players in the pot, it's safe to assume at least one of them has a better low draw than you have. Because at least one of the cards you're looking for is dead, you are not shooting for four or eight cards, but rather seven, six, or even fewer. The news doesn't get any better on the high side of the hand. Many players will have played a pocket pair of Queens and will now have a set. A set of Eights is also a threat. It is also very possible for someone to have played a wrap-style hand containing one each of a Nine, Ten, and Jack. What this *wrap straight draw* does is allow for any of those three cards to give the holder a straight, with the Nine making the nut straight at that moment. You have a runner-runner draw to the nut straight, as a Ten and a Jack give you the best straight assuming no flush is made, but this is a long way to walk for the high half, no matter what possibility you consider.

On the other hand, if the flop is only slightly different, such as 3♠8♥Q♦, your hand is now going to be good for the low much more frequently. While not all that great as a high hand, there are still possibilities. At this point, it becomes necessary to ascertain how many players still in the hand are going for the low along with you. The easy rule of thumb when going for the low is that if there is an even number of players in the hand and half or fewer are in competition for the low, as best you can tell, it is worth staying in. This is especially true if you have any realistic shot at the high as well. To be perfectly honest, this hand does not have much expectation to win the high side of the pot, as you need help on both the turn and the river. The low side is robust because it has the Five as backup in case a Deuce comes on the turn or river, counterfeiting your nut low. The best thing you have going for you is that any Ace-Three is counterfeited, and now only an Ace-Four beats you. While very possible, the good news is that if it's the 2♠, you now have the second-nut flush draw. We did say earlier that this game is all about showing down nut hands, but two second-nut hands isn't as bad as it could be. Try as hard as you can to will the A♠, or especially the 4♠, to come on the river just in case, though.

Seven-Card Stud Fourth Street

In Stud (high only), much more information is available to a player, and decisions may be made based on dead cards. Remember, because no cards are shared, any card an opponent has is by definition not going to be in your hand. As in Omaha, the impact of a hand containing four cards working together, versus only three, can be dramatic. Let's look at some percentages.

In this hand, there are four players: three known hands and a random hand. We ask that you suspend disbelief and assume it contains no cards impacting the three known hands' draws because, believe us, you'll find some hands that seem to have been truly played randomly. Table 9.4 lists the hands and the percentages of total money won.

Table 9.4	Seven-Card Stud Sample Fourth Street
Hand	Percentage of Money Won
A♦A♣8♦T♠	46.1%
J♣9♣T♥4♠	15.2%
6♥6♦K♠J♥	23.5%
Random	15.2%

Because two hands with no cards in common will catch a third card of their pair, a second pair, make a straight, and catch three suited cards in a row to complete a flush in equal amounts over time, the pair of Aces is approximately a 2:1 favorite over the pair of Sixes. The most likely ways for J♣9♣T♥4♠ to win are to catch two cards to make a straight (three of which, the 8♦, the K♠, and the J♥, are dead), to make trips, a better or the only two pair, or preferably to make a club flush. It's still possible to make four of a kind or a full house, but that's even more unlikely than the hands described above. Let's look at what happens, though, if a single card is changed in the second hand (see Table 9.5).

Table 9.5	Seven-Card Stud Sample Fourth Street
Hand	Percentage of Money Won (Q♠ Replaces 4♠)
A♦A♣8♦T♠	33.7%
J♣9♣T♥Q♠	36.8%
6♥6♦K♠J♥	17.8%
Random	11.8%

The massive difference between the synergy of three cards and four cards working together is obvious when comparing Table 9.4 to Table 9.5. With three cards to go, four cards to a straight with a unique flush draw (only this hand is able to make a club flush) is now a slight favorite over the pair of Aces. In this particular example, the straight draw now has three chances to catch a King or an Eight. It could also win by making two pair, if no other known hand does (Aces-up and Kings-up definitely win against this hand) or by catching three consecutive spades. The guy letting his cat play on the random hand still wins about 1/8 to 1/9 of the time, though.

If you are playing a drawing hand, each type of hand it is "working," that is, a four-card straight and two or three to a flush, makes it stronger. Beware the big pocket pair!

Seven-Card Stud High-Low Fourth Street

This game allows for even more control in some ways, as you will be able to see if your or another's hand is the only one eligible to win the low side of the pot when you get to fifth street. Let's assume the guy's cat is off to the litter box and the human is back on the game and gets a good low hand: 2345. For this section we'll explore how well different variations of this fare against two of the three hands we talked about in the last section.

First, 2345 is of four different suits. The results are shown in Table 9.6.

Table 9.6 Seven-Card Stud High-Low Sample Fourth Street: 2345 Unsuited	
Hand	Percentage of Money Won
A♦A♣8♦T♠	22.2%
J♣9♣T♥Q♠	29.4%
2♦3♣4♥5♠	48.4%

Whoever knew Deuce-through-Five could be so strong? If you play high-low Stud, you'll know it's extremely powerful. The main thing working against this hand is that it doesn't have a flush draw, and two of its cards to make a straight: the A♦ and the A♣ are dead. It, therefore, has three chances to catch one of six cards (the remaining two Aces and any of the four Sixes) to make its straight and low simultaneously. The problem with this is that the four-card straight draw in the second hand has one more card it can catch (Seven, as one Eight and no Kings are dead) to make a better straight. In addition, it can be harder than one thinks to make a low in Stud. While this hand will very often make a winning low, it will not always do so. The second hand has no chance of a low, but the first hand can catch three consecutive low cards to qualify. In case no low hand qualifies, as you remember, the highest hand takes the entire pot. The good news here is that the third hand will be contributing 33.3 percent of the total money in the pot, collecting 48.4 percent of it when the hand's over. Poker players thank their lucky stars for this kind of advantage.

Let's now see what happens if the low hand has two suited cards other than diamonds or clubs, as the other hands hold those draws. Table 9.7 has the results.

Perhaps you're surprised the flush draw didn't make that much of a difference. In this hand, three hearts would need to come on the last three cards to make a flush, which this simulation indicates would happen 0.6 percent of the time. That's six times per one thousand opportunities. The good news is that you're still betting and raising all you can because you are still getting back way more than you're investing. Three suited cards are shown in Table 9.8.

Table 9.7   Seven-Card Stud High-Low Sample Fourth Street 2345 with Two Hearts

Hand	Percentage of Money Won
A♦A♣8♦T♠	22.2%
J♣9♣T♥Q♠	28.8%
2♥3♣4♥5♠	49.0%

Table 9.8   Seven-Card Stud High-Low Sample Fourth Street 2345 with Three Hearts

Hand	Percentage of Money Won
A♦A♣8♦T♠	20.6%
J♣9♣T♥Q♠	26.0%
2♥3♥4♥5♠	53.4%

We're above 50 percent now with an increased expectation of 4.4 percent, but we've been unable to really jump into complete dominance. That doesn't happen until all four of the low hand's cards are suited, in which case it will win approximately 70 percent of all money bet. It's interesting to think about: The difference between catching two of the same suit out of three cards is only 4.4 percent more money collected than needing to receive three in the last three cards. Flushes are hard to make in Stud! Still, every little bit helps, and as we've said before, if you're not betting and raising as much as possible with the low hand, you're making a big mistake.

Miller, Sklansky, and Malmuth's Odds-Based Approach to Determining the Correct Action

Part of knowin' when to hold 'em and when to fold 'em when playing rationally comes from knowing your chances of winning the pot in relation to how much you must invest to stay in versus the total money in the pot. David Sklansky and Mason Malmuth have written a large number of poker and general gambling books and articles over the years. We would recommend that you read as many of them as possible. We have! Ed Miller joined their team to write the excellent book *Small Stakes Hold 'Em: Winning Big With Expert Play* (Two Plus Two Publishing, 2004). In this and other books, they discuss the role of odds in a player's decision-making process during hands. They break the discussion down into four key areas: Pot Odds, Implied Odds, Reverse Implied Odds, and Pot Equity. We'll summarize their points here.

When deciding how many cards will either win you a hand or get you one step closer to winning it, you must first come to a conclusion as to what hand or range of hands your opponent(s) is playing.

Pot Odds

Simply put, this divides the amount of the money already in the pot by how much it will cost you to stay in the hand. If there is $10 in the pot and it will cost you $2 to stay in, for example, you are receiving 5:1 pot odds. Table 9.9 lists the odds of completing your draw based on how many outs you have. Pot odds become much more important on the turn and river, so we'll leave the detailed discussion for then.

Implied Odds

Implied odds, the authors say, is current expectation adjusted for future betting. What this means is, it will almost certainly cost you more money to stay in the hand in future rounds. It is here that your betting position plays a large role. Let's say you flop an open-ended straight draw, in which case eight cards will win you the hand, with a 4.75:1 shot on each card to come. Assume you will *only* win the hand if you make your straight but will *definitely* win the hand if you get the straight. If you are last to act, the first player bets, the second player calls, and you are now required to invest $2 into a $10 pot. This is good because it is a 5:1 investment. But wait! This is in fact a 5:1 investment for a 2.375:1 shot at this moment. The reason this is so is because there are two more cards to come, so you get two chances at your draw. This does assume you'll stay in until the river, but in this example, you will definitely win if you make the straight, so it would be hard to get you out. In a real game, you must figure out when it would be best to fold.

Constantly update how worthwhile it will be for you to stay in the hand and how to go about betting. Are you going to win if you hit your draw? Which cards could come on the turn that would guarantee your win or make your hand vulnerable or even a definite loser? What betting position are you in? How can you maximize your profits or minimize your losses by implementing a particular betting pattern?

Table 9.9   Pot Odds Needed to Make Calling Correct

Number of Outs	Break-Even Pot Odds
1	45:1
2	22:1
3	14.3:1
4	10.5:1
5	8.2:1
6	6.7:1
7	5.6:1
8	4.75:1
9	4.1:1
10	3.6:1
11	3.2:1
12	2.8:1
13	2.5:1
14	2.2:1
15	2.1:1
16	1.9:1
17	1.7:1
18	1.6:1

Source: Miller, Sklansky and Malmuth; 2004; p. 30

Let's look at a more realistic example. You are the first to act against two other players. There is $6 in the pot. You hold Q♣J♦, and the flop in Figure 9.25 appears.

You now have an open-ended straight draw, as either an Eight or a King gives you the nut straight. If you *bet for information*, to see how the other players feel about needing to call a bet to stay in, and get raised and re-raised, what should you do? There is now $18 in the pot, and you need to call $4 more to stay in (4.5:1 pot odds).

Figure 9.25 Aggressive players will make you pay to draw to your straight.

First, you need to decide what you are up against. Because there was no raise before the flop, it's unlikely anyone has a pair of Aces. It could be that a player limped in with a pair of Tens or Nines, so you may up against a set. But it's more likely that someone played Ace-Ten or Ace-x. You are assuredly behind in the hand but have some good things going for you. First, because the other players are thought to have Aces, three are accounted for, so only seven cards (the Ace and three remaining Tens and Nines) hurt you. Eight cards give you your winning straight, so you are in the same situation as you were earlier in the chapter: putting 1/3 of the money into a pot you have a better than 50 percent chance of collecting. Assuming you are against competing Aces-up hands, Table 9.10 gives the results.

Table 9.10 Hold 'Em Hand with a Flop of A♥T♣9♠	
Hand	Percentage of Money Won
Q♣J♦	30.4%
A♦T♦	61.0%
A♣9♥	8.6%

Our simulation shows that you will win 30.4 percent of all money with your straight draw versus these hands. As 30 percent is a little less than a third, the money from the first round, and any money bet on the flop, will give you the needed odds to stay in for now. So what turn cards would cause you to change you mind? An Ace is certainly trouble, as is either a Ten or a Nine. Because we have perfect information, we know we are drawing dead if any of these cards come, but do you know that for sure, based on your knowledge of the players you're against? Could they be playing with a set? If you think so, then you'll need to see if other dangers, such as a flush draw, are out there. J8 is a possibility, so if a Seven comes, they get their straight.

Reverse implied odds show how a weak hand does not fare well, even when it is ahead on the flop. The following example is structured after one you can find on page 34 in Miller, Sklansky, and Malmuth's book (if, for example, you are in the big blind and three other players limp in). You hold 7♥3♦, and you get the flop in Figure 9.26.

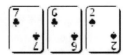

Figure 9.26 Handle the truth: You won't win.

There are so many ways to lose this hand that it's ridiculous. You wisely check, and there is a bet behind you. Folding is certainly the best action. Miller, Sklansky, and Malmuth argue the following:

> With a weak made hand, especially when the pot is small, reverse implied odds sometimes force you to fold when the pot odds seem to support continuing. You will be paying off a better hand for big bets far more often than someone will pay you off. When the pot is small, if there is a high chance you are either already beaten or will be outdrawn, fold marginal made hands (35, emphasis in original).

Pot Equity

Miller, Sklansky, and Malmuth define *pot equity* as "the dollar or bet equivalent to the percentage of the pot that you expect to win. That is, if the pot contains ten bets, and you have a draw to the nuts that will come in 20 percent of the time, your pot equity is two bets" (ibid). They isolate three areas in which this information helps a player decide on the best course of action.

- ✦ Pot equity tells you how much you are giving up if you fold. With 10 bets in the pot, you have a draw that will win you the pot 5 percent of the time. If you must call one bet to stay in, pot equity dictates that you fold, as your equity is only 0.5 of a bet.

- ✦ Pot equity helps you decide whether or not to grant a free card. In this case you must add together all your opponents' combined pot equity. If you are heads-up against a player you believe has an open-ended straight draw to beat you, you must decide if the player will pay you off more in the long run, after granting them a free card on the turn. In other words, if you know they'll fold on the river if they miss their straight, you need to make them pay to chase their draw.

- ✦ A strong drawing hand gives you a large amount of pot equity. For example, with the nut flush draw after the flop, you will have a slightly better than 1/3 chance of making your flush. While it will sometimes lose to a full house or better, that's life. With four opponents, the authors note, you are putting 20 percent of the money into the pot for a 35 percent chance of winning. You are operating at a 15 percent advantage. Get your money in the pot!

Conclusion: How Much Thinking Can One Do in a Minute?

For those of you just beginning your poker career, this may seem like an infinite number of possibilities to consider. In actuality, most of the situations you will run across confront you repeatedly. At the very first, poker can be a little overwhelming, but as you encounter situations you've been in before, you will get more and more comfortable about making your decisions quickly. This is why we suggest that until you are familiar with the game and the online environment that you play at a single table. You'll eventually be good enough to play multiple tables without any problem. After you've memorized that you have eight cards to complete an open-ended straight, you'll instantly know how much money has to be in the pot to call (10.5 bets), and you'll take the appropriate action. The short answer to the question posed in this section's title is that it can surprise you in both directions. When you know how to frame the questions and know what the numbers are, you can go into depth about opponent playing style, for instance. If you don't have the numbers memorized, you will be stuck figuring them out or making the dreaded "Oh, whatever..." call. Bad poker player—bad!

The Turn and Fifth and Sixth Streets

In a board game, we are now halfway through the betting. The initial betting round and the flop are much more wide ranging in their possibilities. With two more cards to come, several things can still happen. In Stud, there are still three betting rounds, but things are beginning to take shape, based on the dead cards from folded and other live hands. While several things can still happen, once you see the fourth of five cards, you should, over time, be able to realize where you are in the hand versus the other players. Through continuing the sample hands we gave you in the last chapter, we'll discuss how your fortunes have changed for better or worse. By the end of this chapter, you will know how to

- ✦ Evaluate how well you hit the turn.
- ✦ Evaluate how much "work" you need to do to make certain hands.
- ✦ Evaluate your hand relative to Sklansky, Malmuth, and Miller's pot-based odds.

The Fourth (or Fifth) Card Comes Out

In the board games, a fourth community card will be placed on the table, while in Stud games a third upcard will be added to each remaining player's hand, as shown in Figures 10.1 and 10.2.

The action in a board game will begin with the first active player to the left of the button. In Stud, as you remember, the highest hand showing begins the betting. So what's the new situation?

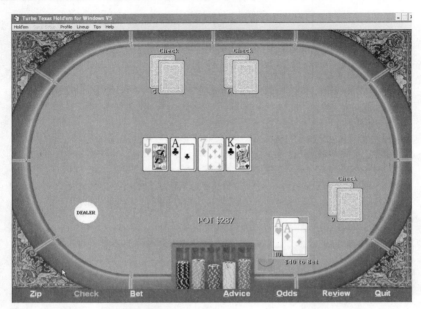

Figure 10.1 A sample Hold 'em turn

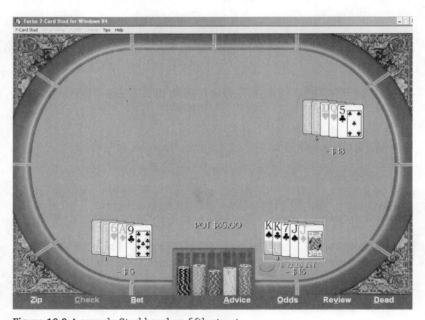

Figure 10.2 A sample Stud hand on fifth street

Hold 'Em Turns

Bingo! Some Hands Play Themselves, Part Deux

Just like on the flop, when this happens it's a real treat. For example, suppose you come in with J♥T♥, and you get the flop shown in Figure 10.3.

Figure 10.3 Can this flop get any better on the turn?

In this situation you had the then-nut straight with a straight flush redraw. This situation is very nice for you, as anyone with two hearts will be staying in if this is a low-limit game. Some players with a Six or a Ten will also likely stay in, just in case a straight card comes. There would have likely been a raise before the flop if someone had pocket Sevens, Eights, or Nines, but if there was enough action in a loose game, you could have certainly justified calling. Let's say you're up against a set of Sevens among other things, and the turn card is the 7♥.

As Vince van Patton says to Mike Sexton on the World Poker Tour telecasts, the "Star Spangled Banner" (or "O Canada" or "God Save the Queen" or another national anthem) is going off in your head! You're online, so you can dance a jig around the room if you want. But how to extract maximum money from the others? First, it depends on your position. If you're in early position, with several players it will often be good to go for a check-raise, as anyone with a full house or flush will certainly bet. A full house might go for a check from early position, but a flush will almost certainly bet to force someone with trip Sevens to pay for their draw. The standard play here would be to go ahead and raise on the turn rather than the river because any hands with high flushes and made full houses will stay in and maybe even re-raise! In online poker, you just never know what someone will call you down with. The other play would be to simply call on the turn. This could be good, especially if someone in front of you raises. It would then be worth it to go for the check-raise on the river because the other player will be convinced their hand is the winner. This is highly debatable because if the river is *checked around*, you will have lost two or three bets; but if you are convinced someone behind you will bet, go for it. Hey, if the hands are high enough, they may just raise you right back! These are indeed the good times.

An absolutely great way to trap people is when you make quads and someone else makes a full house with an overset. Let's say you limp in from late position with 4♣4♠ and the flop comes, as shown in Figure 10.4.

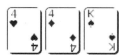

Figure 10.4 Flopping quads can be very profitable or kill your action.

This is a monster flop for you because no raisers before the flop likely means that no one is playing a pair of Kings. Two shots at a single card hits all the time, as in about one out of every 23 times; so while it's a bad beat when you lose, it's not beyond the realm of possibility that someone slowplaying pocket Kings will try to trap you—you're still in good shape. Let's say there are four players left after the flop, in which two players likely to have Kings have bet and someone representing Ace-Four has raised. You decided not to re-raise. The turn card is the K♦.

This card could be a little bit of a *scare card* for you, but the way we see it, if someone makes a higher four of a kind than you, all you can do is type "nh" (nice hand). Please refrain from typing "nhusob" (nice hand you….), as that would be impolite. You may think it as loudly as you want, however. The two players you believe have singleton Kings now believe they will be splitting the pot, unless they pair their other cards on the river. An interesting thing could happen if you are in position between the two Kings. Let's assume the player representing a third Four has nothing and bows out whenever it's their turn. Usually, being *caught in the middle* or *caught in between* two players is not what you want, as they can raise and re-raise after you've already called one bet. In this case, though, you have the absolute nuts, operating under the assumption all four Kings are accounted for on the board and in hands. After you call the first bet, the two Kings will raise and re-raise. At this point you may either call or raise again. If you think re-raising will scare away action on the river, simply call the three bets. If you think they'll keep on betting when a third Four doesn't show up on the river, go ahead and re-raise.

Another situation in which you may get paid is if someone decides to push an overpair on the flop. If you're in the big blind with the same pocket Fours as before and someone in early position raises you, *put them on* a big pair or at least AK. Suppose you hit it big and get the flop shown in Figure 10.5.

Figure 10.5 Wait in the weeds for your opponents to make a hand or bluff.

If one of your opponents holds A♣A♦, there's no way in the world someone would fold in this situation. Smart players will *raise for information* on the flop to see if someone has a Four. But you're deciding to lie low for now and bet and call their raise, or simply call their initial bet. Players with hands like K9s will now be loving their hands as well. The turn brings the A♠, and the trap is sprung. Of course, this could be any card higher than a Nine, as long as it makes the overset full house. Less-attentive or less-experienced players could believe Aces over Fours could now be the best hand. Even if you're going against two full houses (Aces full and Nines full), there are only two cards left in the deck to beat you. That means there is only a 1 in 22 chance either hand will improve. Bet and raise until the pot is capped, or they simply call you.

From the last chapter, you will remember we talked about hands in which you flop a very strong, but not invincible, hand. We'll continue on with the turn and bring in the next level of thinking about the hand. As you recall, you're in a hand with four other players before the flop with Q♥T♥ in the pocket, and you got the flop shown in Figure 10.6.

Figure 10.6 The turn could easily change this hand for the worse.

You now have the nut straight, but the nuts could change. Remember the following:

✦ You could be up against a spade (flush) draw. 5♠6♠ or any two spades would likely stay in, and 7♠8♠ is a straight flush draw.

✦ You could be up against a couple of different straight draws. Any Queen or Ten is drawing to tie you, while any Ace is drawing to beat you if a Queen or Ten comes by the end of the hand.

✦ You may be up against a "double draw," in which a player has to hit only one card to make either a straight or a flush. A♠T♠ makes a winning straight if a Queen comes and has the nut flush with any spade.

✦ You could be up against a set or two pair. If someone is playing K♥J♥, they will likely be in until the end, as any King or Jack gives them a full house.

The real vulnerability with this hand, as you will recognize from previous examples, is that your Q♥T♥ has no redraw. Therefore, you are now simply hoping nothing comes to beat you. Let's assume two other players, A♠T♠ and K♥J♥, are against you after the flop. Table 10.1 gives the percentages of total money won after the flop and after a *blank* (a card that helps no one) comes on the turn.

Table 10.1   Hold 'Em Hand Results

Hand	Percentage of Money Won	
	Flop (9♠J♠K♦)	Turn (2♣)
Q♥T♥	44.6%	66.7%
A♠T♠	37.0%	23.8%
K♥J♥	18.1%	9.5%

Using Miller, Sklansky, and Malmuth's odds-based system, let's explore what the betting and *action strategies* (whether to check, bet, raise, or fold and in what order) might look like in this hand.

Before the flop, it's very likely the A♠T♠ would have raised. Because five players stayed in, we'll assume one of them was the small blind, there are now 10 small bets (five big bets) in the pot. After the flop, the K♥J♥ with two pair would be likely to bet as a show of strength but also for information to see if the straight is out there. The flush draw could *raise on the come* (bet to give the impression they have the straight or perhaps a set) to try to get a free card on the turn. This is especially good in late position, because if the turn is checked around to the draw, it gets to *freeroll* (pay nothing to see) the river. If you have the straight and no redraw, it would likely be the best play to go ahead and get a raise or re-raise out there to force the drawing hands to pay to catch up. Let's assume the action is now three small bets (K♥J♥ bet, A♠T♠ raised, Q♥T♥ re-raised), K♥J♥ is laying about 5.25:1 implied odds (two chances at a 10.5:1 four-out draw) and must pay two more small bets after his initial bet to stay in. Assuming A♠T♠ will call, there will be 17 small bets (8.5 big bets) in the pot, which means calling is correct, as the *profit margin* is 3.25 small bets. (8.5 − 5.25 = 3.25) Two additional small bets will put 9.5 big bets in the pot for the turn.

The turn, as we noted, is a blank. The A♠T♠ flush draw is now a 4.1:1 underdog with nine outs, and the K♥J♥ two pair is a 10.5:1 underdog with four outs. There are now 9.5 bets in the pot. If the straight bets there will be 10.5:1 and 11.5:1 pot odds for the two callers, which justifies calling one bet. A flush draw should never bet after a re-raise on the flop, but if K♥J♥ is not convinced for some reason that their hand is trailing and bets, Q♥T♥ will happily raise. A♠T♠ will always call, which will put 14.5 big bets in the pot. K♥J♥ must now call one more bet for 14.5 pot odds with a 10.5:1 shot, so it doesn't matter that he bet initially, does it?

INCORRECT! K♥J♥ was foolish to bet initially as they could have stayed in for one bet, getting 10.5:1 or 11.5:1 pot odds, while two bets into what would be a 15.5 big bet pot will yield pot odds of only 7.75:1, which means K♥J♥ is now receiving 7.75:1 pot odds for a 10.5:1 draw. You get better odds at blackjack and craps. In the meantime, the made straight will win two-thirds of all money over time, so you will be willing to let anybody bet who wants to. The one caveat we would need to throw in is, if you believe you may be against another QT, it would mean your pot odds are cut in half. We'll talk about how to play redraws next.

The exception to playing K♥J♥ this way is if you have a very good idea your opponent would be willing to bluff with a draw or with an overpair. In that case, a bet could be considered.

Two Made Straights with One Enjoying a Redraw

This is a good opportunity for someone with a made hand to scoop a pot every now and then against a hand with no redraw. The important thing to do is, make certain a better flush draw does not stay in the pot. For example, suppose you play 8♠9♠ against three other players and see the flop shown in Figure 10.7.

Figure 10.7 You can draw to the nuts and improve again if the right cards hit.

You now have an open-ended straight draw and a backdoor flush draw. An aggressive player bets, and you call. Another player folds, and the final player calls. The turn brings the T♥, giving you the absolute nut straight and a redraw to a spade flush. The aggressive player bets, which could mean several things, including that they have a straight right along with you. So what to do? Doug had this happen to him at the Bellagio in a small-stakes ($4–$8) game. An aggressive player was taking a break from what we believe was a $30–$60 game and *playing over* (putting his own chips on the table and playing, while the original occupant is away from the table) his wife's seat. After he bet, Doug determined he likely had a straight along with him or was raising with a lesser hand. Because of the pot odds to call on the turn, the other player folded what we believe was a flush draw. The high-limit player yelled, "Sir, you're scaring away the customers!" But Doug wanted to be heads-up against the straight with no redraw in a small pot. It was a split pot, but Doug knew raising on the turn was correct because the player with the flush draw would either fold (because the pot wasn't big enough to chase) or would make an ill-advised call to go after the flush. Let's look at some numbers.

The first column of Table 10.2 shows the percentage of total money won by the three hands after the flop, if all stay in until the river. The second column shows the percentages if all three stay in after the turn, and the third column shows the percentages if the two straights stay in.

Table 10.2 Hold 'Em Hand Results		
Hand	Percentage of Money Won	
	Flop (4♠6♠7♦)	Turn (T♥ 3-handed)	Turn (T♥ 2-handed)
8♠9♠	16.5%	41.7%	60.2%
8♥9♥	16.2%	41.7%	39.8%
A♠3♠	67.3%	16.6%	(folded)

Because the player with the flush draw played correctly (which is not something you can count on), Doug's expectation increased by almost 20 percent. There were two big bets in the pot before the flop, and everyone checked when the flop came. Therefore, when there was a bet and a raise, there were only five big bets in the pot, which would have given the flush draw 2.5:1 pot odds for a 5.6:1 shot (seven remaining spades). Plus, he had to figure it was likely he would be re-raised. If the gentleman with the flush draw would have seen the rest of the cards, he would have won around 1/6 of the money while having to put in around 1/3 of it. Good fold, sir.

Partial Success Redux

In the last chapter, we talked about what kind of shape you would be in if you flopped hands like three of a kind, two pair, etc. What we'll do now is step you through what you're up against if some of the "danger" from a danger flop is realized!

Three of a Kind in Danger

You'll recall from last week's episode that you held 9♣9♠, and you got the flop shown in Figure 10.8.

Looking good, but there are lots of ways to become an underdog in a hurry. Worst-case scenario first: If the turn brings in the 7♦ or the Q♦, you are now in a lot of trouble. Table 10.3 shows what kind of shape you're in if you need to make a full house against a flush.

Figure 10.8 You're starting strong, but how will you finish?

Table 10.3	Hold 'Em Hand Results	
Hand	Percentage of Money Won	
	Flop (8♦9♦T♥)	Turn (7♦)
9♣9♠	56.1%	21.5%
A♦4♦	26.8%	78.5%
J♠T♠	17.1%	0.0%

The straight is now drawing dead. The good news for you is that any Seven, Eight, Nine, or Ten gives you a winning full house. This totals nine outs, a 4.1:1 shot (it would be 10 outs, but the J♠ is dead). The odds are the same against a made straight, as only a full house wins you the pot. Check and call.

Two Pair Endangered

In this situation, you're not going to be nearly as bad off as you were in the last example, but you will be threatened. You have T♥J♥, and you see the flop in Figure 10.9.

For this example, you're playing against two other players holding A♦5♦ and Q♠K♠.

Figure 10.9 In this scenario, your two opponents can find lots of ways to beat you.

There would likely have been at least one raise before the flop, but JTs is a good hand in a multi-way pot, so you stay in. Your hand is vulnerable in several ways. Most directly, an Ace gives the Ace-Five hand a better two pair, and another Five gives it trips. This hand also has a backdoor flush draw. The Queen-King has a backdoor flush draw, and a Nine or an Ace gives it the nut straight. Table 10.4 shows the difference if the turn comes with the K♦ as opposed to the 3♥.

Table 10.4   Hold 'Em Hand Results

Hand	Percentage of Money Won		
	Flop (5♣T♠J♠)	Turn (K♦)	Turn (3♥)
J♥T♥	46.0%	52.5%	64.4%
A♦5♦	4.3%	9.4%	2.4%
Q♠K♠	49.6%	38.1%	33.3%

If the turn makes a straight or a flush, as we've discussed before, you would need to hit a 4-out, 10.5:1 shot to make a full house. In this example, you're either in good shape or pretty good shape. We'll dispose of the long-shot hand first. The Ace-Five might be under the mistaken impression an Ace will give it a winner, but in reality it is looking for another Five or runner-runner diamonds to win. The two Aces, by the way, are *false outs* (cards you believe will win you the hand but will, in fact, make someone else the favorite or outright winner). In order to win, the Ace-Five hand must have another Five or Ace show up on the river. This is, you guessed it, a four-outer. What are the odds on a four-outer? That's right! 10.5:1.

You've no doubt noticed by now that situations such as four-outers, two-outers, and nine- or eight-outers occur quite frequently. You will soon memorize the odds of these draws coming in. This will speed up your game as well as make it more statistically correct. Don't forget to multiply the odds by some sort of "BS" factor, though, if you think your opponent is bluffing. Don't be afraid to raise someone if you believe they're trying to steal your lunch money.

If the turn is not a diamond, then only one of the two remaining Fives wins the hand.

The Queen-King is in a different situation entirely. It, in fact, has a double draw to a spade flush and the nut straight, which makes it a strong hand to hold, especially if the Ace-Five player decides to put more money in the pot after the turn. If the turn brings the King, any King or Queen will give this hand a winner with a higher two pair than Jacks over Tens. If the Three is on the turn, there is only the double draw to wait for. It could be much worse.

Overpair

In this situation, in which you have a pocket pair higher than the highest card on the board, you can either be in great shape or in horrible shape. Our guy Smitty had a great drawing hand that didn't make in the last chapter. Let's see how some other situations are likely to play out. If you raise with Q♥Q♠ and get two callers before the flop, you can assume one or more of the following will be true:

✦ You are up against at least one overcard. Many players will not call a raise unless they have an Ace or a King with their other card complementing it. If this is the case, you will also know.

✦ You have two of the outs overcards would need in order to make a straight. As an added bonus, if another Queen comes, you have at least a set and maybe a full house!

✦ You could very well be up against a lower pocket pair. Heads-up, a higher pair is about a 4:1 favorite over a lower one. Of course, if you get re-raised…

✦ You could be up against AA, KK, or AK. You're a slight favorite over AK, but a 4:1 underdog against a higher pair.

In hands in which several good hands are butting heads, there's the possibility of big hands beating slightly less-big hands. It's not unusual for an Ace-high flush to beat an Ace-high straight, and a full house will often show up when a flush is made.

> Be very aware when a *make you, make me* situation comes up. For example, Doug recently made an Ace-high flush while playing in Atlantic City. What he failed to realize is that the card giving him the flush also paired the board and gave the winner a full house. Always be aware! This is a very common occurrence. That's a horrible mistake for an (allegedly) good player to make, but make it he did.

We'll now turn to some statistical analysis of how big hands compete against each other. First, we'll set the hands for your two opponents as A♦T♦ and K♣J♣, and the flop as shown in Figure 10.10.

Figure 10.10 Your overpair could hold up against your opponents' hands.

The pocket Queens are still in the lead as of the flop, but it is directly vulnerable to any Jack, King, or Ace, as a Jack will give an opponent trips, and a King or Ace will make someone two pair. As of the flop, however, both hands are either on a draw or are behind. If the turn is the Q♦, you have now made a power set of Queens but are now threatened on the river by *discovered outs* (outs that did not exist on the flop but appeared on the turn). Specifically, any diamond except the Jack or Four gives the Ace-Ten hand a flush. You'll notice that the Jack and Four of diamonds pairs the board and gives you a full house. On the other hand, all the outs from the flop for a higher two pair are now eliminated. The Jack will make it possible for KJ to make quads on the river, but we'll let them go for those every time. If, on the other hand, the turn is the 8♣, you are still in the lead, but there are several things that can go wrong on the river because K♣J♣ now has a flush draw, and A♦T♦ has an open-ended straight draw (see Table 10.5).

Table 10.5   Hold 'Em Hand Results

Hand	Percentage of Money Won		
	Flop (9♦J♥4♣)	Turn (Q♦)	Turn (8♣)
Q♥Q♠	57.8%	64.3%	52.4%
A♦T♦	18.0%	28.5%	14.3%
K♣J♣	24.2%	7.1%	33.3%

Overcards

Playing overcards on the flop isn't that hard to justify, as long as the action is only one small bet. It gets more debatable on the turn if you don't hit. In the last chapter, we held A♣K♦ and saw the flop shown in Figure 10.11.

Figure 10.11 You're drawing to make a pair on the turn.

Notice that A♣K♦ has no chance of making either a flush or a straight. Trips would be the best we could do with one pair being the most likely. Remember from the last chapter that you could be drawing dead if you are against A9 and/or K9, because what gives you one pair would give those hands two pair. Against both A9 and K9, you would have no way to win. Against one of them, you will only win about 13.2 percent of all money. Just for the sake of argument, let's assume you are not reverse dominated but are against two playable but not incredible hands like Q♦9♦ and J♠9♠.

In this case, you stand half a chance because any Ace or King will put you ahead, forcing them to draw for another Nine, Queen, or Jack. First, let's see what happens when all the turn accomplishes is to give someone else a flush draw. In this case it needs to be a diamond, so the 3♦ will suffice. But what happens if you hit an overcard and make top pair going to the river? If the turn is the K♥, you are now looking good. Table 10.6 shows where you are in these hands.

Table 10.6 Hold 'Em Hand Results

Hand	Percentage of Money Won		
	Flop (9♣5♥2♦)	Turn (3♦)	Turn (K♥)
A♣K♦	22.5%	19.1%	83.5%
Q♦9♦	65.0%	76.1%	9.5%
J♠9♠	12.5%	4.8%	7.1%

The real trick here, as we mentioned in the last chapter, is to be able to figure out if you're up against two pair or not. Knowing how your opponents play is one way. Betting for information is another, possibly more expensive, way. One good clue would be the action before and on the flop. If there hasn't yet been a raise, you may well have the best hand. Calling one bet would be good here, but it becomes marginal if there is a raise. If you think they're semi-bluffing with a Nine or with a King with *kicker issues* compared to your Ace, get on in the pot, but raise with extreme caution.

Flush Draws and Straight Draws

These were talked about by themselves in the last chapter, but they have been covered quite extensively in our discussions of other types of hands earlier in the chapter. To see where you are with these draws, we ask that you place yourself in the role of the opponents in those hands.

Love Those Aces, But It's Like a Nightmare. . .

And it just keeps getting worse, as the famous "right back at you" between Tom Cruise's character and Grady Seasons went in *The Color of Money*. There will be times on the flop when you are likely in trouble, but there will be plenty of times on the turn when you should know without a doubt that you are mortally wounded. You look down and see A♣A♠, so you raise and get three callers. You are against two pretty good hands: J♣9♣ and 6♥6♦.

If the flop comes as shown in Figure 10.12, you'll be a slight underdog.

If the turn is an Eight or a Queen, you are drawing dead, as the best you do is make trip Aces. If the turn is the 6♣, you are also drawing dead because you cannot beat a flush or a full house. The random hand is long gone, of course. The best you can hope for is a blank, such as the 4♥. Table 10.7 shows the percentages with this turn of events.

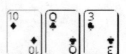

Figure 10.12 Aces are great, but only until you see the flop.

Table 10.7   Hold 'Em Hand Results

Hand	Percentage of Money Won	
	Flop (T♦Q♣3♣)	Turn (4♥)
A♣A♠	44.7%	64.5%
J♠9♠	51.2%	33.2%
6♥6♦	4.1%	2.4%

The double draw now has one shot to hit either a straight or a flush, so it has its customary 1/3 chance to make. The pair of Sixes is still waiting for another Six, and you're praying hard for a blank on the river. The only real way you could be in trouble is if someone made two pair playing any two suited cards or a semi-quality hand like QTs. The meek shall inherit the Earth, but only after the brave leave it to them in their wills. Get in that pot!

Omaha High and High-Low (Twists and) Turns

In both varieties of Omaha, some key questions to answer are the following: How close am I to the nut hand and how far do I need to go to get there? If I have the nut hand on the turn, do I have a *redraw* that can make me even better? How many players am I against? What do I know about how they play? Finally, the biggest key question:

What are the chances I'm playing for half or less of the pot?

You will recognize that this is exactly the same opening paragraph from the last chapter, with the exception of the word "turn" being substituted for the word "flop" in the second sentence. We did this intentionally. In a full 10-person game, you need to be planning on showing down the nuts far more often than not.

Omaha High Turns

We won't bother to go over the first hand from the last chapter, as the nut straight would either hold up or it wouldn't. Instead, let's look at the second hand we discussed. Table 10.8 has the hands listed out as well as the relevant statistics. In this case, you will remember that the underdog hand with the pair of Sixes is now the strong favorite against the other two hands because it has the only set. In fact, no other hand even has two pair. Let's make things a little more interesting, though, and put the T♦ on the board for the turn.

Everything changes again! One hand folds as soon as possible, leaving three players. The new percentages are in Table 10.8.

Table 10.8   Omaha High Hand Percentages

Hand	Percentage of Money Won	
	Flop (6♠8♣K♦)	Turn (T♦)
A♦A♣8♦T♠	16.0%	36.0%
J♣9♣T♥4♠	15.2%	16.7%
6♥6♦K♣J♥	62.2%	47.3%
K♠Q♠7♦7♣	6.5%	(folded)

While the set of Sixes is still the favorite, it will win less than 50 percent of all money, according to our simulation. That's a really tough thing to see, but it all adds up. The hand with the pair of Aces is now able to win in several different ways. First, it could catch an Ace on the river, giving the player the best set. No one is holding JQ or 79, so there is no straight out there. The 6♦ and the 8♦ are already accounted for, so any diamond left in the deck is a winner. The hand now also has two pair, Tens and Eights, which means that the four (three, really, as the T♥ is dead) Tens and Eights still out would give this hand a better full house than the Sixes full 66KJ would make. J9T4 is drawing to a non-diamond Seven or Queen, which gives it six outs (actually, it's five outs, as the Q♠ is dead).

Since Omaha is about suffering, let's talk about another turn card that really throws everything for a loop. In this case, let's make it the 7♥.

Hey, that means the player with the pocket Sevens is now the dominant hand, right? Nope. In fact, it is now only good for about 12.5 percent of the money over time. Table 10.9 explains.

Table 10.9   Omaha High Hand Percentages

Hand	Percentage of Money Won	
	Flop (6♠8♣K♦)	Turn (7♥)
A♦A♣8♦T♠	16.0%	0.0%
J♣9♣T♥4♠	15.2%	84.4%
6♥6♦K♣J♥	62.2%	3.1%
K♠Q♠7♦7♣	6.5%	12.5%

The board is of four different suits, so there will be no flushes. The hand now comes down to a nut straight versus draws to full houses and quads, which makes it a huge favorite. The pair of Aces has no draw to a straight and cannot make a winning full house. The set of Sixes is now hoping for the fourth Six to come out, as that is the only way for it to win. What about a King to give it Kings full of Sixes? Good catch, but notice the hand with the pocket Sevens also has a King. If a King came on the river, the Sevens hand would use the King and one Seven to make Kings full of Sevens. Anything other than a Six pairing the board gives the set of Sevens the win, which the money says will happen 1/8 of the time. Everything else gives the straight the win.

We strongly suggest playing on practice software, such as Wilson Software or another maker's product, a *bunch* or at least play at the lowest limit tables available, until you get a good grip on this and Omaha high-low. They are very tricky games, and the odds change drastically from card to card.

Omaha High-Low Turns

For this discussion, we'll first look at a hand with a lot of capacity to win the low and a good but not huge chance to win the high. For example, you hold A♣2♣4♦5♦, which is a pretty good starting hand. You have a chance at the nut flush and can make all kinds of low combinations work. The flop comes, as shown in Figure 10.13.

Figure 10.13 The best draws are just that—draws.

This flop is very good in some ways and mediocre in others.
The good news is that if a low makes, you will by definition have the nut low, as the A4, A5, or 45 combination will be best no matter what happens. The other good news is that an Ace or a Six will give you a straight. The bad news is that the low is not yet made, and you have only a Five-high, runner-runner flush draw. Let's say you are up against one decent hand and one outrageously lucky one, such as A♥5♥J♠Q♠ and 4♠5♠T♦T♣.

This is exactly the insane kind of situation in which you will find yourself in an online card room, so get used to stuff like this happening. It drives you crazy. Let's say the turn card brings the 7♥ or the 6♥.

What a difference a card's rank can make! Table 10.10 shows how the money is distributed.

In either case, the second hand will be picking up the nut flush draw and will make the second nut low. Unfortunately, neither is good as of the turn, and both need to rely on the river to improve in order to collect any money. Because the third hand already has a set of Tens and can split the low if an Ace counterfeits the first hand on the river, it is in great shape to win the majority of the money. If the 6♥ comes, though, it's an entirely different situation. In this case the first hand will have made the *nut-nut* hand as of the turn, in that it will have the best low and high hand (A2 and Six-high straight). It needs to dodge a heart and a card that pairs the board, but it will, at worst, split the low, and in this case, it will split the high because the idiot who played 45TT will also have the best straight. Wow…but what can you do?

Table 10.10   Omaha High-Low Hand Percentages

Hand	Percentage of Money Won		
	Flop (2♦3♠T♥)	Turn (7♥)	Turn (6♥)
A♣2♣4♦5♦	32.8%	33.3%	63.9%
A♥5♥J♠Q♠	13.6%	10.5%	9.7%
4♠5♠T♦T♣	53.6%	56.2%	26.4%

A much more common occurrence is for a flop to hit you pretty well but not perfectly. For instance, assume you have A♥2♥K♠5♠, you are against A♦2♦J♠Q♠ and 9♥T♥A♠K♥, and you get the flop shown in Figure 10.14.

Table 10.11 lists the percentages if the turn brings the K♣.

Figure 10.14 You're doing well, but you're not there yet.

Table 10.11   Omaha High-Low Hand Percentages

Hand	Percentage of Money Won	
	Flop (3♠8♥Q♦)	Turn (K♣)
A♥2♥K♠5♠	42.1%	48.6%
A♦5♦J♠Q♠	44.6%	16.0%
9♥T♥A♠K♥	13.3%	35.4%

This is one of those uncommon hands in which no one will likely make a straight or a full house. The simulation shows that the top hand will win the entire low half of the pot, unless a two comes on the river, in which case it will get quartered. Amazingly, it will also be in line to split the high with the bottom hand, with a pair of Kings and an Ace kicker. If a Nine or Ten comes, the bottom hand wins with Kings and Nines/Tens. If a Deuce or a Five comes, the first hand wins with Kings and Deuces/Fives. The second hand will tie the low if a Deuce comes and will win the high if a Ten comes, giving it a straight. It will also win if a third Queen or a second Jack comes, which would give it trips and Queens over Jacks, respectively.

Seven-Card Stud Fifth and Sixth Streets

There's an extra round of betting in Stud, so we're going to talk about both fifth and sixth streets in this chapter. The next chapter deals with the river.

We'll assume there are our customary three players still in the hand. The random fourth hand from the previous chapter will not figure into the rest of the hand. Table 10.12 lists the hands and the percentages of total money won.

Table 10.12	Seven-Card Stud, Sample Fifth Street		
Hand		**Percentage of Money Won**	
	Fifth Card	**Fourth Street**	**Fifth Street**
A♦A♣8♦T♠	9♦	46.1%	33.2%
J♣9♣T♥4♠	Q♣	15.2%	21.8%
6♥6♦K♠J♥	K♣	23.5%	45.0%

The hidden pair of Aces is now in a decent amount of trouble, but assuming all players stay in until the end, the Aces will still be putting in 1/3 of all money with the expectation of winning all but 0.1 percent of it back. Given the size of the pot going into fifth street, calling is justified. The trick here is to determine if the player has a pocket pair or a much more dangerous third King, which would make that hand a 73.5 percent winner over time. In this case they have the pocket pair (6♥6♦). Putting ourselves in the situation of playing the Aces, what do we have to hope for? It goes without saying that we would first want another Ace. The T♦ would be a great card for us in this case, as it would give us a higher two pair, Aces-up versus Kings-up. It would also give us redraws to an Ace-high flush and a full house. The second hand is *drawing thin* in that two or possibly three of the Kings it would need to make its straight are gone, as is one of the Eights. In this example, only two other clubs are dead, so there are still seven clubs left in the deck. Unfortunately, the clubs would need to come runner-runner. The hand with the Kings is in a good position, but as the Aces would certainly have raised by now, some alarm bells should be going off.

The important thing to note here is that even with a double draw, the drawing hand is a major underdog against two made hands. The pot must be substantial to stay in. Be certain you are getting at least 4:1 odds in a hand like this if you stay in. Other players will likely be raising with their strong hands, so you will need to decide if one or both of them is bluffing.

As the old saying goes, though, every dog has his day. Let's say sixth street brings blanks for the Aces and Kings hands but makes the straight for the second hand. The new percentages are in Table 10.13.

Table 10.13 Seven-Card Stud, Sample Sixth Street				
Hand		Percentage of Money Won		
	Sixth Card	Fourth Street	Fifth Street	Sixth Street
A♦A♣8♦T♠9♦	2♥	46.1%	33.2%	0.0%
J♣9♣T♥4♠Q♣	8♥	15.2%	21.8%	88.2%
6♥6♦K♠J♥K♣	4♥	23.5%	45.0%	11.8%

The lucky so-and-so has now made the straight and is now an 8:1 favorite versus a 4:1 underdog. Approximately one-ninth of the time, a King or Six will come and make the straight a loser. Also notice that the J♣9♣ is in the pocket, which means only three of the straight cards are in view. If four straight cards were out (or four cards for any hand, for that matter), then it would not be a stretch to conclude the straight had likely been made. With three cards, though, the made straight has the advantage of being concealed, which means aggressive players may be willing to raise to see if it's a bluff. It's not, so here comes the re-raise!

Seven-Card Stud High-Low Fifth and Sixth Streets

Finally, we'll continue with the discussion of how nut-low/straight draw hands fare against high hands with little or no chance for low. You'll remember we are playing 2345. Your low hands will, of course, not always be this good, but if it's against only one low card showing (the 8♦), you'll play *any* low draw *every* time!

First, 2345 is of four different suits. The results are shown in Table 10.14.

The main theme of this hand is that the 2345 hand that started off so well will now only win around 1/6 of all money. Of course, because it was so large a favorite earlier in the hand, the holder would likely have raised so much there will be enough in the pot to get 5:1 pot odds to stay in! The bad news is that a lot of it is your money. Pot equity will dictate that you stay in, though, as you will have put in around 25 percent of the pot yourself, which means you need to stay in for your 16.1 percent chance, because if you fold, it will be inefficient by 8.9 percent. Compounding the problem is that you now have no chance for the high side of the pot, as you can't beat the Queen-high straight held by the second player.

Table 10.14   Seven-Card Stud High-Low, Sample Fifth and Sixth Streets

Hand	Sixth Card	Percentage of Money Won		
		Fourth Street	Fifth Street	Sixth Street
A♦A♣8♦T♠7♦	2♥	32.7%	37.4%	10.9%
J♣9♣T♥4♠Q♣	8♥	11.6%	23.0%	73.0%
2♦3♣4♥5♠K♣	4♦	55.6%	39.7%	16.1%

Remember, having two and even three suited cards does you negligible good. As you go for your low, however, if you can get to four suited cards, with one or even two cards to go, your winning percentages will go up dramatically.

Bonus! Remember that a pair does not need to be showing for someone to have a full house. It would necessarily have to come on the river because, with only two cards unseen, the most there could be is three of one rank. Keep that in mind.

Conclusion

Most of your losses will come from making inefficient plays on the flop and fourth street, where the possible outcomes make memorizing all combinations difficult. On the turn and on fifth and sixth streets, a player above a rank amateur should begin to see what is possible and what is probable with their hands. The main thing to realize is that a player does not master the situations all at once. Instead, over time the sheer repetition of seeing the same and similar situations over and over again will ingrain them in your head. The next chapter talks about the river, when the dealin's done.

Playing the River

After all the cards have come out, you need to decide how to end the hand with the most virtual chips in your stack, whether that means raising to make money or folding to save money. The tactics you'll use vary somewhat from game to game, but it's crucial that you know how to determine the best possible hand and how close you are to having that hand. Be prepared for the unexpected, though, because the most unlikely of hands can become winners when that last card comes out. After all, if there were no river, there would be no fish.

Playing the River in Hold 'Em and Pineapple

When you get to the river in Hold 'em and Pineapple, you should take a few seconds to determine the best possible hand incorporating the five shared cards and any other two hole cards. We put a couple of Hold 'em practice hands in Chapter 4, but you should take the time now to play online for free at the play money tables, or with your computer software, to get as much practice as you can reading the board. Once you're confident in your ability to recognize the best possible hand, continue on through this chapter.

Playing When You Have the Nuts

There's no better feeling than seeing that last card come out and realizing you have the best possible hand. When you have the hand locked and can't be beaten, you should think about how you can convince your opponents to put in as much of their money as possible. As an example, consider the hand in Figure 11.1.

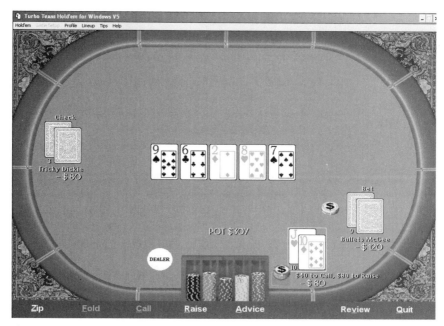

Figure 11.1 You snuck up on your opponents in this hand, so they might put in money on their own.

You were in the big blind in this hand. The small blind folded before the flop, but four other players called, leaving five players in the hand. You stayed in with your two overcards after another player bet on the flop, called on the turn with your overcards and a straight draw, and backed into the nuts on the river. What's even more attractive about this hand is that the board contains four cards to the straight, the 6♣7♠8♥9♠, so any of the four remaining players with a Five or a Ten has made a straight as well. Of course, your straight is the best possible straight on a board where no flush or full house is possible, so you're hoping that another player made a Ten-high straight, two pair, or a set. But how do you get the most money from your opponents in this case?

You could check and hope someone else bets the hand for you, giving you a chance to check-raise, but when you're playing at lower limits ($10–$20 and below), the surest way to get money out of the other players is to bet. The other folks know, or should know, what the best possible hand is, but they might not be willing to believe you have the absolute nuts of JT when you bet from early position. In this dream sequence, the pot has the uncalled small blind, 10 small bets, and three large bets in it after the turn (in a $5–$10 game, that amounts to $79 after the $3 rake is taken out), so a player with two pairs or a set might call you, and someone with a Ten might raise you.

In general, you should avoid clever plays when you're playing Hold 'em at $10–$20 limits and below online. The players at these levels are more skilled than they used to be, but for the most part the less-skilled players aren't aggressive enough to try to bet into a board where they don't have the nuts, and the more-skilled players aren't foolish enough to bet into a board where they don't have the nuts. If you know one or two of your opponents habitually bluff, or are insanely aggressive, you might be able to get in a check-raise every now and then, but why not let them raise your bet and try to bluff you out that way?

You should always pay attention to the texture of the board and your opponents' betting patterns before you make your move with the nuts. Some players refuse to believe that their previously unbeatable hand has been overtaken by events. Some may fail to realize that there's a flush or straight possible (they're easy to overlook if you don't take a second), or they may be steaming from a previous hand and want to soothe their savaged ego by winning the next hand with a show of aggression. If they want to try to knock you off the best hand, so be it. Thank them for the chips if you win it all, and don't be too disappointed if you have to split the pot.

Playing When You Have a Strong Hand

Playing the river's easy when you have the best possible hand, but things get a bit more complex when you have a strong hand that's not the nuts. As an example, consider the hand in Figure 11.2.

There's a lot going on in this pot. You have the best two-pair hand, but you're beaten by any set or any QT that makes a straight. But how much do you have to worry about the straight? Assuming you've been betting the whole way and nobody raised you on the turn, you have a pretty good chance of winning this hand. You always have to be on guard when there's a straight on board; but in this type of situation, where someone would had to have paid a small bet and a big bet to get one of the four Jacks, you'll have to accept that you'll have to pay off a raise and that you got beat while you were almost a 7 to 1 favorite after the flop and a 9 to 1 favorite after the turn.

Notice how the situation changes if that last J♦ were the J♥, though. Instead of drawing at four outs, an opponent holding a reasonable hand, such as Q♥T♥, could win by drawing any of the remaining nine hearts or any of the three non-heart Jacks on either the turn or river. In that case you're only a 3 to 2 favorite after the flop and a 3 to 1 favorite after

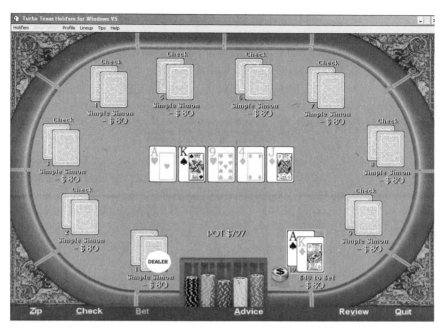

Figure 11.2 How do you play when you're not guaranteed part of the pot?

the turn, so you can expect to take your share of losses. When that final heart hits on the river, you should check and, if you feel you have a shot at the pot, go ahead and call.

The math for deciding when to call in limit Hold 'em is relatively simple. If there's any doubt that your opponent has you beat, you can check the pot odds to see if it's correct to call. For example, if it would cost you $10 to call for a shot at a $90 pot, you need to decide whether your opponent would bluff one out of 10 times. If your opponent would bluff every now and then, you should call.

Playing When You Have a Marginal Hand

You need to start thinking about folding on the river when your hand isn't close to the strongest possible hand. Again, however, you need to take both your opponents' tendencies and the texture of the flop into account when deciding whether or not to bet or call on the river. Remember the hand in Figure 11.1, but give yourself two pairs instead of the one-card straight made possible by the board. You can assume with some certainty that none of your opponents can beat your two pair with another two pair or a set, but there's a very good chance that someone caught a straight on the end. If a fairly solid player who hadn't bet before the river suddenly bets, you should give them credit for a hand and fold. If you're uncertain about whether you're beat, go ahead and call. It's better to lose the $10 it'll cost you to call than the $90 in the pot.

Another situation you need to look out for is when you have top pair but another player has raised consistently throughout the hand. For example, if you have A♠J♠ in the big blind and called a pre-flop raise, you're pretty much stuck checking and calling when the board comes J♥3♦7♣. You lose to anyone who has 33, 77, JJ, QQ, KK, or AA (J7 and 73 are unlikely given the raise), but you have to be on guard against giving away a pot to an aggressive player who is pressing with AK.

Playing When You Have a Weak Hand

This situation is easy to play. If you're drawing at a flush or straight and didn't hit it, fold, unless you backed into top pair, and the player who drove the betting through the turn checked on the river. Even then, you should check, unless you're last to act and you have top pair with a decent kicker.

Playing the River in Omaha High

If you think watching the river card come out in Hold 'em is hard on your nerves, wait until you play Omaha. As an extreme example of what can happen when the last card hits the table, take a look at the hand in Figure 11.3.

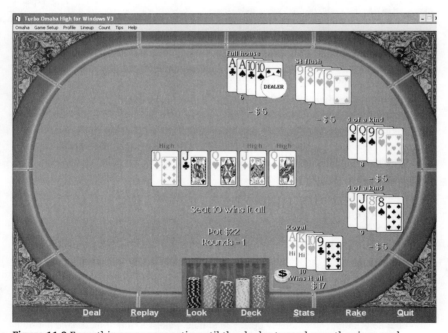

Figure 11.3 Everything was copasetic until the dealer turned over the river card.

This hand features a Royal Flush, four Jacks, four Queens, a Queen-high straight flush, and Tens full of Queens. The eventual winner was in front with an Ace-high straight on the flop, but the Jacks pulled way ahead by making quads on the turn, only to be beaten in not one, not two, but *three* places on the river.

> ♠♥♣♦ **Note**
>
> Be sure to drop by the Gambler's General Store at 800 South Main Street the next time you're in Las Vegas. There's a similar hand painted on the exterior wall facing the parking lot.

The fantasy hand shown in Figure 11.3 provides an important lesson to the Omaha high player: Small full houses can cost you a lot of money on the river. The player with Tens full of Queens simply refused to let his hand go, and what started out as the best hand before the flop took a lot of that player's chips with it when it went down in flames. And please remember that winning Omaha hands tend to be a lot stronger than Hold 'em hands! Those extra two hole cards make a huge difference. If you're not sure whether you're beat or not, it'll only cost you one bet to find out at limit Omaha. If you're in a pot-limit or no-limit game, you'll need nerves of steel and good judgment to call. We can't help you there; it's all about experience at that point.

Playing When You Have the Nuts

If you have an almighty lock on an Omaha hand, you are bound to get paid off, particularly when your lock is well disguised. For example, you might have played A♥J♥J♦7♦ and flopped a Jack-high straight flush in diamonds. We've already shown you how to extract the most money from your opponents on the flop and turn, but how should you follow up those tactics on the river? The secret comes in noticing whether and how the board changed from the turn to the river. As an example, consider the board in Figure 11.4.

This board changed from a flush board to a full house board on the river, but where you'll find full houses, you might also find quads. How you extract the most money from your opponents depends on how many players remain in the hand and what they were doing before the river. If a player bet what must be the nut flush draw, and one other player called along with you, you can figure the player with the flush will fold to a bet, and the player who called along with what had to be two pair or a set will call a bet, or even raise, after you bet. In general, though, you should avoid making any fancy moves and bet the nuts, unless your notes on your opponents tell you that you can rely on them to bet the second-best hand for you to check-raise. Don't cost yourself a big bet on the end by trying for two; the move doesn't work often enough to make up for the river bet you missed.

Figure 11.4 The texture of this hand changed radically on the river.

Playing When You Have a Strong Hand

The texture of the board matters a great deal when you don't quite have the nuts but do have a strong hand in Omaha high. One common example of a strong hand that isn't the nuts is a King-high flush, as shown in Figure 11.5.

According to a 100,000-hand simulation in Turbo Omaha, you are still just about a 2 to 1 favorite to win a hand with a King-high flush against nine random hands, where no one folded before the river. By comparison, you have a 42 percent chance of winning when you have a Queen-high flush, which is still a pretty good shot at the money. As always, though, you need to do a reality check and pay attention to anyone who comes out betting or raising on the river, particularly because the flush draw has been available since the flop. You must rely on your knowledge of your opponents and your gut instinct to know when you are beat.

Another common hand is when you have a set against a possible straight. As before, you need to decide whether your opponent backed into a straight on the river or whether they were drawing for it from the flop. In general, the lower the cards on the board, and the more gaps between them, the less likely it is that your opponent has the straight they're representing. As an example, consider the hand in Figure 11.6.

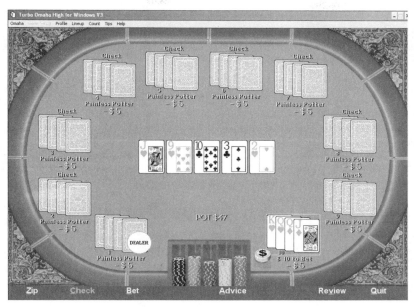

Figure 11.5 The second nut hand will get you in trouble, but a King-high flush is still a winning proposition with no pair on board.

Figure 11.6 The card ranks and the gaps between them make a straight less likely.

In this case, your opponent would need to hold either T7 or 75 to have a straight. Neither hand is particularly likely if you're going up against rational players in an Omaha high game, but there's always the chance someone played two pairs or a couple of suited Aces and hit the straight on the river.

Playing When You Have a Marginal or Weak Hand

In a word: Don't. We've seen hands won by Ace-high, but they're few and far between. If someone bets on the river, and they were betting from the start of the hand, give 'em credit for a hand and save your money.

> ♠♥♣♦ **Note**
>
> If Omaha isn't crazy enough for you, check out the rules for Chowaha, the world's wildest poker game, at www.coonrod.com/scot/poker/chowaha.html. We don't think you can play it anywhere online, but you never know.

Playing the River in Omaha High-Low

In general, the rules for playing the high side of an Omaha high-low hand are the same as they are when you play straight Omaha high, when the board has cards ranked Nine or higher, but you have to be more willing to believe that an opponent can make a low straight or hit a small full house when there's a possible low. You should also tend to discount straights and full houses that require middle cards, such as Sevens, Eights, and Nines, as most players usually toss those cards before the flop.

As a general rule, you should bet and raise aggressively with any high hand you feel is the likely winner, particularly if you have a flush or straight that can't be tied. You do need to be careful of how you play your hands on the low side, though.

Playing When You Have the Nut Low

You're assured some money when you have the nut low, but there's absolutely no guarantee that you're assured half the pot. Because flushes and straights don't count against you for low, ties on the low side are much more common than ties on the high side. As an example, consider the board in Figure 11.7.

When three players remain in a hand at the river, odds are good that at least two of the players are going for the low and that the third may have a shot at the high, in addition to a low draw with an A4 or similar that would have been worth something if a Deuce or Three hit on the turn or river. When you have no shot at the high half of the pot, you need to play your nut low cautiously. Don't raise with it, because you're likely to only get one-quarter of the money

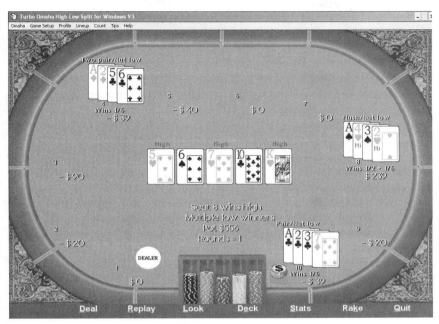

Figure 11.7 Who *doesn't* play an Ace and a Deuce in Omaha high-low?

back. If you're in the enviable position of having both the high and low locked (called *nut nut*, because you've got the nuts twice) and can't be tied on the high side, raise all you want.

Playing When You Have the Second Nut Low

Otherwise rational Omaha high-low players lose a lot of money chasing with the second nut low when they're sure, absolutely sure, that there's a better low out there. It's one thing to keep calling when you have a good shot at the high half and the second nut low, but it's quite another when you're only gunning for low and you're against two or three opponents. All we can tell you is to read your opponents as best you can, go over their hand history in your mind, and be tempted to call only if there's one other player in the pot. If two or more players call on the river, you're very likely beaten on the low side. It's hard advice to follow; we know, because we go against our better instincts from time to time and call anyway. We're right part of the time, particularly when the low only became possible when the turn and river were low cards, but we're wrong sometimes as well. What's worse, when we're right, we get, at most, half the pot; sometimes it's only a quarter or a sixth.

Playing When You Have an Emergency Low

An *emergency low* is a low hand that sort of happened by accident. You weren't planning on going for low, you didn't plan on winning any money on the low side, but suddenly three low cards appeared on the board, and you qualified. Of course, your low hand may be something like 8♣7♥6♦5♣2♦, but it's better than nothing. Or is it? Most of the time a rough low hand you backed into won't win even a quarter of the pot, but sometimes it'll make you money. Whatever you do, don't bet unless you've got the high side covered! The best-case scenario is when no one bets on the river, and you get to turn over your cheese for a shot at half the money. You can save a lot of money by folding on the river if someone does bet, unless you are absolutely, positively, 100 percent certain they're only going for high.

Playing the River in Seven-Card Stud

Unlike the river card in a flop game, you don't gain any new information when the last card comes out in a Stud game. You can, however, use the probability, pot odd calculations in Chapter 9 and 10, and your opponents' betting patterns to help you determine their likely hands. This section walks you through the hands you can have and offers advice on how to play in each situation.

Playing When You Have a Full House or Higher

Full houses just win, baby. We put the worst full house possible (Twos full of Threes) through a 100,000-hand simulation in Turbo 7 Stud and came out the winner 87 percent of the time, when everyone stayed to the river. Tens full of Deuces, on the other hand, won a whopping 93 percent of the time. When none of your opponents have a pair on board, and don't appear to be threatening a straight flush, you can turn your attention to moving as many chips as possible from their stacks to yours.

You should bet your hand for value in most low-limit games. If you made your full house on the river, you can take a shot at the pot and make your opponents think you only have trips, *particularly when you only have a pair showing on board and you hesitate a few seconds before you bet.* You hesitate to make your opponents think you're deciding whether or not to bet your set. If your opponents suspect you just have trips, they are more likely to raise if they have a higher set, a straight, or a flush. If they can't beat trips, they probably won't call anyway.

If one or more of your opponents have a pair showing, you have to be a little concerned over whether they might have a full house or not. If someone has trips showing on the board, their set had better be smaller than yours, or you're in trouble. Sure, you'll call any bets on the river, but nothing slows you down like TTT on another player's board when you have 99988.

If you have quads, bet and raise until they make you stop. Quad Deuces with the 3♥3♠3♣ as kickers (we used all Threes to allow the rest of the ranks to form quads) won 98.7 percent of hands when everyone stayed to the river. Unless you see trips or quads on someone else's board, and their visible set is higher than yours, just keep going. You'll lose about one hand in a hundred, but that likelihood isn't significant enough to worry about. If you're playing at a table where you can win a bad beat jackpot, be thankful your quads came up second best!

Playing When You Have a Straight or Flush

You should be very happy when you have a straight or, even better, a flush in seven-card Stud, but even an Ace-high flush with a weak second card is vulnerable to a higher flush or a full house. Straights are even more vulnerable. To play a straight or a flush well, you must examine your opponents' boards and determine whether they stuck around trying to improve their two pair or trips, or whether they believed they have the straight or flush you're representing beat. As an example, consider the hands in Figure 11.8.

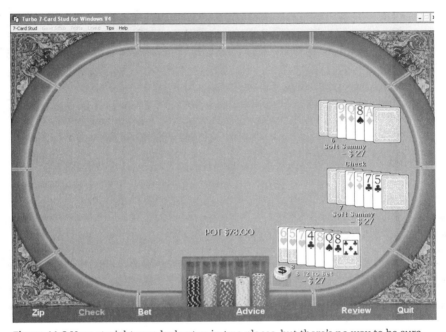

Figure 11.8 Your straight may be beaten in two places, but there's no way to be sure.

Your opponents checked and called on fifth and sixth streets, but you should suspect you're up against a full house when the player showing the pair bets on the river, and only one or two of the cards they would need to make the full house are gone. Your board more or less gives away the fact that you have a straight and not a flush; you have just two cards of the same suit showing, the suited cards were the last two cards to appear on your board, and your upcards contain three cards to the straight. The other opponent called the bet as well, but you might not be as worried about that hand. If the player at the bottom right of the table has a straight, it can't beat yours. It's possible the player at the bottom right has a flush, but it would had to have come on the last card.

It's worth your while to call in this situation, for a couple of reasons. First, you can call because an observant and aggressive opponent will likely bet trips against a board showing three to a straight, particularly when two of the straight cards are two ranks apart, like the Nine and the Queen in this example. You would need to have exactly a Ten and Jack in the hole to make the straight, which you do, but that's the sort of uncertainty that can convince an aggressive player to take a chance on betting their set.

Playing flushes is easier because your hand is so much stronger, but you must consider whether your high cards beat other potential flushes. Figure 11.9 shows a typical situation where your flush is in some danger.

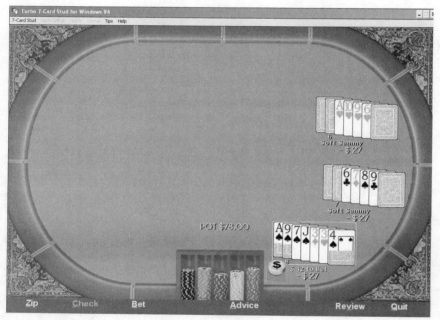

Figure 11.9 An Ace-high flush is great, but not when your second card is a Nine and there's another Ace-high flush draw around.

Both you and your opponent show three cards to the flush, but your opponent shows A♥T♥, and your second highest flush card is the 9s. You should still play the hand to the end, but you might consider not betting, unless you've seen three of your opponent's flush cards go into the muck. The aggressive play is to bet and call any raise, of course, but let your experience and knowledge of your opponent be your guide.

Playing When You Have Trips or Two Pair

We're not exaggerating when we say that you will win and lose more money at seven-card Stud with two pair than you will with any other hand. Figure 11.10 shows a typical scenario.

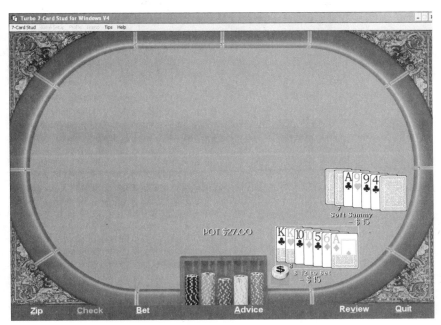

Figure 11.10 It's no fun playing two pairs against an Ace and another pair.

Your Kings and Tens don't look very strong in this situation, but there's still hope. If your opponent bet after the Ace hit, you may very well be up against Aces and Nines. On the other hand, if your opponent checked and called after the Ace hit, two pairs smaller than Aces seems more likely. When you're in this type of situation, think back through the hand and glean what you can from the betting pattern. Raising the bring-in signals a big pair, or at least a pair bigger than any remaining upcards. In that case, you might be up against Queens and Nines instead of Aces and Nines. Our advice? Call, unless your opponent's visible pair outranks your larger pair.

You're in much better shape when you have trips, but you're still not out of the woods. Straights just seem to pop up when you have three of a kind. As an example of what can go wrong, check out the hand in Figure 11.11.

In this hand, your opponent made the bring-in bet, and three players called *but did not raise*. The last bit is important: Because no one put any pressure on the bring-in, there could be any three cards underneath. If your opponent raised on sixth street, you're probably going against a straight. You should call opponents who you know tend to bluff with scary boards, but if you're sure you're beat, go ahead and save your money for another hand. However, if you don't see a likely straight or higher pair on another player's board, go ahead and bet your set on the river.

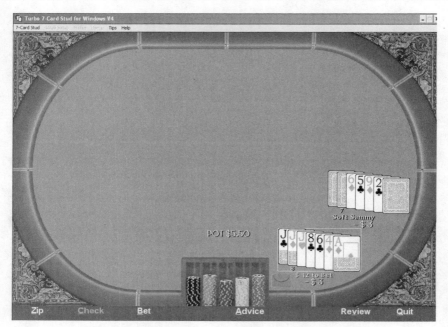

Figure 11.11 Surely there can't be a straight hiding under there.

Playing When You Have One Pair or Worse

One pair rarely wins in seven-card Stud, but it can happen. If no one has been driving the betting, and you don't see a higher pair on anyone's board, check and call on the river. You may be up against a small two pair, but your bigger pair may still take down the pot. Of course, if you miss your straight or flush draw entirely, and don't think you can drive your opponent out of the pot with a bet, check and fold.

Playing the River in Seven-Card Stud High-Low

Seven-card Stud high-low can be a tough game to figure out on the river. Players don't need to declare whether they're going high, low, or both, so your hand-reading skills need to be sharp. You also need to remember dead cards accurately in order to calculate odds as appropriate. Playing the high side in seven-card Stud high-low requires the same skills as when you're playing the standard version of the game, but you should give more credence to players who might have caught low trips and straights. If you do have the best possible high hand, however, bet and raise aggressively to force any competing low draws to put in extra dollars.

Regardless of what hand you have, you should always determine the best possible low hand an opponent could have and whether you have a cinch hand for either high or low. Figure 11.12 shows one possible scenario.

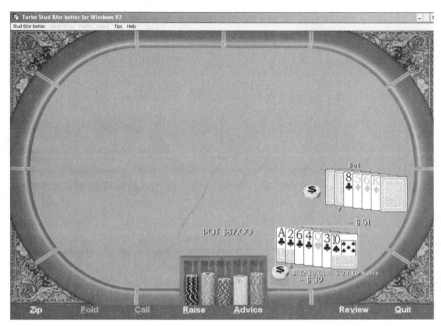

Figure 11.12 No hole cards can beat you for low, so bet and raise to build your half of the pot.

In this example, you have 6432A for low and your opponent shows no card lower than a Five, which means your opponent can have no better hand than 6532A, which you beat. When no set of three hole cards can beat you, you have what's known as a *board lock*, but it can be tough to figure out whether you have all of your opponents locked on either the high or low side. You typically get 30 seconds to act when you play online, so be sure to take some time on each street to update your reads. Use your opponents' thinking time, too! Ignore the television, ignore your friends sending you instant messages, and ignore the cat when money's on the line.

Playing When You Have the Nut Low

When you have the single best possible low hand of the remaining hands, rejoice and bet until they make you stop. However, if one of your opponents could tie you for the low, and the action indicates they are going for low, check and call if you don't have a credible shot at winning the high side of the pot. Figure 11.13 shows one hand where you should consider checking and calling.

The opponent at the top left of the screen doesn't have a reasonable high draw, so you have to figure that player went for low and probably got there. The best possible low hand ties yours with 7632A, but the open trips to your right indicate that you have absolutely

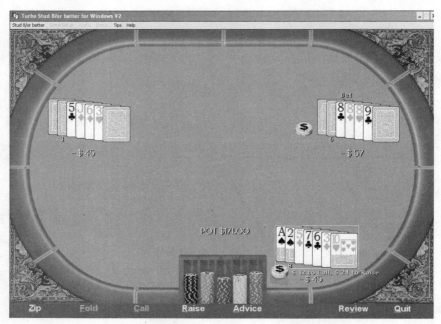

Figure 11.13 The succession of unsuited low cards tells you this player was going for low.

no shot at the high half of the pot. The high hand is sure to bet, so your best option is to check if possible and call if you have to. You can win, at most, half the pot, but winning half, or even a quarter, of the pot is better than winning none of it.

Playing When You Have the Second or Third Nut Low

Judging your opponents' hands in seven-card Stud high-low is trickier than it is in Omaha high-low because players have only two down cards until the third one arrives on the river. Experienced Omaha high-low players make a lot of money off of players who stay with the second and third best low hands, but it's less wrong to stay with the second and third nut low in seven-card Stud high-low. As an example, consider the hand in Figure 11.14.

Neither you nor your low opponent can beat quads, so all you have to worry about is whether you can win on the low side. You have a 7654A low, so your opponent needs either an Ace or a Deuce in the hole to win. Of course, your opponent doesn't know that you have A4 in the hole, so you might get lucky and be able to flat call the big hand's bet on the river. But what do you do if the high hand bets, you call, and your opponent for low raises? Now you have to consider the odds and the player. On the mathematical front, your opponent has three shots at one of the remaining seven Aces or Deuces. There are 20 dead cards that don't count against the draw (the seven you hold, the eight your two

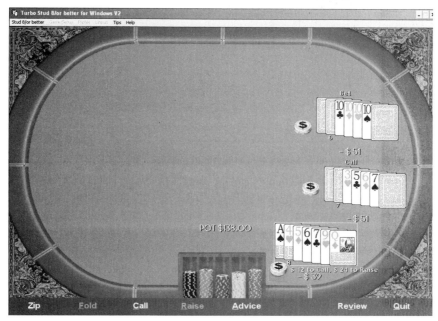

Figure 11.14 It's hard to call with this low hand, but you probably should.

opponents hold, and the five that were discarded on third street), so the probability of each of your opponents' hole cards *not* being an Ace or Deuce is

$$25/32 \times 24/31 \times 23/30 = 13,800 / 29,760 = 46.37\%$$

In purely mathematical terms, you're a very slight underdog in this situation. The high hand is sure to make it three bets, though, so you're in for at least three, and maybe even four, bets if the other low player caps it. It's all down to your judgment at this point. Does your opponent want to blow you off the hand, or do they have you locked out?

Do note how the numbers change if another of the Aces or Deuces is gone. With only six cards to draw to, you become a slight favorite.

$$26/32 \times 25/31 \times 24/30 = 15,600 / 29,760 = 52.42\%$$

Each additional dead Ace or Deuce adds 6.05 percent to your chances of winning, but you still stand to win a few extra bets or lose a bundle. Good luck.

Playing When You Have an Emergency Low

Emergency lows, where you back into a hand such as 87653 while you're drawing to complete a high hand, are easier to play in seven-card Stud high-low than they are in Omaha because you have more information about which cards are out. The calculations in the second- and third-nut discussion apply here as well. If you have a high hand or a low hand that can compete with the other players' hands, go ahead and call. Just remember that if an opponent needs one card to beat you, they only need seven outs to be a mathematical favorite. For example, if your opponent raised before the flop with a good low card showing and called a pair's bet on fourth street, you might want to jettison the hand and cut your losses.

Playing the River in Razz

If you bought a ticket to the river in Razz, you probably have a good read on your opponent's hand and figure to have them beat or to have the odds in favor of you making your draw. As in seven-card Stud high-low, you should check for board lock, where your hand at least ties the best possible hand your opponent can have. Of course, with three hidden cards that could be A23, you could always be in trouble. Just remember that you read low hands from the highest card to the lowest card, so an 86543 beats an 8732A. In general, you should bet if you hit your draw or figure to have the best hand, raise if your opponent bets into you and they need two or more perfect cards in the hole to beat you, and fold if you missed your draw or if you figure your opponent has you locked out.

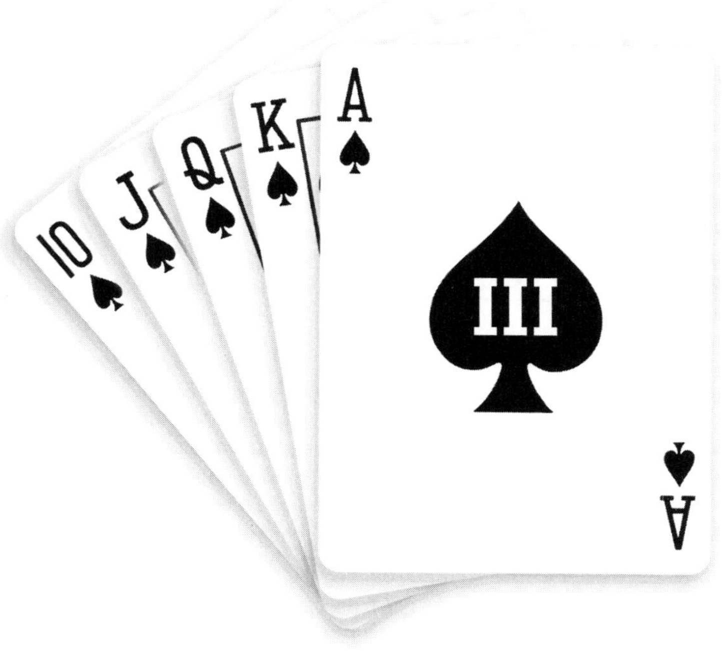
10
J
Q
K
A
III
A

Evaluating Your Play Using Spreadsheets

Knowledge is power, particularly at the poker table. You need to know how to play your cards, of course, but you need lots of self-knowledge to play well and to continuously improve as a player. In this chapter, we'll show you what records to keep, how to summarize them in a spreadsheet program, and what questions to ask of the data you've kept.

Keeping Detailed Written Records

Even if you don't plan to glean too much information from your play, you should still strongly consider writing down the following information in a notebook every time you play:

- ✦ Site
- ✦ Date
- ✦ Game
- ✦ Level
- ✦ Number of players
- ✦ Time in
- ✦ Time out
- ✦ Total time played
- ✦ Buy-in
- ✦ Cash-out
- ✦ Win/loss

You can use this information to derive your total wins or losses, your average win or loss per hour, your hourly win rate, and to determine how much your win rate fluctuates from game to game and hour to hour. Be sure to record each game's results in its own column (e.g., Hold 'em in one column, Omaha high-low in another, and so on) so you don't have to pick through the table to find the values you want. Maintaining written records instead of electronic records means you have to do a lot of math by hand, but it's better than nothing.

Using Statistics Kept by the Poker Sites

If your site offers statistics on your current session, you should copy them down at the end of a session and analyze them when you're done. On PartyPoker, for example, you right-click your player name and choose Show Statistics to display a box like the one shown in Figure 12.1.

In Figure 12.1, there is one set of statistics for flop games, such as Omaha and Hold 'em, and another set for Stud games. The percentage of hands won statistically is interesting in that it shows you how well you're doing in relation to the expected win rate, based on the number of players at your table. If you're at a Hold 'em table with 10 players, you should expect to win about 10 percent of the hands. If you're at a Stud table with eight players, your average win rate should be around 12.5 percent.

Figure 12.1 These statistics may not seem very important, but they tell you a fair amount about how you played during a session.

Obviously those rates will fluctuate based on the number of players at your tables, but they're still worth paying attention to.

The Flop Seen or 4th Street Seen percentage, on the other hand, tells you a great deal about how you're playing. If you play the system we advocate, you'll end up seeing the flop or fourth street about 33 percent of the time, when you play at a full table. Obviously, when you're at a short-handed table, such as one of the six player maximum flop tables or five player maximum Stud tables available on some sites, those percentages will go up because you don't need as good a hand to play against fewer opponents. By the same token, you could log on for a short session and get an incredible run of cards that entice you to see 45–50 percent of the flops or fourth streets. You could also receive no playable hands for an hour and log off having seen just 11 percent of the flops or fourth streets. We've each gone through a three hour Hold 'em session and ended up seeing only 8 percent of the flops. It's frustrating, but it happens to everyone.

Finally, the Win% if 4th Street Seen and Win% if Flops Seen percentages tell you a lot about how well you're running. If you play quality hands, you should expect to win about a third of the time that you pay to see the flop or fourth street. What's a third of one third? One ninth, or 11 percent. That's above your target win rate in a flop game and right around your target win rate in a Stud game. Throw in the hands where you raise before the flop and win or complete the bring-in and take the pot in a Stud game, and you're ahead of the game.

What you want to watch out for are discrepancies between the number of hands you play and the number of hands you win after you pay to see the flop or fourth street. For example, if your Flops Seen percentage is 50 percent and your Win% if Flops Seen score is 20 percent, you know that you're probably going in with some subpar hands and are putting your money at unnecessary risk. If you want to play that loose, that's fine, but be sure you know exactly what you're getting into before you try it.

Tracking Your Play in a Spreadsheet Program

Spreadsheet programs make it possible for you to record and summarize your data much more efficiently than you could dream of doing by hand. We'll focus on Excel, the world-leading spreadsheet program, but if you can't afford, or don't want to buy, a copy of Microsoft Excel, you can turn to OpenOffice, an open source software alternative, which includes a mostly Excel-compatible spreadsheet program named Calc. To download OpenOffice, visit openoffice.org and find the build for your operating system. Windows, Linux, and FreeBSD are well supported, but the Macintosh implementation only works with Mac OS X and has some bugs.

Tracking Your Play in More Detail

When you play poker seriously, you must be willing to examine every aspect of your game. Just as studying the strategies and tactics of poker improves your skill at the game's mechanics, studying your habits and tendencies will point out your strengths and help you identify correctable leaks in your game. We recommend tracking your results by the hour, rather than by the session, to get a better view of your tendencies. Of course, you need to get your data into a spreadsheet before you can analyze it. The following sections show you the basics of entering data into a spreadsheet quickly.

Creating a Data List Efficiently

You'll get the most value out of entering your data as a data list, shown in Figure 12.2.

The data list in Figure 12.2 contains all of the data points we recommended you record by hand with one addition. Instead of recording your buy-in and cash-out for a session, you should record your hourly win or loss (not your total bankroll or cash on the table). Yes, it's a little extra work, but the insights you gain from recording your hourly progression make it worth the effort.

One key point to note about data lists is the row at the top, which contains column headings that are centered in their cells and displayed in bold type. You need to format your column headings distinctively so your spreadsheet can distinguish the column headings from the data.

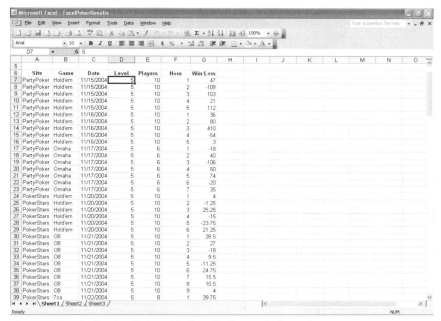

Figure 12.2 It looks simple, but this data list forms the base for some pretty advanced data views.

Taking Advantage of AutoComplete

There are a few techniques you can use to enter data more quickly. For example, if you've already entered a value into a column, both Excel and Calc offer to complete the value for you. As shown in Figure 12.3, each program waits until it can distinguish your potential entry from all other entries in the column and suggests a candidate value for the cell. You can press the Enter key to accept the suggestion or keep typing and complete your new entry.

Copying a Value into Multiple Cells

Of course, entering the same value time after time can wear on you, particularly if you have to type most of a cell's contents before AutoComplete kicks in. For example, if you play Omaha and Omaha high-low, you have to get all the way through "Omaha" before your spreadsheet program offers to complete the entry. Fortunately, there is a way to type a text value in a single cell and duplicate the entry across a cell range.

To copy a cell's text value into a cell range, follow these steps:

1. Type the value to be copied in a cell and press Enter.

2. Click the cell that contains the value to be duplicated.

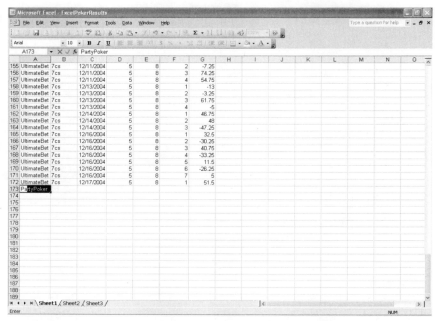

Figure 12.3 AutoComplete, as it's called in Excel, streamlines data entry.

3. Grab the black square at the bottom right corner of the cell (called the *fill handle* in Excel), and drag it until it covers the range of cells into which you want to copy the value.

Extending a Series Quickly

You can also use the fill handle to enter a series of numbers quickly. When you enter a series using the fill handle, you enter the first two series values to define the series' progression and extend the series. Typing the same value in two cells and selecting them puts the same value into the cells you cover when you drag to extend the series.

♠♥♣♦ Note

Extending a series of dates doesn't work the same in Calc as it does in Excel. In Excel, when you type the same date into two adjacent cells, select the cells, and extend the series, Excel puts the repeated date in the new cells. By contrast, following the same process in Calc increases the date by one day in each new cell below the cell at the end of the original selection.

A Quick and Dirty Intro to Spreadsheets

This isn't a heavy-duty spreadsheet book, so we'll go through some of the data management tasks quickly. Following are a couple of tips that can help if you're unfamiliar with Excel and Calc.

To enter data into a cell, just click the cell and start typing. If you want to clear your entry without saving it, press the Esc key. Press Enter or Tab when you're done. To delete the contents of a cell, click the cell and press either the Delete key or the Backspace key.

You use formulas to summarize your worksheet data. To create a formula in either Excel or Calc, click the cell where you want to enter the formula, type an equal sign, and type the rest of the formula. You can find the available formula functions in the programs' Help files, but we discuss the formulas we use in the chapter.

Most formulas summarize the data in one or more cells. You refer to cells in Excel and Calc using the cell reference, which consists of the cell's column followed by the cell's row. For example, cell A4 is the fourth cell down in column A. You refer to ranges of cells by typing the first cell in the range, a colon (:), and the last cell in the range. For example, you would refer to the cells from A1 to A4 with the range reference A1:A4. You can span rows and columns in a row reference, too. The range reference A1:B4 is perfectly valid and encompasses eight cells.

In Excel, you can refer to every cell in a row or column by repeating the row number or column letter around the colon. For example, you would refer to every cell in row 2 as 2:2 and every cell in column G as G:G.

To enter a series of values in cell range, follow these steps:

1. Type the first series value in a cell and press Enter.
2. Type the second series value in the active cell and press Enter.
3. Select the two cells.
4. Grab the fill handle and drag it until it covers the range of cells into which you want to extend the series.

For example, if you wanted to enter a series of five hours in the cell range C2:C6, you would type 1 in cell C2, 2 in cell C3, select cells C2:C3, grab the fill handle, and drag it down until it covers cell C6. The last step of this procedure appears in Figure 12.4.

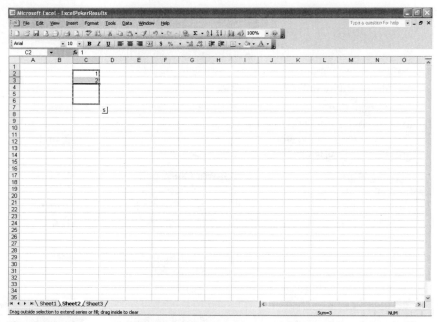

Figure 12.4 After you establish the series progression, you can extend it as far as you like.

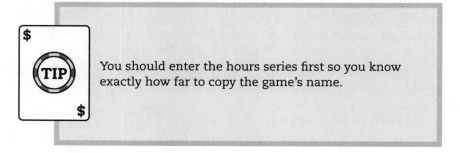

You should enter the hours series first so you know exactly how far to copy the game's name.

Sorting a Data List

Now that you've entered your data into the worksheet, you can start your analysis. The simplest way to analyze your data is to sort it by game, date, and hour so all of your Hold 'em results will be together, followed by your Omaha results, Omaha high-low, and so on. An example data list appears in Figure 12.5.

To sort a data list in Excel or Calc, follow these steps:

1. Click any cell in the data list.

2. Choose Data, Sort to display the Sort dialog box (shown in Figure 12.6).

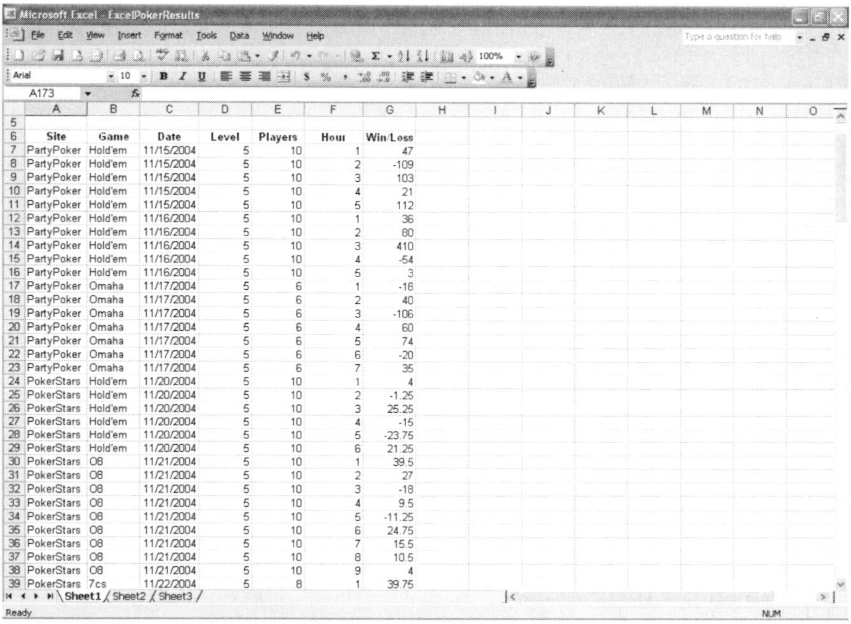

	Site	Game	Date	Level	Players	Hour	Win/Loss
7	PartyPoker	Hold'em	11/15/2004	5	10	1	47
8	PartyPoker	Hold'em	11/15/2004	5	10	2	-109
9	PartyPoker	Hold'em	11/15/2004	5	10	3	103
10	PartyPoker	Hold'em	11/15/2004	5	10	4	21
11	PartyPoker	Hold'em	11/15/2004	5	10	5	112
12	PartyPoker	Hold'em	11/16/2004	5	10	1	36
13	PartyPoker	Hold'em	11/16/2004	5	10	2	80
14	PartyPoker	Hold'em	11/16/2004	5	10	3	410
15	PartyPoker	Hold'em	11/16/2004	5	10	4	-54
16	PartyPoker	Hold'em	11/16/2004	5	10	5	3
17	PartyPoker	Omaha	11/17/2004	5	6	1	-18
18	PartyPoker	Omaha	11/17/2004	5	6	2	40
19	PartyPoker	Omaha	11/17/2004	5	6	3	-106
20	PartyPoker	Omaha	11/17/2004	5	6	4	60
21	PartyPoker	Omaha	11/17/2004	5	6	5	74
22	PartyPoker	Omaha	11/17/2004	5	6	6	-20
23	PartyPoker	Omaha	11/17/2004	5	6	7	35
24	PokerStars	Hold'em	11/20/2004	5	10	1	4
25	PokerStars	Hold'em	11/20/2004	5	10	2	-1.25
26	PokerStars	Hold'em	11/20/2004	5	10	3	25.25
27	PokerStars	Hold'em	11/20/2004	5	10	4	-15
28	PokerStars	Hold'em	11/20/2004	5	10	5	-23.75
29	PokerStars	Hold'em	11/20/2004	5	10	6	21.25
30	PokerStars	O8	11/21/2004	5	10	1	39.5
31	PokerStars	O8	11/21/2004	5	10	2	27
32	PokerStars	O8	11/21/2004	5	10	3	-18
33	PokerStars	O8	11/21/2004	5	10	4	9.5
34	PokerStars	O8	11/21/2004	5	10	5	-11.25
35	PokerStars	O8	11/21/2004	5	10	6	24.75
36	PokerStars	O8	11/21/2004	5	10	7	15.5
37	PokerStars	O8	11/21/2004	5	10	8	10.5
38	PokerStars	O8	11/21/2004	5	10	9	4
39	PokerStars	7cs	11/22/2004	5	8	1	39.75

Figure 12.5 These results are jumbled, but there are ways to make sense of them.

3. Click the Sort By down arrow, and select the first column by which you want to sort your data list.

4. Select the first Ascending or Descending option button to put lower values at the top of the sorted list (ascending order) or at the bottom of the list (descending order).

5. Repeat Steps 3 and 4 for the remaining two sort levels if desired.

If you sorted the data shown in Figure 12.5 by win/loss in descending order, and then by game, which emphasizes your best hours as a player, you would get the results shown in Figure 12.7.

Figure 12.6 Use the Sort dialog box to specify how you want to arrange your data.

Figure 12.7 This data view focuses on your best hourly wins.

Filtering a Data List

Sorting a data list can provide useful information, but a sort leaves all of your data displayed on screen for you to pick through. If you'd rather limit the data that appears on the screen, you can create filters to display just the data you want to review. Excel and Calc offer several types of filters, from the very simple to the somewhat complex. Neither program's filters are hard to use, once you've gone through the process once or twice.

Creating an AutoFilter

The simplest type of filter you can create is the AutoFilter, where you select the value you want to use as your filter criterion from a list of values in a column. To create an AutoFilter in either Excel or Calc, follow these steps:

1. Click any cell in your data list.

2. Choose Data, Filter, AutoFilter. Filter arrows appear at the right edge of the column header cells.

3. Click the filter arrow on the column by which you want to filter your data in order to display a list of the column's values, as shown in Figure 12.8.

4. Select the value to use as your criterion to filter the list.

Figure 12.8 You can select any value to filter your data list.

Filtering a data list removes the data you don't want from your worksheet while retaining any sorting or other processing you've done. Filtering the data list in Figure 12.7 to display just your Omaha results produces a much more readable output, as shown in Figure 12.9.

You can create compound filters when AutoFilter is turned on. To create a compound filter, click a filter arrow to filter your data list by the entries in one column, and then click another filter arrow to filter the remaining records by any additional criteria.

> **TIP**
>
> You'll also find the Sort Ascending and Sort Descending options in the filter down arrow list, if you'd like to sort your filtered data list.

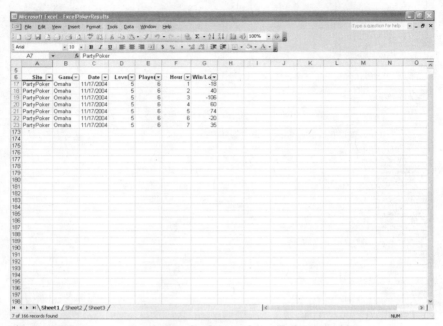

Figure 12.9 Focus your attention on the data you're really interested in.

Creating a Top or Bottom 10 Filter

One of the more interesting ways you can filter your data is to determine what impact your best and worst performances have on your bottom line. It's no secret that the key to playing winning poker is to lose as little as possible while waiting to win the occasional big pots that come along. Your results really take off when you win two or three big pots in a row, but you'll have to play quite a while for that to happen. When you track your results by the hour, you can get a very good idea of how your best and worst hours affect your results.

To display the top or bottom values in a data list column in Excel, follow these steps:

1. Click any cell in your data list.

2. Choose Data, Filter, AutoFilter. Filter arrows appear at the right edge of the column header cells.

3. Click the filter arrow on the column by which you want to filter your data and choose Top 10. The Top 10 AutoFilter dialog box appears (as shown in Figure 12.10).

Figure 12.10 Find the best and worst values using the Top 10 AutoFilter dialog box.

4. Click the first down arrow and select either Top or Bottom.

5. Click in the middle field and type the number of values you want to display.

6. Click OK.

If you're interested in displaying the top or bottom percentiles of a data list column's values in Excel, follow these steps:

1. Click any cell in your data list.

2. Choose Data, Filter, AutoFilter. Filter arrows appear at the right edge of the column header cells.

3. Click the filter arrow on the column by which you want to filter your data and choose Top 10.

4. In the middle field, type the percentage of values you want to see.

5. Click the third down arrow in the Top 10 AutoFilter dialog box and choose Percent.

6. Click OK.

If you wanted to see the top 25 percent of your hourly wins, for example, you would choose Top from the first down arrow list, type **25** in the second field, and choose Percent from the third down arrow list.

The procedure to display the top or bottom data list values in Calc is a bit different than it is in Excel. You can still choose Data, Filter, AutoFilter, and then choose Top 10 from any column's filter list, but that option only displays the top 10 values, not a dialog box where you can choose an arbitrary number of top or bottom values. The dialog box does exist, though.

To display the top or bottom values in a Calc data list, follow these steps:

1. Click any cell in your data list.

2. Choose Data, Filter, Standard Filter to display the Standard Filter dialog box, shown in Figure 12.11.

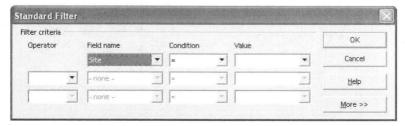

Figure 12.11 Calc lets you find the top and bottom value sets in a data list, but the procedure's a bit different.

3. Click the first Field down arrow, and choose the field by which you want to filter your data list.

4. Click the first Condition down arrow and choose Largest to display the top values or Smallest to display the lowest values.

5. In the Value field, type the number of values you want to display.

6. Click OK.

To display the top or bottom percentile values in a list, choose Largest % or Smallest % from the Condition down list and then, in the Value field, type the percentage of values to display.

Creating a Custom Filter in Excel

The filters we've discussed so far let you find rows that contain a specific value, such as the name of a game, or the top or bottom range of values in a list column. What these filters don't let you do is to find list rows that contain values that fall within a range of values. For example, you can't use a Top 10 filter to display your results from December 11 to December 17..However, you can use a custom filter in Excel, or an advanced filter in Calc, to filter your results according to that type of criteria.

To create a custom filter in Excel, follow these steps:

1. Click any cell in your data list.

2. Choose Data, Filter, AutoFilter. Filter arrows appear on the top row of your data list.

3. Click the filter arrow of the column by which you want to filter the list and choose Custom. The Custom AutoFilter dialog box appears, as shown in Figure 12.12.

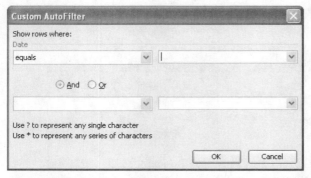

Figure 12.12 In Excel, you can use the Custom AutoFilter dialog box to find rows that meet complex criteria.

4. Click the down arrow at the right edge of the field at the top left of the dialog box, and choose the comparison operation you want to use.

5. Click the down arrow at the right of the field at the top right of the dialog box, and choose the value to use in conjunction with the comparison operator.

6. If you're done, click OK. If you'd like to create compound criteria, continue to the next step.

7. Select the AND option button to require the column's value to meet both criteria you set, or select the OR option button to require the column's value to meet either criterion you set.

8. Click the down arrow at the right edge of the field at the bottom left of the dialog box, and choose the comparison operation you want to use.

9. Click the down arrow at the right of the field at the bottom right of the dialog box, and choose the value to use in conjunction with the comparison operator.

10. Click OK.

When you create a custom filter in Excel, you can choose from the following comparison operations: equals, does not equal, is greater than, is greater than or equal to, is less than, is less than or equal to, begins with, does not begin with, ends with, does not end with, contains, and does not contain.

CAUTION

The begins with, does not begin with, ends with, does not end with, contains, and does not contain comparison operations only work with text values, not dates or numbers. If you apply one of those operations to a column that contains dates or numbers, the filter will hide all of the rows in your data list.

If you wanted to filter your data list so it only shows your results from November 21 to November 27, you could do so by following this procedure:

1. Click any cell in the data list.

2. Choose Data, Filter, AutoFilter.

3. Click the Date filter arrow and choose Custom.

4. Click the down arrow at the top left of the dialog box, and choose is greater than or equal to.

5. Click the down arrow at the top right of the dialog box, and choose the date starting with 11/21.

6. Click the down arrow at the bottom left of the dialog box, and choose is less than or equal to.

7. Click the down arrow at the bottom right of the dialog box, and choose the date starting with 11/27.

8. Click OK.

Creating a Custom Filter in Calc

You can also create a custom filter in Calc, but the steps are slightly different. In this case, you use the Standard Filter dialog box, which you encountered earlier. You're also limited to the following operations: equals, does not equal, is greater than, is greater than or equal to, is less than, and is less than or equal to.

To create a custom filter in Calc, follow these steps:

1. Click any cell in the data list.

2. Choose Data, Filter, Standard Filter. The Standard Filter dialog box appears (shown in Figure 12.13).

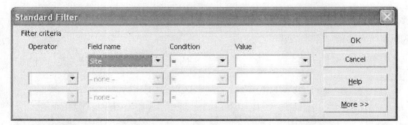

Figure 12.13 The Standard Filter dialog box pulls double duty in Calc.

3. Click the first Field Name down arrow, and choose the field by which you want to filter the data list.

4. Click the first Condition down arrow, and choose the operation to use in the condition.

5. Click the first Value down arrow, and choose the value to use in the condition.

6. If you're done, click OK. If you'd like to create a compound condition, continue to the next step.

7. Click the first Operator and choose AND to require the column's value to meet both conditions you set, or choose OR to allow the column's value to meet either condition you set.

8. Repeat Steps 3 through 5 with the second set of condition controls in the Standard Filter dialog box.

9. If you're done, click OK. If you'd like to add a third condition, do so by repeating Steps 3 through 5 with the third set of condition controls.

10. Click OK to apply the filter.

Removing a Filter

To remove your AutoFilter and turn off filtering in Excel or Calc, choose Data, Filter, AutoFilter. To remove your filter while keeping filtering turned on, choose Data, Filter, Show All in Excel, or choose Data, Filter, Remove Filter in Calc.

Copying Only Visible Rows in a Data List

One of the annoying things about Excel is that when you select the contents of a filtered data list, you actually select all of the rows from the top left corner of your drag area to the bottom row, not just the visible cells.

To copy and paste just the visible cells in Excel, follow these steps:

1. Select the cells you want to copy.

2. Choose Edit, Go To.

3. Click the Special button to display the Go To Special dialog box, shown in Figure 12.14.

4. Select the Visible Cells Only option, and click OK.

5. Choose Edit, Copy.

6. Select the upper-left cell of the paste area.

7. Choose Edit, Paste.

When you select filtered data list cells in Calc you select the visible cells by default, so there's no need to go through the procedure listed for Excel.

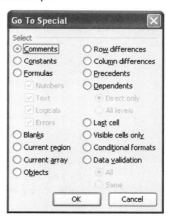

Figure 12.14 The Go To Special dialog box lets you select subsets of the cells in your worksheet.

Copying Visible Cells with a Single Mouse Click

If you do a lot of filtering in Excel and would rather select the visible cells with a single mouse click, you can add the Select Visible Cells button to a toolbar to ease the process.

To add the Select Visible Cells button to a toolbar, follow these steps:

1. Choose Tools, Customize to display the Customize dialog box.

2. Click the Commands tab to display the Commands tab page, shown in Figure 12.15.

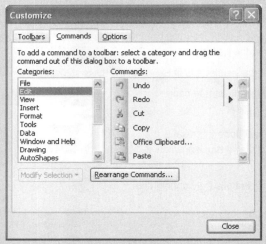

Figure 12.15 There are all manner of interesting and useful toolbar buttons in the Customize dialog box.

3. In the Categories list, click Edit.

4. Scroll down the Commands pane until you see the Select Visible Cells toolbar button.

5. Drag the Select Visible Cells button to a toolbar and release the left mouse button. When you drag the button to a valid spot on a toolbar, an insertion point appears on the toolbar.

Recalling Filters with Views

Creating filters isn't that difficult, but it can be a little time consuming to go through the motions to re-create a filter you use frequently—assuming you remember all the little settings, of course. If you use Excel, you can save the filter settings you like and display that view with a few mouse clicks. For example, you could create a filter to display just your Hold 'em results on UltimateBet, save the filter, and recall it whenever you want to revisit your data.

To save a filter as a view, follow these steps:

1. Create the filter you want to save.

2. Choose View, Custom Views to display the Custom View dialog box.

3. Click the Add button to display the Add View dialog box, which is shown in Figure 12.16.

Figure 12.16 Here's where you define the custom view you want to save.

4. Type a name for the view (such as UBHoldem) in the Name box.

5. Ensure the Hidden Rows, Columns, and Filter Settings check box is selected.

6. Click OK.

To recall the view, follow these steps:

1. Choose View, Custom View.

2. Click the name of the view you want to display.

3. Click Show.

Summarizing Data Lists Using SUBTOTAL Formulas

Every spreadsheet program we know of lets you summarize your data using formulas that you type into cells. For example, if you are using Excel and want to display the sum of the values in the cell range G14:G18, you would type the formula =SUM(G14:G18) in the cell where you want the result to appear. The problem with standard formulas, such as SUM, AVERAGE, MAX, MIN, and so on, in Excel is that they operate on all of the cells in the range named in the formula, regardless of whether the cells are visible in the worksheet or not. It's the same problem you run into when you copy and paste cells in Excel: Unless you tell Excel you only want to operate on the visible cells in the range, the program assumes you want to summarize all of the cells in the range.

Creating a SUBTOTAL Formula

Fortunately, you can create SUBTOTAL formulas that summarize just the visible cells in a range. The SUBTOTAL formula has the following syntax:

```
SUBTOTAL(operation, range1, range 2...)
```

In an Excel SUBTOTAL formula, the operation *argument* (information the formula needs to work) represents the function with which you want to summarize the data named in the range arguments. Table 12.1 lists the summary operations available to you. Note that some of the operations affect all of the cells in the range and that others affect only the visible cells in the range. Be sure to use the proper code!

Table 12.1   Excel SUBTOTAL Formula Summary Operations

Function	All Values	Visible Values	Description
AVERAGE	1	101	Finds the arithmetic mean (average) of the values.
COUNT	2	102	Counts how many cells in a range contain a number.
COUNTA	3	103	Counts all non-blank cells in a range.
MAX	4	104	Finds the largest value in a range.
MIN	5	105	Finds the smallest value in a range.
PRODUCT	6	106	Multiplies the values in a range together.
STDEV	7	107	Finds the standard deviation of a sample from data in a range.
STDEVP	8	108	Finds the standard deviation of all values in a range.
SUM	9	109	Finds the sum of all values in a range.
VAR	10	110	Finds the variance of a sample from data in a range.
VARP	11	111	Finds the variance of a sample from data in a range.

The range arguments are simply the cells that contain the values you want to summarize in the formula. For example, to summarize the visible values in column G of an Excel worksheet, you would type the formula =SUBTOTAL(109, G:G).

When you create the same formula in Calc, you replace the comma in the formula with a semicolon and use the summary operation code from Table 12.1's All Values column to create the SUBTOTAL formula. Calc's SUBTOTAL formula only considers the visible cells in a data range, so you don't need to worry about two sets of functions.

One Shortcut That's Not in Calc

One of Calc's limitations is that you can't use the shortcut notation G:G to include every cell in a column in a cell range, which means you have to name the cells at the beginning and end of the range. To find the sum of the visible cells in column G of a Calc data list, for example, you would create a formula such as =SUBTOTAL(9;G6:G10000). We set the cutoff at row 10,000 because you can track five years of full-time play (40 hours a week multiplied by 50 weeks of play a year, which allows you a two-week vacation each year) in that space.

Summarizing Data Lists with SUBTOTAL Formulas

There's more to designing a worksheet that contains a SUBTOTAL formula than just slapping the formula into any cell and calling it good. Take a look at the worksheet in Figure 12.17 as an example.

The SUBTOTAL formula is in row 3. But if you invoke a filter that hides the values in row 3, you hide the SUBTOTAL formula's result! You also don't want to put the formulas at the bottom of the data list because you'd have to insert a new row every time you wanted to enter another hour's results. You'd also need to scroll to the bottom of the data list to see your results, which is a pain.

The trick to including SUBTOTAL formulas in a worksheet is to have a number of blank rows above the row where your data list starts. The worksheet in Figure 12.18 is one possible configuration.

Calculating Averages and Standard Deviations

Readers with a statistical bent can no doubt find all manner of ways to measure their data, but we'll focus on two particularly useful summaries: the average and the standard deviation. To find the average of the visible values in column G of an Excel data list, you would create this formula:

=SUBTOTAL(101,G:G)

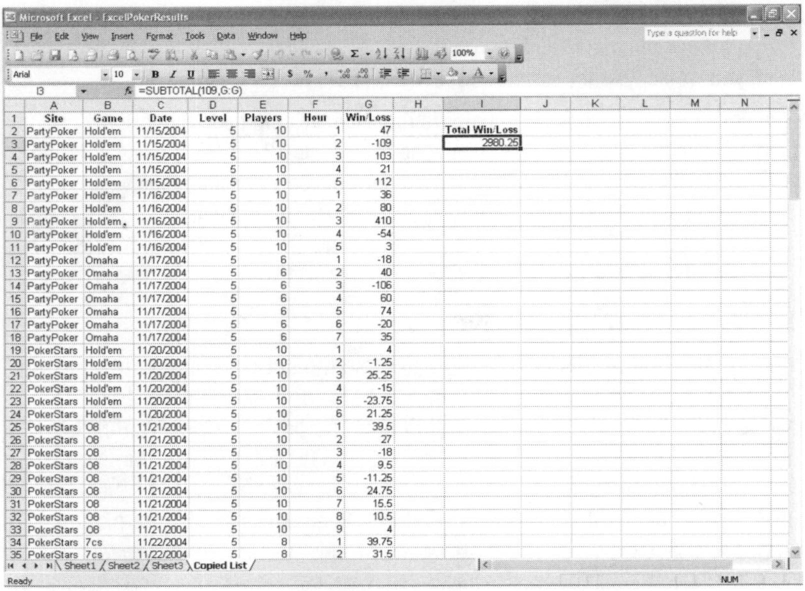

Figure 12.17 Trouble lurks in the depths of this subtotaled worksheet.

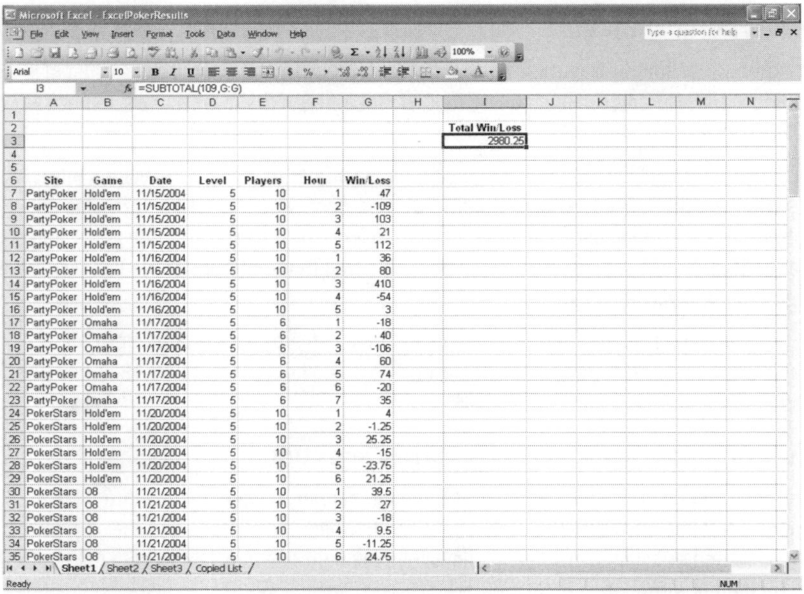

Figure 12.18 Putting a SUBTOTAL formula above the data list it summarizes keeps the result in full view.

The same formula in Calc, where you can't use the G:G column reference, would be

`=SUBTOTAL(1;G6:G10000)`

To make the Excel formula consider all values, regardless of any active filters, you would change the formula to

`=SUBTOTAL(1,G:G)`

Because Calc's version of the SUBTOTAL formula only considers visible cells, you need to create an AVERAGE formula, such as the following:

`=AVERAGE(G6:G10000)`

We assume you're familiar with averages, but you might not be familiar with how you calculate and interpret a data set's *standard deviation*. Simply put, standard deviation is a measure of how much your data set tends to vary from the average. A data set such as 1, 2, 3, 4, 5 has an average of 3 (1 + 2 + 3 + 4 + 5 = 15/5 = 3) and a very low standard deviation. By contrast, a data set such as –30, 45, –6, 7, –1, which also has an average of 3, contains values that vary significantly from the average, resulting in a much higher standard deviation.

The paper-based method to calculate a data set's standard deviation goes like this:

1. Find the data set's average.

2. Subtract the average from each value in the data set.

3. Square the difference.

4. Add the squares of the differences.

5. Divide the differences by the number of values in the data set minus one (e.g., if there are five values in the data set, divide the sum of the squared differences by four).

6. Calculate the square root of the result from Step 5.

Table 12.2 lists the first few calculations for the data set 1, 2, 3, 4, 5.

Table 12.2   Calculating a Standard Deviation

Value	Value – Average	Square the Difference
1	–2	4
2	–1	1
3	0	0
4	1	1
5	2	4

The sum of the differences is 10. Dividing 10 by 4 gives the result 2.5. The square root of 2.5 is about 1.6, so the standard deviation of the data set is about 1.6.

Table 12.3 lists the calculations for the data set –30, 45, –6, 7, –1.

Table 12.3   Calculating the Standard Deviation of Another Data Set with an Average of 3

Value	Value – Average	Square the Difference
–30	–33	1,089
45	48	2,304
–6	–9	81
7	4	16
–1	–4	16

The sum of the differences is 3,506. Dividing 3,506 by 4 gives the result 876.5. The square root of 876.5, and the standard deviation of this data set, is about 29.6.

In Excel, the formula you use to calculate the standard deviation of the visible cells in column G is

```
=SUBTOTAL(108,G:G)
```

The same formula in Calc, where you can't use the G:G column reference, would be

```
=SUBTOTAL(8;G6:G10000)
```

To make the Excel formula consider all values, regardless of any active filters, you would change the formula to

```
=SUBTOTAL(8,G:G)
```

Because Calc's version of the SUBTOTAL formula only considers visible cells, you need to create a STDEVP formula, such as the following:

```
=STDEVP(G6:G10000)
```

 Note

You should use the STDEVP formula, and its corresponding summary functions 8 and 108 in the SUBTOTAL formulas, so your spreadsheet calculates your data's standard deviation based on all values in the list, not a sample.

Interpreting Standard Deviations

These two data sets share an average, but their different standard deviations point out the variability of the data they contain. But what does a data set's standard deviation really tell you? It tells you how closely your data set's values correspond to the set's average. It also tells you, on average, how many of your data points are within a certain distance of the average. In general, you can expect 68 percent of your data points to be within one standard deviation of the average, 95 percent of your data points to be within two standard deviations of the average, and 99.7 percent of your data points to be within three standard deviations of the average.

As an example, consider the following hourly results from 94 hours of $5–$10 Hold 'em play:

> 0, 47, −109, 103, 21, 112, 0, 36, 80, 410, −54, 3, −45, −18, 40, −106, 60, 74, −20, 35, 63.75, 4, −1.25, 25.25, −15, −23.75, 21.25, 7.25, 39.5, 27, −18, 9.5, −11.25, 24.75, 15.5, 10.5, 4, 74, 39.75, 31.5, 69.25, −18.75, 22, 42.75, −14.25, 51, 52.25, 9.5, 23.75, 2, −22.25, 70.25, 50.25, −30.5, 38.75, −40.5, 45, 53.25, 57, 7.75, 43.25, 14, 4.25, 22.75, −41.25, 46.25, 22.25, −41.5, 55.5, −39, −18.75, −15.25, 55.75, 62.25, 74, 67.25, 32.25, −6, 45.75, −1, 33.75, −7.5, −21.25, −46, 4.75, 49.75, 16.75, −46.5, 23.5, −21.25, 58.75, 0.75, 40.5, 29.25, 68, 32, 27.75, −50, −9, 44.5, 70.5, −24, 56, 2.25, −14.25, 62.5, 9.25, −25.25, 41.5, 18.75, −5.25, 67, 34.5, 73.75, 49, 50.5, −28, 62.5, 67.25, −14, 29.75, 9.5, −7.5, 25, 2, −3.5, 32, 22, 2.5, −28.75, 61.75, 2, 14.75, −15, 0, 19.25, 19.5, 69.5, 9, 61.75, −10, 14.25, −39.75, −19.25, 40.5, −3.5, −5.75, 1.25, −48, −1.5, 23.75, 69, −46, 53, −25.25, 41.75, 17.75, −19.5, 3, 9, −33.75, 13.5, 5.75, 48.75, 55.75, 31, 55.25, 31.25, −27.25, 20.25, −49.5, 4.25, −7.25, 74.25, 54.75, 50, −13, −3.25, 61.75, −5, 43, 46.75, 48, −47.25, −12.25, 32.5, −30.25, 40.75, −33.25, 11.5, −26.25, 5, 62.25, 51.5

According to Excel, the data set's average is 18.41, which means that this player, on average, wins just over $18 an hour at $5–$10 Hold 'em. The data set's standard deviation is 46.46, which means that

- ✦ 68 percent of the time the player's hourly result will be between a $32.05 loss and a $64.87 win.

- ✦ 95 percent of the time the player's hourly result will be between a $78.51 loss and a $111.33 win.

- ✦ 99.7 percent of the time the player's hourly result will be between a $124.97 loss and a $157.79 win.

The variation in the values may surprise you at first, but they'll be of no surprise to anyone who tracks their results.

Obviously, you should strive to increase your hourly average, but should you worry about your standard deviation? It depends on the type of games you play in. If you play in loose games where everyone stays to the end, your opponents are bound to catch cards that beat you, increasing your losses. Of course, you might flop a couple of locks in a row and get five callers on the river each time, jacking up your hourly win. By contrast, tight games drive down your standard deviation because there's less money in each pot.

In general, as long as your hourly average is positive after 100 hours of play, you must be doing something right. Just work on keeping your losses small while you wait for the big hands to come along.

Summarizing Your Data Visually

The Chinese philosopher Confucius actually said that a picture is worth ten thousand words (thanks to comedian George Carlin for setting me straight on that). In Excel and Calc, you use charts to present your data visually.

Choosing the Best Chart Type for Your Data

The chart type you choose depends on your data and the type of information you want to gain from that data. Following are some of the basic charts you can create in Excel and Calc, with descriptions of how the charts summarize your data.

Bar and column charts (a column chart appears in Figure 12.19) are good for comparing values across categories. For example, you could compare how you do at Hold 'em, Omaha, and seven-card Stud.

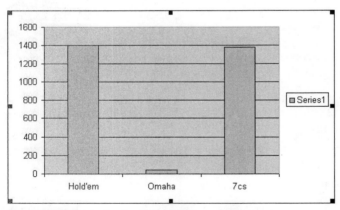

Figure 12.19 Bar and column charts compare different categories of data.

A line chart, shown in Figure 12.20, is good for comparing values that change over time. You could use a line chart to plot your bankroll's growth over time.

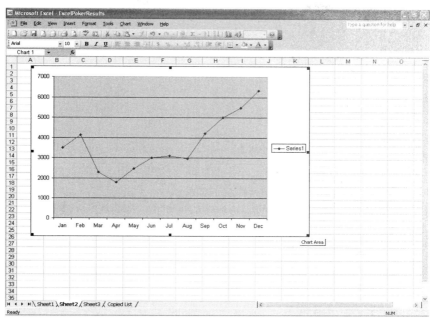

Figure 12.20 Data changes over time; use a line chart to track it.

Pie charts, such as the one shown in Figure 12.21, show how much a particular data category contributes to a whole. You could use a pie chart to plot how much of your time you spend playing various games. Pie charts can't handle negative values, though, so you'll need to use a bar or column chart if you need to plot a negative number.

XY scatter plots, such as the one shown in Figure 12.22, help call out a range of values in a category. Unlike pie charts, which only display each category's total, XY scatter plots display all data points in a series. XY scatter plots don't display totals, but you can create a worksheet formula to calculate that information.

> ♠♥♣♦ **Note**
>
> Both Excel and Calc create charts based on the visible, selected cells in a filtered data list, so you can just select the cells you want to summarize and start creating your chart.

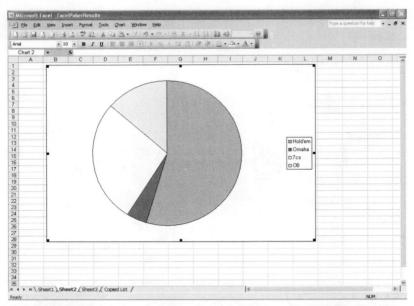

Figure 12.21 Pie charts provide easy-to-read summaries of how much a category of data contributes to a total.

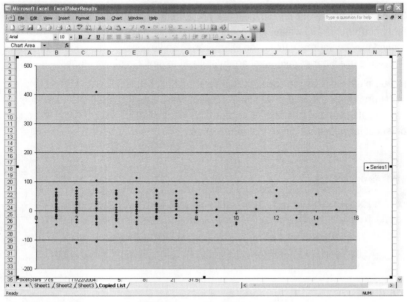

Figure 12.22 XY scatter plots show lots of helpful details.

Creating Charts in Excel

One of the nicest features of Excel and Calc is that they partially automate the chart cre-ation process. All you, the user, need to do is figure out which type of chart you want to create and choose the proper menu item.

To create a chart in Excel, follow these steps:

1. Select the data you want to plot, including the header row (if any).

2. Choose Insert, Chart to run the Chart Wizard. The first page of the wizard ap-pears in Figure 12.23.

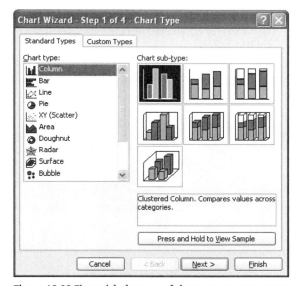

Figure 12.23 First, pick the type of chart you want to create.

3. Click the chart type you want to create and click Next.

4. Verify that the sample chart that appears in the second wizard page is correct. If the chart doesn't look right, click the Series tab to display the Series tab page (as shown in Figure 12.24).

5. In the Series list box, click the name of the series you want to check.

6. Verify that the cell ranges in the Name, X Values, and Y Values fields are correct. If the ranges aren't correct, type an equals sign, followed by the cell range that contains the values for those fields.

7. Click Next.

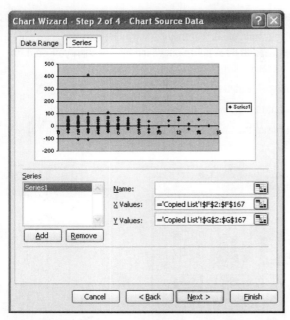

Figure 12.24 If necessary, tell the Chart Wizard which data to put where.

8. If desired, type titles for the chart and the horizontal and vertical axes in the appropriate fields.

9. Click Next.

10. Select the desired location for your new chart.

11. Click Finish to create the chart at the specified location.

You can create the default chart type, which is a column chart if you haven't changed anything, by selecting your data and pressing F11.

Creating Charts in Calc

Creating a chart in Calc is similar to the procedure you follow in Excel. Here are the details:

1. Select the data you want to plot, including the header row (if any).

2. Choose Insert, Chart to start the AutoFormat Chart tool.

3. Verify that the data range that appears in the Range field is correct. If not, correct the range.

4. If desired, click the Chart Results in Worksheet down arrow, and select a new location for the chart.

5. Click Next to display the second AutoFormat Chart page, shown in Figure 12.25.

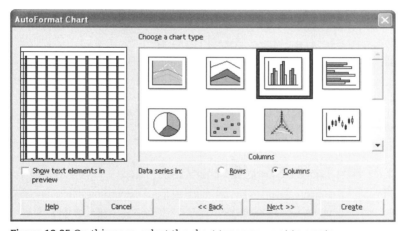

Figure 12.25 On this page, select the chart type you want to create.

6. Click the chart type you want to create.

7. Click Next.

8. If desired, change the grid line, data location, and chart subtype settings.

9. Click Next.

10. If desired, type titles for the chart and the axes in the appropriate fields.

11. Click Create.

Analyzing Your Results

Now that you can get your data into a spreadsheet program, sort it, filter it, and chart it, you can get down to brass tacks and ask specific questions about how you're playing. The following example questions are just that: examples. You know your play better than we ever will, so be creative in finding new ways to look at your results. Remember, every insight you gain means more money in your account.

How Do You Do in Specific Games?

One of the simplest questions you can ask is how much money you have won or lost in Hold 'em, Omaha, seven-card Stud, and so on. You can create SUBTOTAL formulas with the SUM operation to get the results after you filter your data list, and then use bar and column charts to summarize your results in particular games.

How Many Hours Have You Played?

To find the number of hours you've played, create a SUBTOTAL formula that counts the number of cells in your win/loss column that contain a numeric value. The formula you'd use for the example worksheet used in this chapter would be =SUBTOTAL(109, G:G) in Excel and =SUBTOTAL(9; G6:G10000) in Calc. As mentioned earlier, a pie chart is a natural fit when you want to display the share of time you've spent playing a particular game or a particular limit.

How Do You Do at Specific Limits?

You need to create a compound filter to answer this question. First, you need to display the results of a particular game. Only then can you create a second filter based on the limit you played at. You'll probably find that Hold 'em is more competitive at a given limit than seven-card Stud, which is in turn more competitive than Omaha high-low at the same limit.

How Do You Do on Specific Sites?

This one's easy: Just filter based on the site you're interested in summarizing and create a SUBTOTAL formula.

How Do You Do in the First Few Hours?
After a Few Hours?

You can gain a lot of insight into how you play when you examine your results on an hourly basis. For example, do you like to sit down at a table and play aggressively at first, then back off later? If you do follow that strategy, your first-hour results might vary significantly more than your other results. Do you start to get bored or tired over time and play more hands later in the session? Make a few loose calls you might otherwise not make? Filtering and charting your results to show how you do during particular hours can help point out these trends. In particular, try creating an XY scatter plot, with the hours on the X axis and your results on the Y axis. You might be surprised to see what pops up.

How Do You Do at Shorthanded Tables?

If you tend to play in the early morning hours, you might end up at Omaha high-low tables with only six players and Stud tables with only five players. How do you do at those games?

How Did You Do on Particular Dates?

Do you play better on weekends against the players who don't play during the week, or do you tend to win against the hard-core crowd that's there punching the clock every day? Did you play poorly because you were worried about work, a test, or a relationship? The easy solution is not to play when you're ill at ease, but it's not that easy to do when you can lose yourself in a game. Of course, you'll be tempted not to play when you see how much of yourself you're losing.

How Did You Do During the Past Week? During the Past 30 Days?

The book industry is big on what it calls *trailing* results: how well a book has done over the last week, month, quarter, six months, or year. They update their results every day or week to update those values. You should take a look at your weekly and monthly trailing results as well. To do that, filter your data list so the last seven or 30 days appear, and start asking questions!

Analyzing Your Game Using Poker Software

Using Excel or another spreadsheet program to analyze your results provides important insights into how you play at different times, but that sort of analysis tells you nothing about the individual hands you play. What's more, it tells you nothing about how you should play Ace-Nine suited before the flop. Should you raise with A9s when you're under the gun? Just call? Play it at all? And for that matter, how do you do overall when playing A9s? Excel can't help you answer those questions, but the resources and programs in this chapter can.

In this chapter, we show you how to determine the winning percentages of hands using a Web-based hand analyzer, how to play and simulate situations in the most popular poker variants using the Wilson Software Turbo Poker series, and how to analyze your own (and your opponents') play in intricate detail using the PokerTracker software program.

Determining the Winning Percentages of Hands

One interesting aspect of Late Night Poker, the World Poker Tour, and the World Series of Poker broadcasts is that the shows display each player's winning percentage, if they stay to the river. It's useful to know these percentages so you can see the psychology and tactics that go into high-stakes poker, but you can also use the percentages to determine how much of a favorite or underdog you are when you face similar situations.

If you've thought about programming your own software to determine various hands' winning percentages in the games you play, you don't have to. Seattle-area programmer Paul Deeds beat you to it. Just point your Web browser to www.twodimes.net/poker/ and use the Poker Odds Calculator, shown in Figure 13.1 evaluating a pair of Hold 'em hands.

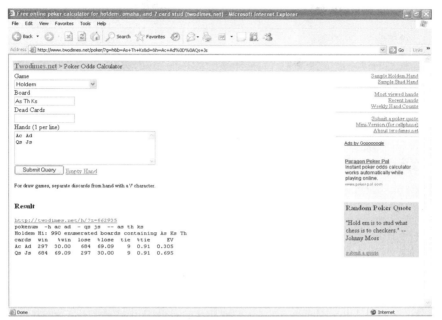

Figure 13.1 The Poker Odds Calculator calculates competing hands' winning percentages instantly.

To use the Poker Odds Calculator, follow these steps:

1. Open www.twodimes.net/poker/ in your Web browser.

2. Click the Games down arrow and select the game you want to evaluate.

3. If you want to evaluate a hand in a flop game on the flop or turn, type the cards in the Board field. For example, the board in Figure 13.1 is A♠T♥K♠ (the Ace of spades, Ten of hearts, and King of spades).

4. Type any dead cards, such as cards that were folded in a Stud game, in the Dead Cards field.

5. Type the hands to be evaluated in the Hands box. Put a space between each card and press the Enter key after you enter each hand.

6. Click Submit Query.

The hands' expected win, loss, and tie rates appear at the bottom of the Results area. The last result, expected value (EV), is the percentage of total money bet that a particular hand can expect to win.

> ♠♥♣♦ **Note**
>
> If you're a programmer and would like to build your own poker application, you can use the open source code available at SourceForge. The project's direct link is http://sourceforge.net/projects/pokersource/.

Using Wilson Software's Turbo Products

The Poker Odds Calculator lets you evaluate one known hand against one or more other known hands, but you can't see how a known hand stacks up against random hands. It's no problem to see how A♠K♠ stacks up against A♥K♦ before the flop (for the record, A♠K♠ is a 52.5 to 47.5 percent favorite heads-up), but you can't tell how A♠K♠ will do against nine random hands over the course of 100,000 deals. You need to use other programs for that sort of analysis, the best of which is the Wilson Software Turbo Poker series. No, playing against computer opponents is not the same as playing against real humans. No, playing against computer opponents doesn't re-create the atmosphere of playing when there's something at stake. But here's the most important point, which drowns out the objections: Investing $85 or so in a Wilson Software Turbo Poker program will save you far more than $85 when you start playing for real money. Seriously. We paid far more than $85 to learn how to win at Hold 'em. We paid far more than $85 to learn how to win at Omaha high-low. What's even better, of course, is that you can use the Turbo Poker programs as simulation tools for years after you don't feel you have anything more to learn from playing the game. That's far more bang for your buck than beating Halo 2 twice in 24 hours.

Playing a Turbo Poker Game

To start a Turbo Poker game with the current settings, choose the left-most menu heading (which corresponds to the name of the game), and click Begin a New Game to display the Deal Options dialog box, shown in Figure 13.2.

If all you want to do is play the game without changing any settings, which we recommend until you want to run high-speed simulations, click Done to display the game screen, and then click Deal (or press D) to deal the first hand. Figure 13.3 provides a typical look at the game's interface after you start playing.

You can check, bet, raise, call, or fold by pressing the first letter of the action (note that the check and call options will never be available at the same time) or left-click the action you want. If you want to fold and complete the hand without waiting, press Z or click Zip to display the hand result, and press D to deal another round.

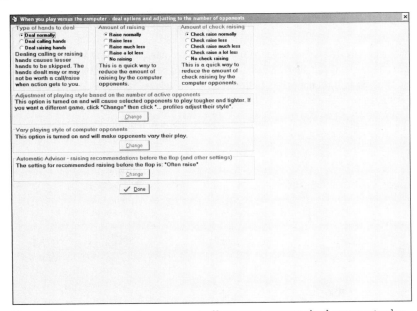

Figure 13.2 You can control every aspect of how your computerized opponents play.

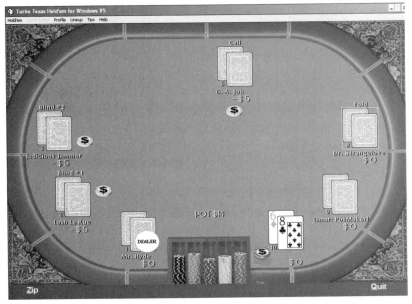

Figure 13.3 The Turbo Poker programs offer consistent and easy-to-understand play interfaces.

Changing a Game's Settings

Playing or simulating a poker game only works well when you can replicate your game's conditions exactly. The online poker rooms we frequent have a standard three-raise limit and two blinds, but if you play in brick-and-mortar card rooms, you might have different rules. California card rooms have a button charge that acts as a blind, for example, and MGM/Mirage poker rooms, such as the Bellagio, allow four raises instead of three.

To change the rules in a Turbo Poker game, choose Game Setup, Modify Game Settings to display the Game Settings dialog box. The Games Settings dialog box from Turbo Texas Hold 'em 5.0 appears in Figure 13.4.

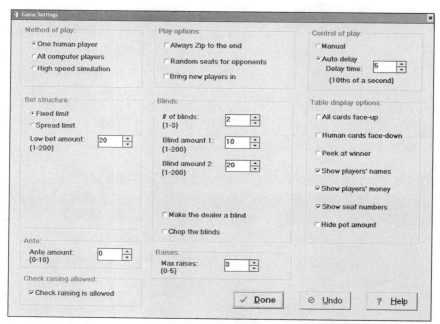

Figure 13.4 You can change the Turbo Poker games to match your favorite game's rules.

The default settings in Turbo Texas Hold 'em give you a good game, but we recommend making a few changes to these defaults. Specifically, we recommend that you turn on the following options:

- ✦ Always Zip to the End
- ✦ Random Seats for Opponents
- ✦ Bring New Players In
- ✦ Hide Pot Amount

Turning on the Always Zip to the End option moves you to the next hand after you fold. Turning on the other three options makes the game more realistic for playing when you know nothing about your opponents and have to keep track of the money in the pot yourself. You should also consider turning off the Show Players' Names options so that you have to deduce a player's profile over time from their play and not know exactly how they'll play from very start based on their name.

To end a game, press Q or click Quit at the bottom-left corner of the program window. You can then save your game or exit the program by choosing Exit from the left-most menu. In Turbo Texas Hold 'em, for example, you would choose Hold 'em, Exit.

Turning the Advisor On or Off

When you play one of the Turbo Poker software programs, you'll see all but one of the play options (check, bet, call, raise, or fold) at the bottom of the program window displayed in red. The option displayed in yellow is the automatic advisor's recommended action, but we feel that having a recommended action at the bottom of the screen takes away from the game's play. You can't have the programs not recommend actions, but you can choose which player advises you. We like to have the worst player available advise us, so it's no big deal to ignore a recommendation to check with the nuts on the river.

To choose the advisor profile with maximum ignorability, follow these steps:

1. Choose Game Setup, Advisor Settings to display the Advisor Settings dialog box.

2. Select the Manual option button and click the Change button that appears. Clicking the Change button displays the list of available profiles, shown in Figure 13.5.

3. Click the advisor that corresponds to the game you're playing:

   ✦ In Turbo Texas Hold 'em, click #38, Simple Simon.

   ✦ In Turbo Omaha High or Omaha High-Low, click #52, Painless Potter.

   ✦ In Turbo Stud, click #52, Soft Sammy.

   ✦ In Turbo Stud 8/or Better, click #38, A. Pismo Clam.

4. Click Done to finalize your selection.

5. Click OK to accept your changes.

To set the advisor back to normal, choose Game Setup, Advisor Settings, and select the Automatic option button.

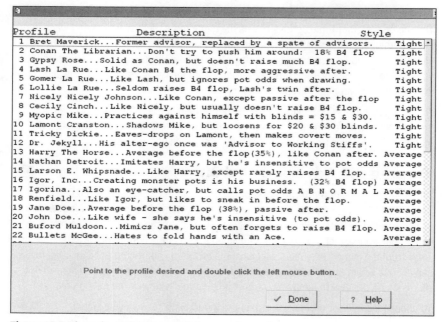

Figure 13.5 It's easier to ignore an advisor you know is wrong.

Changing the Rake

Every online card room takes a few dollars from each pot as its profit. A maximum of three dollars per pot may not seem like a lot of money, particularly when you compare the online rake to physical card rooms that often take up to five dollars from each pot ($4 as the rake and $1 for a bad beat jackpot); but if you play 60 hands per hour, even the relatively low online rake takes $120 or so off the table every hour. If you want to see how you do in a game on an hourly basis, you need to simulate the rake accurately.

To change the rake in a Turbo Poker game, follow these steps:

1. Choose Game Setup, Rake Options to display the Rake Options dialog box.

2. Select the Drag the Pot During Play option button.

3. Click Settings to display the Rake and Toke dialog box, shown in Figure 13.6.

4. Select the options to reflect the game you want to simulate.

5. Click Done.

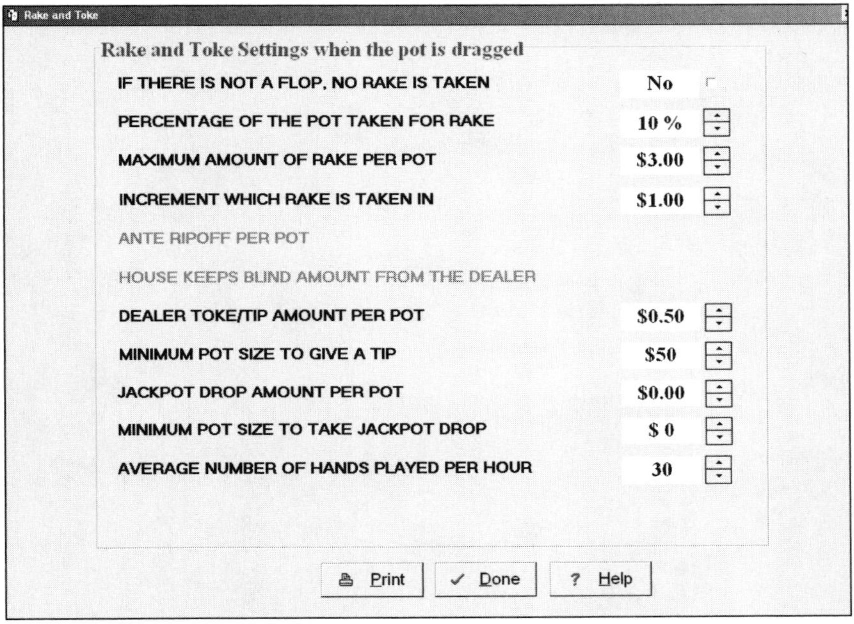

Figure 13.6 Make the rake match your game so you know how much money the house takes off the table.

Changing the Number of Players

Another way you can customize your Turbo Poker game is to set up a shorthanded table so you can play against five opponents at a flop game or four opponents at a Stud game. Each program alters the computer opponents' strategy and your advisor (if set to Automatic) to reflect the game's shorthanded status.

To change the number of players in a game, follow these steps:

1. Choose Game Setup, Change Number of Players.

2. In the Change Number of Players dialog box, shown in Figure 13.7, click the up and down arrows to set a new number of players.

3. Click Done.

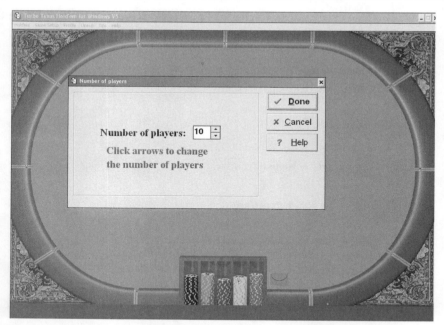

Figure 13.7 How you play changes when there are fewer players in the game, so it pays to practice when there's no money on the line.

Changing the Lineup

Literally thousands of players play online poker at a given site, so you won't always face the same level of opposition. Sometimes the tough players all congregate at your table, but sometimes you'll have one or two tough players, a couple of solid players who occasionally put in too much money, and some soft players who chase with anything. If you play a lot at $3–$6 limits and below, you have no doubt run into the loose wild games that used to be the exclusive province of California card rooms. And, yes, once in a great while, you will be the only decent player at a table where almost everyone calls and no one but you raises before the flop, but those tasty and very profitable games are few and far between.

The Turbo Poker games come with a wide variety of built-in lineups for average, aggressive, and passive games. Don't worry about memorizing which lineup has which players in it; the lineup names indicate what type of players you'll face.

To load an existing lineup, follow these steps:

1. Choose Lineup to display the Lineup dialog box, shown in Figure 13.8.

2. Click Load to display the Load a Lineup dialog box.

3. Click the lineup you want to use in your game.

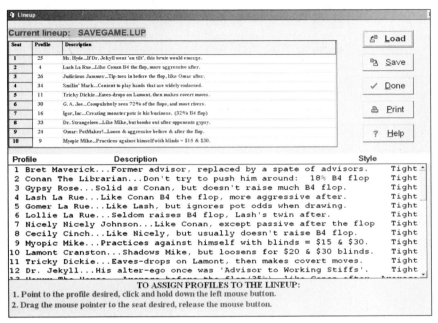

Figure 13.8 Pick the lineup that most closely approximates your game.

    4. Click OK.

    5. Click Done.

The existing lineups are fine for most purposes, but you might want to create a lineup with mostly strong players and one or two soft spots or to test how a particular strategy works against a mixed field. To create and save a new lineup, follow these steps:

    1. Choose Lineup to display the Lineup dialog box.

    2. Click the lineup that's closest to the lineup you want to create.

    3. For each player you want to replace, drag the replacement profile from the list at the bottom of the dialog box to the lineup position of the player you want to replace.

    4. Click Save to display the Save Lineup dialog box.

    5. Type a name for your lineup in the File Name field. You don't need to add the .lup extension; the program adds it for you.

    6. Click OK.

    7. Click Done.

Creating a New Player Profile

Playing the Turbo Poker games is fun and can give you great insights into how you should play against different lineups. You can extend those benefits by defining your own custom player profiles to practice specific strategies and tactics against various lineups. Which options you set depends on which Turbo Poker program you play. Figure 13.9 shows the first of many settings pages for a Turbo Texas Hold 'em profile.

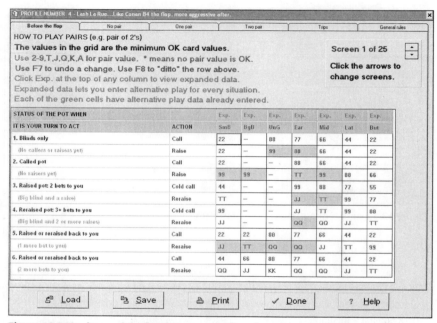

Figure 13.9 You have a lot of options to consider when you create a new profile.

Don't panic! There's no need to define every play option from scratch when you create a new profile. Instead, you should pick the profile that plays the way you want it to play, except for one thing. For example, when we tested in Chapter 8 whether it made sense to call before the flop and under the gun with the Hold 'em hand KTo, we used the Lash La Rue profile as our base and changed his starting hand requirements so that he would call under the gun with KTo. Yep, that's it: one change. Most of the time you'll be able to make one or two changes to an existing profile and either run a simulation or play against your new profile to hone your skills in given situations. For example, if you want to see how you should play against an aggressive Hold 'em player who will call in any position with Axs, you can change the Lash La Rue profile to make that decision and save the profile as a new player.

To create a new profile, follow these steps:

1. Choose Profile to display the Profile dialog box.

2. Double-click the existing profile upon which you want to base your new profile.

3. Change the necessary options to implement the desired strategy.

4. Click Save.

5. Double-click a custom profile number to display the Save the Profile dialog box, shown in Figure 13.10.

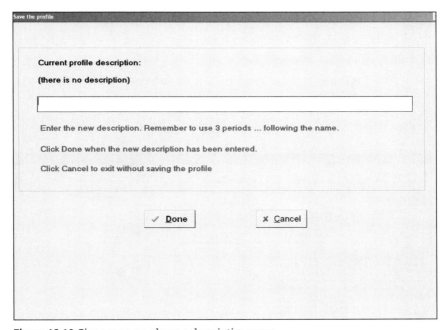

Figure 13.10 Give your new player a descriptive name.

6. Type a description in the text field. The entry must have the player's name, followed by three periods, and a description. For example, you might type **KTo Caller . . . Calls under the gun with King-Ten offsuit**.

7. Click Done to save the new profile.

8. Click Done to close the Profile dialog box.

Challenging the Advisor

Many players find that they disagree with the advisor program on the best course of action in a given situation. You can run a simulation to see whether you or the advisor program is right in that one circumstance over the long haul, or you can challenge the advisor directly. No, you won't play the advisor head-to-head. Instead, you and the advisor play the exact same hands against the exact same opponents and see who wins the most (or loses the least) money over the course of 50, 100, or 200 hands.

♠♥♣♦ Note

The challenge routine tells you the deal code it used to generate the simulation, which makes it possible for you to replay the hands and revisit your decisions.

To challenge the advisor, follow these steps:

1. Choose Game, Challenge, where Game is the first menu header (which reflects the name of the game you're playing, such as Hold'em) and Challenge is the menu item that starts with that word. The Challenge the Advisor dialog box, shown in Figure 13.11, appears.

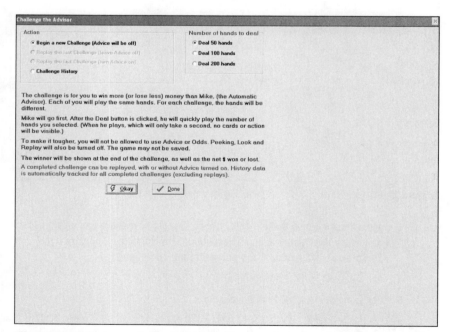

Figure 13.11 Select your challenge and see if you can beat the advisor.

2. Select the Begin New Challenge option button.

3. Select the option button representing the number of hands you want to play.

4. Click Okay.

5. Click Deal or press D.

After you play through the challenge, the Turbo Poker program compares your results to the advisor's. You can then re-run the challenge with advice turned off or with advice turned on by choosing Game, Challenge, and selecting the appropriate option button in the Challenge the Advisor dialog box.

Running Simulations in Turbo Poker Games

A lot of programs let you play poker, but the Turbo Poker series lets you run simulations where more- or less-skilled opponents make decisions every step of the way. Yes, you can run your simulations in "goldfish" mode where your opponents never bet or fold, but those results don't help when you want to determine whether betting or going for a check-raise earns more money in a given situation.

We'll show you how to run both types of simulations: those where your opponents make intelligent decisions and those where no one folds. It's actually easier to show you how to set up a full simulation first, so we'll start there.

Setting Up a Simulation

The first thing you need to do to create a simulation in a Turbo Poker program is to decide which elements of the game you want to change. Earlier in this chapter we showed you how to change the number of players, change the rake, and randomly seat your opponents. Go ahead and make those changes now.

Stacking the Deck and Freezing the Button

After you change the game settings, you need to stack the deck so that the player representing you gets the same hand every time in the simulation. In a flop game, the player in the tenth seat represents you. In a Stud game, the player in the eighth seat represents you.

To stack the deck in a Turbo Poker flop game, follow these steps:

1. Choose Game Setup, Stack the Deck.

2. Click the Change button to display the Stack the Deck/Freeze the Button dialog box, shown in Figure 13.12.

3. Drag the first card in the hand you want to test to the left opening for Seat 10.

4. Drag the second card in the hand you want to test to the right opening for Seat 10.

5. Drag cards to any other seats to set up hands they play against your assigned hand.

6. Drag cards to the board area (three openings for the flop, one for the turn, and one for the river) to represent the board you want to test.

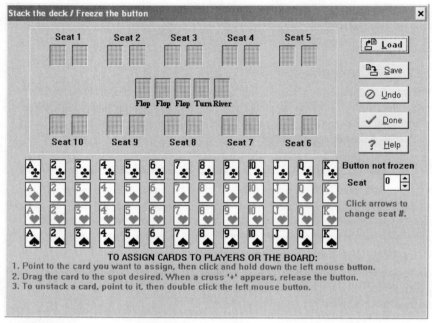

Figure 13.12 Assign cards to each player's hand and to the board to begin setting up your simulation.

♠♥♣♦ Note

You may assign only one card to a hand. For example, if you want to test how much expected value always having an Ace adds to a hand in Hold 'em, you could drag one of the Aces to the left Seat 10 slot and leave the other slot empty. You may also assign unequal numbers of cards to different hands.

7. If you want Seat 10 to act in at a particular time, such as under the gun, click the Seat spin control to freeze the button on a particular seat.

8. Click the Save button.

9. Double-click a Stack Setup number to display the Save the Deck Stacking dialog box.

10. Type a description in the text field.

11. Click Done to close the Save the Deck Stacking dialog box.

12. Click Done to close the Stack the Deck/Freeze the Button dialog box.

CAUTION

If you don't save your stack, Turbo Poker will forget it as soon as you quit the current game. You'll get the results for your current simulation, but you'll have to re-create the stack to use it again.

When we tested the effect of calling with KTo under the gun, we froze the button on Seat 7, so Seat 8 had the small blind and Seat 9 had the big blind.

Stacking the deck for a Stud game uses a similar Stack the Deck/Freeze the Button dialog box, shown in Figure 13.13.

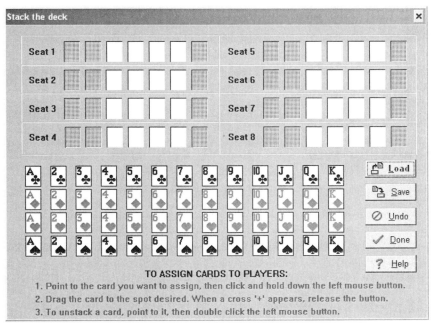

Figure 13.13 The deck stacking interface is a bit different for Stud games, but it should look familiar.

As in the flop game simulations, you can assign unequal numbers of cards to different hands. For example, if you wanted to see how a player holding A♥A♣2♦ would fare against seven opponents with random hands, you could assign those three cards to Seat 8, save your changes as you would for a flop game, and run your simulation.

Loading a Saved Deck Stack

If you want to run a simulation using a deck stack you saved earlier, you can load the stack into your program quickly. To load a saved deck stack, follow these steps:

1. Choose Game Setup, Stack the Deck.
2. Click the Change button to display the Stack the Deck/Freeze the Button dialog box.
3. Click the Load button to display the Load the Deck Stacking dialog box.
4. Double-click the deck stack you want to use.
5. Click Done to close the Save the Deck Stacking dialog box.
6. Click Done to close the Stack the Deck/Freeze the Button dialog box.

Repeating a Deal

You know, it's all well and good to simulate two different strategies, but it's not a fair test unless the strategies face exactly the same hands. For example, assume you have 9♠9♥ in Hold 'em and the board comes J♦9♣4♥. Is it more profitable to bet your set or to check and hope for a check-raise opportunity? Even if you run a 100,000-hand simulation, you have no idea how similar the hand mixes are. The Turbo Poker programs eliminate that problem by letting you choose one of 50,000 repeatable deals. If you choose the same deal code for two simulations, the trials will use exactly the same cards.

To repeat a deal, follow these steps:

1. Choose Game Setup, Stack the Deck to display the Stack the Deck/Freeze the Button dialog box.
2. Type the repeatable deal code (1 through 49,999) in the Deal Code Number field.
3. Click Done.

Limiting Which Hands Count toward Your Simulation Results

Simulating how A♠K♠ does versus A♥K♦ is all well and good, but you can perform that simple analysis with the Poker Odds Calculator at twodimes.net. The Turbo Poker programs don't limit you to determining how sets of hole cards measure up against each other. For example, you might want to find out how J♦T♦ performs when at least three players see the turn after a flop of 9♦8♥8♠, or determine whether AQo plays better against one opponent or four.

To require a minimum, maximum, or exact number of players to count a hand toward simulation results, follow these steps:

1. Click the left-most menu header, which reflects the game you're playing, and choose Automatic Test Capability.
2. Click the Test Using # of Opponents button to display the Specify the Number of Opponents dialog box, shown in Figure 13.14.

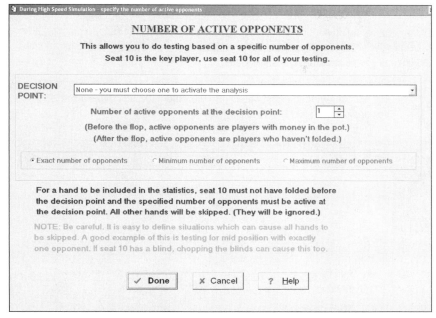

Figure 13.14 You can require a minimum, maximum, or exact number of players before the program counts a hand in your simulation.

3. Click the Decision Point down arrow, and select the point in the hand where you want the program to count the number of active players in the pot. The three most useful decision points are

   ✦ Flop is dealt and Set 10 has not folded

   ✦ Turn is dealt and Set 10 has not folded

   ✦ River is dealt and Set 10 has not folded

4. Click the Number of Active Opponents at the Decision Point spin control to set the desired number of opponents.

5. Select the Exact Number of Opponents, Minimum Number of Opponents, or Maximum Number of Opponents option button to qualify the value in the Number of Active Opponents at the Decision Point spin control.

6. Click Done.

Running Advanced Simulations

By now, you've put in a lot of work to get your simulation ready to run, but now it's time to select your settings and generate some results. To run a simulation using deck stacks and lineups you've saved, follow these steps:

1. Click the left-most menu header, which reflects the game you're playing, and choose Automatic Test Capability. The Automatic Test Capability dialog box appears, as shown in Figure 13.15.

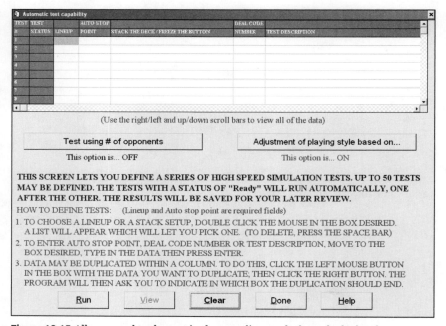

Figure 13.15 All you need to do now is choose a lineup, deck stack, deal code, and the number of hands to be dealt.

2. Double-click in the first Lineup field to display the Pick a Lineup dialog box.

3. Click the lineup you want to use in the simulation.

4. Click OK.

5. Click in the first Auto Stop Point field and type the number of hands you want to generate.

6. Double-click in the first Stack the Deck/Freeze the Button field to display the Load the Deck Stacking dialog box.

7. Double-click the stack you want to use.

8. If desired, type a deal code number in the first Deal Code Number field.

9. Type a description in the Test Description field.

10. If desired, repeat Steps 2 through 9 in the second row to define another simulation.

11. Click Run.

12. Click OK to clear the information box that lets you know the simulation(s) ran successfully.

After you run a simulation, its status in the Automatic Test Capability dialog box changes from Ready to Complete.

CAUTION

When you click the Run button, the Turbo Poker programs will run any simulations with a Ready status. You will need to delete a test to keep it from running.

Viewing and Analyzing Simulation Results

After you've run your simulations, you can display a series of reports that summarize the simulation's results. The Turbo Poker programs generate the following reports:

✦ Win/Loss History

✦ Hands Held

✦ Best Hand Distribution

✦ How Often the Best Hand Held Up

✦ Starting Hand Analyzer

✦ Pot, Money, and Activity Statistics

✦ Player Aggressiveness

✦ Win/Lose Analysis by Stage

✦ Recap of Tightness

✦ Jackpot Frequency Analysis

✦ Totals

The last report, Totals, provides the real bottom line: how much each player won or lost in the simulation. Figure 13.16 shows the Totals report for one test.

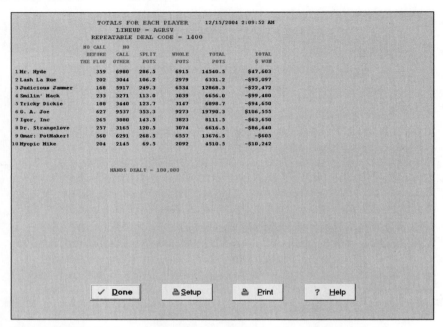

```
              TOTALS FOR EACH PLAYER     12/15/2004 2:09:52 AM
                     LINEUP = AGRSV
               REPEATABLE DEAL CODE = 1400

              NO CALL     NO
              BEFORE     CALL    SPLIT    WHOLE     TOTAL      TOTAL
              THE FLOP   OTHER    POTS     POTS      POTS      $ WON
 1 Mr. Hyde        359    6980    286.5    6915    14540.5    $47,603
 2 Lash La Rue     202    3044    106.2    2979     6331.2   -$95,097
 3 Judicious Jammer 168   5917    249.3    6534    12068.3   -$22,472
 4 Smilin' Mack    233    3271    113.0    3039     6656.0   -$99,480
 5 Tricky Dickie   100    3440    123.7    3147     6898.7   -$94,650
 6 G. A. Joe       627    9537    353.3    9273    19790.3   $106,555
 7 Igor, Inc       265    3080    143.5    3823     8111.5   -$63,650
 8 Dr. Strangelove 257    3165    120.5    3074     6616.5   -$86,640
 9 Omar: PotMaker! 560    6291    268.5    6557    13676.5      -$605
10 Myopic Mike     204    2145     69.5    2092     4510.5   -$10,242


               HANDS DEALT = 100,000
```

Figure 13.16 The Totals report presents the simulation's bottom line on hands and money won.

The How Often the Best Hand Held Up charts, one of which appears in Figure 13.17, show you how often the best hand holds up, but the charts break down the data by the number of players remaining in the hand and the stage of the hand (e.g., on the flop or the turn) when a player has the best hand.

The best way to learn about the other charts and reports is to display them for each simulation. Be sure to choose all of the options to display all aspects of the simulation data. For example, when you view the How Often the Best Hand Held Up charts, you can click the middle list box's down arrow and select Board = All Hands to summarize every hand in the simulation, or select Board = No Pair to see how often the best hand held up on the turn or river when there was no pair on the board.

To display simulation results, follow these steps:

1. Click the left-most menu header, which reflects the game you're playing, and choose Automatic Test Capability. The Automatic Test Capability dialog box appears.

2. In the Status field of the row representing the simulation that generated the results you want to view, click Complete.

3. Select the option button next to the report you want to view.

4. Click Show.

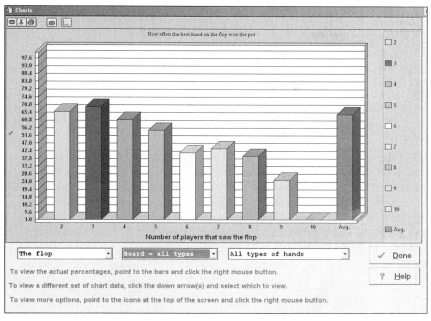

Figure 13.17 The How Often the Best Hand Held Up report tells you how often you can expect to win (or get chased down from behind) when you have the best hand on the flop or turn.

5. Click Done three times to close the report, the report list, and the Automatic Test Capability dialog boxes.

When you view a report, you can print it by clicking the Print button at the top left of the interface. The button with the scissors icon, which looks like the Cut button in Microsoft Office programs, copies the current report's data to the Windows Clipboard as text so you can paste it into a document.

To re-run a simulation with the same settings, double-click in the Lineup field of the simulation you want to run, and click Cancel to close the Pick a Lineup dialog box. The program will think you modified the simulation and will change the test's status from Complete to Ready.

Deleting Your Simulations

To delete your simulations, follow these steps:

1. Click the left-most menu header, which reflects the game you're playing, and choose Automatic Test Capability.

2. Click Clear to delete all of the simulations in the dialog box.

3. Click Done.

Running a "No One Folds" Simulation

Betting aggressively to get other players to lay down the best hand takes skill and judgment. At limit poker, it's difficult to make other players fold when it will only cost them $10 at $5–$10 to call and keep you honest. If you choose your spots judiciously, you can make money by being aggressive. Simulations can help you discover when aggression works and when it might not. Comparing the results of an intelligent simulation, where your opponents might lay down a better hand against the results of a simulation and where everyone plays every hand to the bitter end, offers great insights into how your tactics might work.

To run a showdown poker simulation where no player folds, follow these steps:

1. Click the left-most menu header, which reflects the game you're playing, and choose Automatic Test Capability. The Automatic Test Capability dialog box appears.

2. Click Deal or press D. The simulation's progress, shown in Figure 13.18, appears in the Turbo Poker program window.

3. When the program has simulated enough hands (100,000 is always enough), click Pause or press P. The Resume, Stats/Rake, and Quit options appear at the bottom of the program window.

4. Click Stats/Rake or press S to view the reports list.

5. Click Done to close the Reports dialog box.

6. Click Quit or press Q to exit the simulation.

7. Click Yes to verify you want to quit.

8. Click No to exit the simulation without saving the results, or click Yes to save the results.

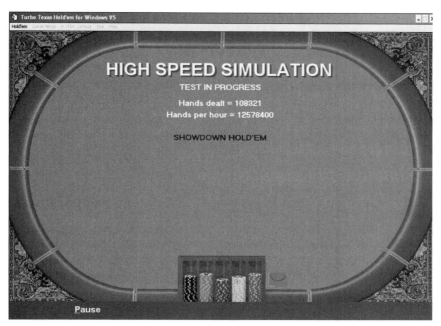

Figure 13.18 You can't define a stopping point for a showdown simulation, so you'll have to tell the program when to stop.

♠♥♣♦ Note

Yes, you can run a simulation with computer opponents by stacking the deck and choosing the Showdown menu option, but you won't be able to save your results or re-run the simulation without reloading your settings. If you have any doubts as to whether you should run the simulation as a saved test or as a one-off showdown simulation, use the Automatic Test Capability dialog box to save your work.

Analyzing Your Results with PokerTracker

The Turbo Poker software programs let you examine various strategies, but they don't help you analyze how you actually played online, unless you look up a hand's history and program in the action. Of course, when you play poker in a brick-and-mortar card room, you need to write down the hands you want to examine later. If you stay to the river, you need to write down your hand, the other cards you saw, the board, and the action while you decide what to do with your next set of hole cards. It's a pain, and taking notes marks you as a knowledgeable player and might kill your action.

When you play online, your poker client software tracks every hand in minute detail; all you need to do is get that information out of your hand histories. It's hard to do on your own, but PokerTracker, which you can buy from www.pokertracker.com/ for $55, automates the process. You can import Hold 'em hand histories from all of the major online poker sites and analyze the files to your heart's content.

♠♥♣♦ Note

We couldn't find a reliable program with which to analyze your seven-card Stud play. We chose not to recommend PokerStat, a competing program that does handle Omaha and Omaha high-low hands, because it only works for hands played at Paradise Poker and PokerStars.

Importing Hand Histories Automatically

Bringing your hand histories into PokerTracker is pretty easy, as long as you have configured your poker client software to save your hand histories on your computer. The steps you need to take in order to store your histories vary from program to program, but the process for PartyPoker is typical.

To store your PartyPoker hand histories on your local computer, follow these steps:

1. Choose Options, Hand History Logs Configuration. The Hand History Configuration dialog box appears, as shown in Figure 13.19.

2. Click the Hand History Logs Should Be Stored Locally on the Machine down arrow and select Yes.

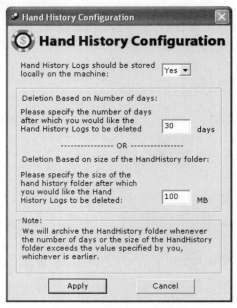

Figure 13.19 Storing your hand history logs on your computer makes it easier to process your results with PokerTracker.

3. Type a value in either of the next two fields to limit your hand history storage, based on an expiration date or total storage space used.

4. Click Apply.

Once you're sure your client software stores your hand histories on your computer, you can import them into PokerTracker. To import your hand histories into PokerTracker, follow these steps:

1. Choose File, Auto-Import Hand Histories/Tournament Summaries – Setup. The Auto-Import Hand Histories dialog box appears, as shown in Figure 13.20.

Figure 13.20 The Auto-Import Hand Histories dialog box

2. Click the Use down arrow and select Look for a File (or Files) on My PC.

3. Select the All Text Files in Folder option button.

4. Click Configure to display the Configure Auto-Import dialog box.

5. Click Add Folder.

6. Select the folder, then click OK three times to accept your changes and start the import.

After PokerTracker imports your hand histories, the program might display a message box indicating you should compact the databases. Go ahead and click OK to clear the message box; you'll compact the databases later.

Viewing Ring Game Statistics

Now that you've imported your hand histories into PokerTracker, you can view the results. To display the statistics from your ring games, choose File, Ring Game Player Statistics. The statistics dialog box, shown in Figure 13.21, appears.

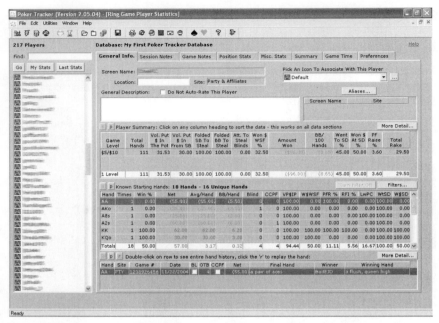

Figure 13.21 Here are the details of how you and your opponents chose to play Hold 'em.

The General Info tab page of the Ring Game Player Statistics dialog box shows how many times you have faced particular players, how they fared overall, how they did in individual sessions, and how they played specific hands.

All of the tab pages provide useful information, and it is worth your time to work through them, but you'll get a lot out of the Position Stats tab page, shown in Figure 13.22.

To view a player's play record by position, click the player's name in the Players list and click the position you want to view. When we looked through our own stats by position, we were shocked to learn how often we played suited Kings and Queens from middle position. Needless to say, we didn't win money playing those hands. Lesson learned. That single insight will probably save us the money we spent to buy PokerTracker.

Replaying a Hand

Unless you have an incredible memory, viewing lists of hands and their results doesn't help you recall how a hand was played out. One of the nicer PokerTracker features is the ability to replay a hand with a table, chips, and the player's names displayed. The replay screen's interface lets you pause the replay to recall what you were thinking, figure out what your opponent was or wasn't thinking, and write down the hand's status so you can simulate different strategies in a Turbo Poker program or using the Poker Odds Calculator at twodimes.net.

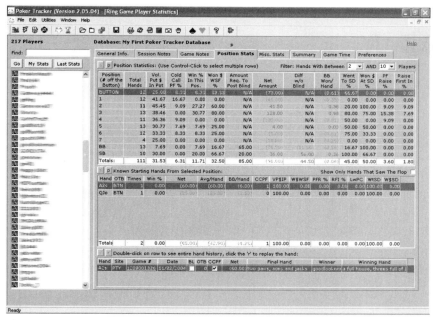

Figure 13.22 Breaking down how a player plays in a given position provides terrific insight into their overall game.

To replay a hand, follow these steps:

1. Choose File, Ring Game Player Statistics to display the Ring Game Player Statistics dialog box.

2. If necessary, click the General Info tab.

3. In the Player List pane, click the player whose hand you want to replay.

4. In the Known Starting Hands list, click the starting hand the player had in the hand you want to analyze.

5. In the Hand History list at the bottom of the dialog box, click the hand you want to replay.

6. Click the R button just above the Hand History list to display the Playback dialog box, shown in Figure 13.23.

7. Click the Play button to start replaying the hand. You can drag the Speed slider to speed up the replay and use the familiar VCR controls to pause, fast-forward, and jump ahead in the replay.

8. Click the Close box at the top-right corner of the Playback window to close it.

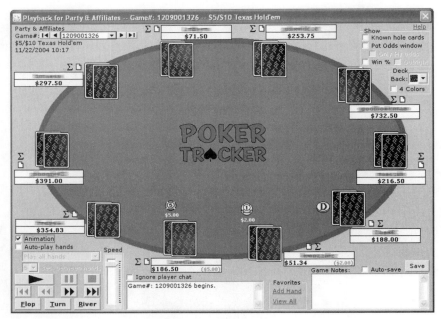

Figure 13.23 Use the VCR-like controls to play back a hand.

Printing and Saving Reports

To print any list from a dialog box, click the P button just above the list, and click the Print button at the bottom right of the window that appears. To save a list as a text file, click the S button just above the list, then choose where to save it and under what name. That's all there is to it.

Compacting Databases

There's a lot going on under PokerTracker's hood. The underlying database consists of multiple tables and queries, many of which must be combined to display the data you see in the program interface. PokerTracker uses the Microsoft Access database engine to store its results, one side effect of which is that the database can grow much larger than it needs to be when tables are combined. Why? Who cares. But you should care about keeping your database's size down, which you can do by compacting the database. Here's how you do it:

1. Choose File, Close a Database and close each open database.

2. Choose Utilities, One Step Compact to compact the databases.

The program will ask permission to create a backup copy of the database and to over-write any existing backups. Both actions are safe, so click OK.

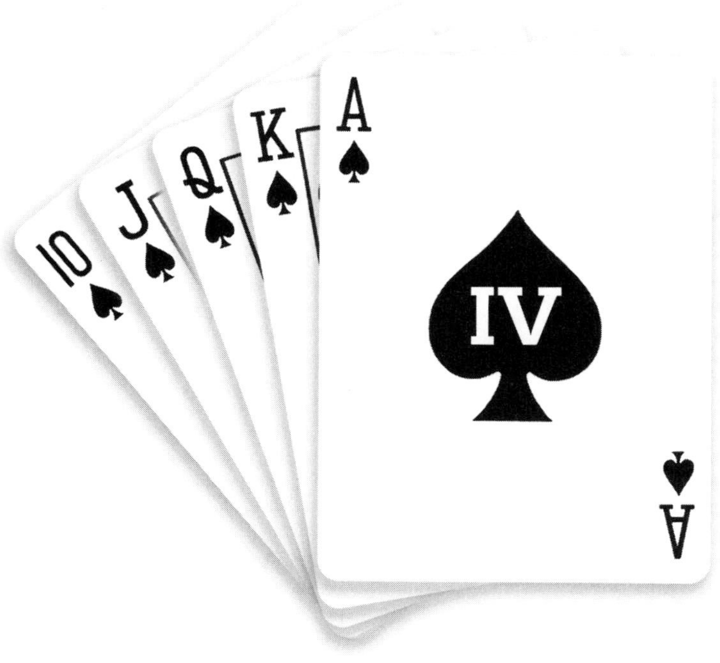
IV

Turning Data into Discipline

Spreadsheet programs and poker tracking databases are good at storing data lists, but the raw data doesn't do you much good unless you know the type of questions to ask. In Chapter 12, we listed a series of questions you can ask of your spreadsheet data. In this chapter, we'll try to find actionable intelligence from that data to help you make specific changes to your game.

Examining an Excel Hourly Play Example

Suppose you've been playing poker for a few months. You spend a couple of hours a night playing during the week, but on the weekends you find the time to play for eight or ten hours at a sitting. Is there anything about that pattern you should change? Maybe. Figure 14.1 shows the results tracking worksheet that reflects your results for those sessions.

We haven't set a filter yet, so the subtotal of the visible cells, shown in cell K2, is the same as the total of all cells in the data list, which appears in cell K3. A good first step in analyzing your hourly results data is to find out where you're losing money, which means you should display your worst five hours and see if a pattern emerges. Figure 14.2 shows the worst five hours in the data list.

The first characteristic that jumps out from this filtered data set is that the hours are all five or higher, which indicates that you probably lose concentration as you play longer in a session. It's a common malady: Many poker players visiting Las Vegas play for two or three days with little or no sleep. But lack of sleep is like alcohol: It degrades your performance while simultaneously blinding you to its effects. The local players there, and the

Subtotal $ 143.00
Total $ 143.00

Row	Site	Game	Date	Leve	Playe	Hour	Win/Lo
5	PartyPoker	Hold'em	3/10/2005	5	10	1	47
6	PartyPoker	Hold'em	3/10/2005	5	10	2	101
7	PartyPoker	Hold'em	3/10/2005	5	10	3	22
8	PartyPoker	Hold'em	3/10/2005	5	10	4	31
9	PartyPoker	Hold'em	3/10/2005	5	10	5	-80
10	PartyPoker	Hold'em	3/10/2005	5	10	6	-40
11	PartyPoker	Hold'em	3/10/2005	5	10	7	1
12	PartyPoker	Hold'em	3/10/2005	5	10	8	-35
13	PartyPoker	Hold'em	3/10/2005	5	10	9	-70
14	UltimateBet	Hold'em	3/11/2005	5	10	1	103
15	UltimateBet	Hold'em	3/11/2005	5	10	2	-3
16	UltimateBet	Hold'em	3/11/2005	5	10	3	87
17	UltimateBet	Hold'em	3/11/2005	5	10	4	67
18	UltimateBet	Hold'em	3/11/2005	5	10	5	-3
19	UltimateBet	Hold'em	3/11/2005	5	10	6	0
20	UltimateBet	Hold'em	3/11/2005	5	10	7	-45
21	UltimateBet	Hold'em	3/11/2005	5	10	8	-63
22	UltimateBet	Hold'em	3/11/2005	5	10	9	-101
23	UltimateBet	Hold'em	3/11/2005	5	10	10	30
24	UltimateBet	Hold'em	3/11/2005	5	10	11	-75
25	PartyPoker	Hold'em	3/12/2005	5	10	1	26
26	PartyPoker	Hold'em	3/12/2005	5	10	2	209
27	PartyPoker	Hold'em	3/12/2005	5	10	3	91
28	PartyPoker	Hold'em	3/12/2005	5	10	4	87
29	PartyPoker	Hold'em	3/12/2005	5	10	5	-5
30	PartyPoker	Hold'em	3/12/2005	5	10	6	-91
31	PartyPoker	Hold'em	3/12/2005	5	10	7	-70
32	PartyPoker	Hold'em	3/12/2005	5	10	8	68
33	PartyPoker	Hold'em	3/12/2005	5	10	9	-103
34	PartyPoker	Hold'em	3/12/2005	5	10	10	-43

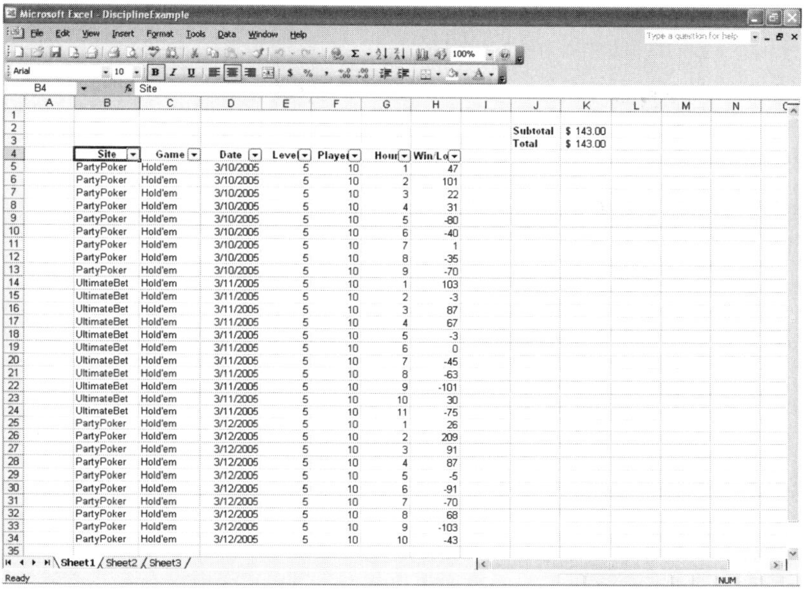

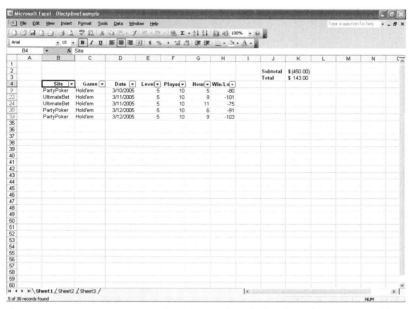

Figure 14.1 This data tells a story; you just have to know how to ask for it.

Subtotal $ (450.00)
Total $ 143.00

Row	Site	Game	Date	Leve	Playe	Hour	Win/Lo
9	PartyPoker	Hold'em	3/10/2005	5	10	5	-80
22	UltimateBet	Hold'em	3/11/2005	5	10	9	-101
24	UltimateBet	Hold'em	3/11/2005	5	10	11	-75
30	PartyPoker	Hold'em	3/12/2005	5	10	6	-91
33	PartyPoker	Hold'em	3/12/2005	5	10	9	-103

5 of 30 records found

Figure 14.2 Here are your worst five hours. What do they have in common aside from a minus sign?

better online players, know that they should play a set number of hours during the time of day when they feel most awake and energetic.

You can verify your preliminary result by removing the first filter and creating an advanced filter so your data list only displays your results from hours five and later. Figure 14.3 shows the result of setting that filter.

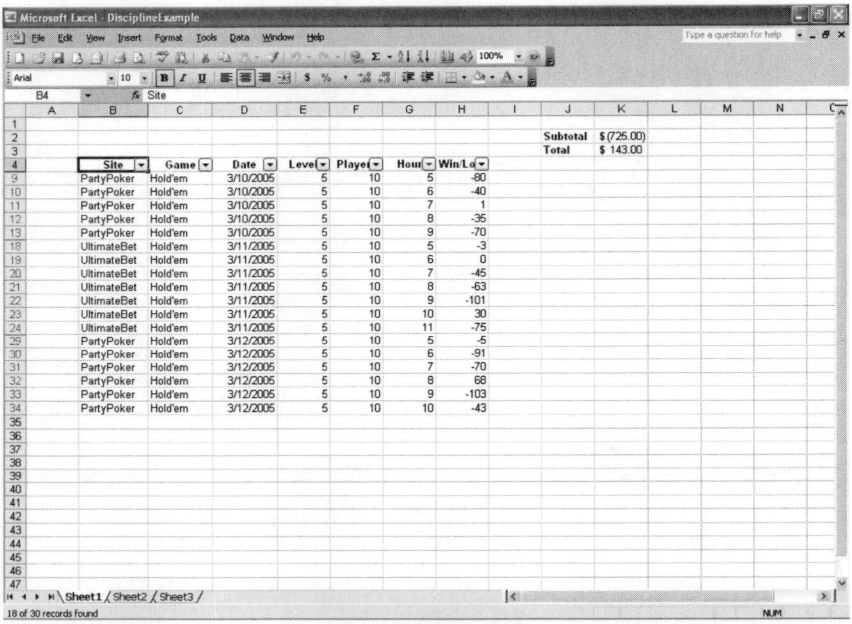

Row	Site	Game	Date	Level	Players	Hour	Win/Loss
9	PartyPoker	Hold'em	3/10/2005	5	10	5	-80
10	PartyPoker	Hold'em	3/10/2005	5	10	6	-40
11	PartyPoker	Hold'em	3/10/2005	5	10	7	1
12	PartyPoker	Hold'em	3/10/2005	5	10	8	-35
13	PartyPoker	Hold'em	3/10/2005	5	10	9	-70
18	UltimateBet	Hold'em	3/11/2005	5	10	5	-3
19	UltimateBet	Hold'em	3/11/2005	5	10	6	0
20	UltimateBet	Hold'em	3/11/2005	5	10	7	-45
21	UltimateBet	Hold'em	3/11/2005	5	10	8	-63
22	UltimateBet	Hold'em	3/11/2005	5	10	9	-101
23	UltimateBet	Hold'em	3/11/2005	5	10	10	30
24	UltimateBet	Hold'em	3/11/2005	5	10	11	-75
29	PartyPoker	Hold'em	3/12/2005	5	10	5	-5
30	PartyPoker	Hold'em	3/12/2005	5	10	6	-91
31	PartyPoker	Hold'em	3/12/2005	5	10	7	-70
32	PartyPoker	Hold'em	3/12/2005	5	10	8	68
33	PartyPoker	Hold'em	3/12/2005	5	10	9	-103
34	PartyPoker	Hold'em	3/12/2005	5	10	10	-43

Figure 14.3 Filter your data again to confirm the data pattern fits your original guess.

A quick glance at cell K2 shows that you have lost a total of $725 when you play past the fourth hour of a session. In other words, if you'd quit after playing for four hours in each session, you would be ahead $868 instead of $143. That's quite a difference. It's also interesting to note that the trend continues as you go along. If you filter the table again to just show your results for hours seven and later, you find that you lost $506 when you played beyond six hours. If you thought you got better as you went deeper into your play sessions, you were wrong.

The chart in Figure 14.4 graphically illustrates how your results trend down over time.

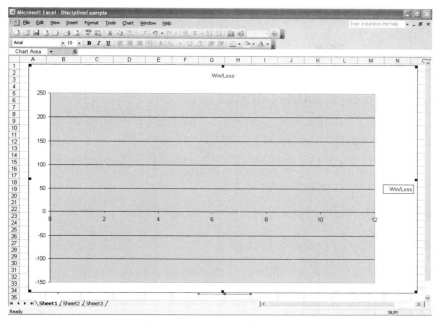

Figure 14.4 This XY scatter chart shows how much you lose when you play beyond six hours.

Examining a PokerTracker Example

It's easy for players to fall in love with a hand, or a type of hand, after they've won with it a few times. Probably the worst thing that can happen to a poker player is to hit a huge pot with 6♠9♣ early in their career. Not only do they get to make a sexual reference as they virtually wave the hand around for everyone to see after they win, they rationalize their losses later on as having been paid for by their earlier good luck. The problem, of course, is that nostalgia for the win pushes the reality of mounting losses with a trash hand to the side.

The first step to solving a problem is to admit that you have a problem. In that light, consider the following words:

> Hi. My name's, um, Mark, and I'm a flushaholic. (Hi, Mark!) I love the look of
> any suited Ace or King in Hold 'em. I love sneaking up on people with the nut or
> second-nut flush draw and occasionally catching two pair or trips when I don't hit
> my flush. But I'm tired of throwing perfectly good money and my self-respect onto
> a fire fueled by greed and the desire to see the looks of disbelief on my opponents'
> faces as I rake in the chips with a sub-par hand. I need your help to keep my bank-
> roll intact and my discipline in place. Thanks for listening. (Thanks, Mark!)

And how does calling with any King or Ace suited in any position work out? Well, it's not going all that well, to be honest. After you fire up PokerTracker and display your hands, you can follow these steps to filter the data so the program only summarizes hands containing an Ace suited with a card below a Ten or a King suited with a card below a Nine:

1. Open the PokerTracker database as shown in Chapter 13.

2. In the Players list, click your user name.

3. Click the Filters button, located just above the top-right corner of the Known Starting Hands list. The Known Hands Filter box appears.

4. Click the Select Specific Hands button to display the Specific Hand Filter, shown in Figure 14.5.

Specific Hand Filter

AA	KK	QQ	JJ	TT	99	88	77	66	55	44	33	22
AKs	KQs	QJs	JTs	T9s	98s	87s	76s	65s	54s	43s	32s	
AKo	KQo	QJo	JTo	T9o	98o	87o	76o	65o	54o	43o	32o	
AQs	KJs	QTs	J9s	T8s	97s	86s	75s	64s	53s	42s		
AQo	KJo	QTo	J9o	T8o	97o	86o	75o	64o	53o	42o		
AJs	KTs	Q9s	J8s	T7s	96s	85s	74s	63s	52s			
AJo	KTo	Q9o	J8o	T7o	96o	85o	74o	63o	52o			
ATs	K9s	Q8s	J7s	T6s	95s	84s	73s	62s				
ATo	K9o	Q8o	J7o	T6o	95o	84o	73o	62o				
A9s	K8s	Q7s	J6s	T5s	94s	83s	72s					
A9o	K8o	Q7o	J6o	T5o	94o	83o	72o					
A8s	K7s	Q6s	J5s	T4s	93s	82s						
A8o	K7o	Q6o	J5o	T4o	93o	82o						
A7s	K6s	Q5s	J4s	T3s	92s							
A7o	K6o	Q5o	J4o	T3o	92o							
A6s	K5s	Q4s	J3s	T2s								
A6o	K5o	Q4o	J3o	T2o								
A5s	K4s	Q3s	J2s									
A5o	K4o	Q3o	J2o									
A4s	K3s	Q2s										
A4o	K3o	Q2o										
A3s	K2s											
A3o	K2o											
A2s												
A2o					Select All	Clear All		OK		Cancel			

Figure 14.5 Use this dialog box to view specific hands in PokerTracker.

5. Check the check boxes that represent the cards you want to view (A9s, A8s, A7s, A6s, A5s, A4s, A3s, A2s, K8s, K7s, K6s, K5s, K4s, K3s, and K2s).

6. Click OK to close the Specific Hand Filter dialog box, and again to close the Known Hands Filter dialog box.

The PokerTracker analysis shown in Figure 14.6 demonstrates that playing suited Aces and Kings without regard to the rank of the kicker can be a dicey proposition.

As the Known Starting Hands list shows, playing suited Aces with kickers below a Ten and suited Kings with kickers below a Nine 43 times accounts for $171 of the total $480.75 loss

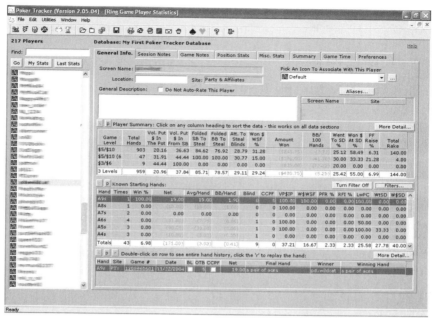

Figure 14.6 PokerTracker can dispel your illusions in a hurry.

shown in this summary. That's over one-third of the loss, so playing those hands has to go. It's been a nice habit, but it's time to get on with life and leave the old ways behind.

Developing a Style

What sort of poker persona should you take on? To start, think of the players you hate to play against: the maniac, the rock, the player who always raises when they enter a pot, and the tight aggressive player you have a hard time getting a read on. While the tight aggressive style is probably the best way to play, there are ways to modify that style to fit your personality.

Borrowing from the Maniac

You know them. You love them. You hate them. They're the maniacs, the players who raise at every opportunity. Sometimes they have nothing. Sometimes they make quads. You can't put them on a hand because they might not know what they have, either.

If you're not playing like a maniac, how is it possible to integrate elements of their style into yours? You can always raise more at the start of the hand, when it costs you one bet instead of two, but raising all the time means other good players are likely to raise behind you in the hope that everyone else will fold, and they can play you heads-up. You, on the other hand, would like several other players to call so you can make a lot of money if you hit your hand.

The secret to playing like a maniac is to do it when you're playing with several known players at a lower limit than you usually play. For example, if you usually play $5–$10, drop down to $1–$2 and, if you recognize other $5–$10 players waiting for a seat in their preferred game, go to town.

Borrowing from the Entry Raiser

The entry raiser sits one step below the maniac on the ladder of annoying players to play against. If they get involved in a pot, they raise so you have to decide whether you want to invest two or more bets in your hand instead of just one. One problem with this strategy is that the entry raiser doesn't scare players who play well within their bankroll. After all, when you have $1,500 in your online account, it's no big deal to call an extra $5 to try to win with AQo. What's more, raising all the time reduces each raise's impact. Raises from solid players are a shock because they're so infrequent and signal that the player has a good hand. Raises from someone who always raises contain no additional information and have little shock value.

The other big problem with this strategy is that the extra money in the pot often makes it mathematically correct for players to go after most any draw they pick up early in the hand. As an example, consider what happens when five players call two bets before the flop in Hold 'em. If you're playing $5–$10 Hold 'em, the pot contains $47 after the rake. Suppose you flop an inside straight draw and are certain the pre-flop raiser has a big pair, such as Aces, and no flush draw. Four out of the 45 unseen cards fill your inside straight, so the odds are 41 to 4, or 10.25 to 1, against you making your straight. If no one bets, you get to draw to your inside straight for free. If, however, someone bets, there will be $52 in the pot, which gives you 10.4 to 1 on your money and makes it mathematically correct for you to draw to your inside straight.

You can play the entry raising game at lower limits as well, but it's also a nice change from the usual at your normal limits. Just remember that you can revert to your standard strategy at any time.

Borrowing from the Rock

It's no fun to sit at a poker table and not play. We've both gone through four-hour sessions where we literally did nothing but pay antes, bring-ins, and blinds. Yes, we can truthfully say that we both have gone through a four-hour session where we didn't make an unforced bet. If you've played for a while, you've probably gone through a similar stretch, and maybe more than one. It's easy to get a reputation as a rock when you're getting crap for cards, but there's also something to be said for battening down the hatches and refusing to budge, unless you have a terrific starting hand or a lock on the hand.

But how in the world can you make money being a rock? Well, it depends on how you use the time when you're not playing. If you use the time to watch your opponents, you're fine, because you're learning while not wasting money. If you're watching television, reading e-mail, or catching up on a little light reading, you're not furthering your poker career one bit.

The other aspect of playing like a rock for a while is that players begin to toss their hands when you raise in the first betting round. If you've tossed hands for a while, try a mid-position ante or blind steal with a decent but not outstanding hand such as JTs in Hold 'em or A♠K♠3♣ in seven-card Stud if your upcard's either the Ace or King. You can also take advantage of your rock image by semi-bluff raising on the turn or fifth street, which we told you is a warning flag. If the board doesn't look too threatening, you might win the hand right there against one opponent or buy yourself a free card the next time around. Just remember that you will need a draw to fall back on, just in case anyone calls.

Personalizing the Tight Aggressive Approach

Phil Helmuth calls them eagles. Doyle Brunson calls them solid players. Alan Schoonmaker, the author of *The Psychology of Poker* (Two Plus Two Publishing, 2000), calls them stone killers. Whatever the name, they're the players you don't want at your table because they're just too good. They know their game inside and out and seem to know yours almost as well. That's the player we're all trying to be, but only a few of us will ever get there. Neither of your authors is there yet, but we're trying to improve a little bit every day.

Playing the tight aggressive game means that you don't get involved in that many pots, but when you do, you go for it. That approach doesn't mean you go crazy and raise with your pocket 88 when there's TJQKA with four of a suit on the board, though. What it means is that you know the numbers, can identify when you're a favorite in the hand, know when you're drawing, and know when to give it up because you're beat.

Be sure to mix up your game, though, so you don't become too predictable. That's another of your authors' faults: We don't change our games enough, which lets our opponents get a good read on our hands. As Doyle Brunson, the grand old man of poker, wrote in *Poker Wisdom of a Champion* (Cardoza, 2003):

> *Shifting gears means playing super-aggressively, then changing to a slower, more selective game while your opponents continue to play according to the pace you've set. They're not aware that you've shifted—only you know for sure.*

Brunson's advice applies best to no-limit games, but it's true at every limit. You want your opponents to have to guess what you have, because sometimes they'll guess wrong.

Maintaining a Stable Playing Environment

Poker is perhaps above all a mental game. Not only does a player need to know the odds and strategies to be successful, but they should also create for themselves an environment conducive to success rather than one that allows unnecessary distractions. In this chapter we will discuss how to create

✦ An appropriate *external* environment for playing winning online poker.

✦ An appropriate *internal* environment for playing winning online poker.

The Two Environments

True, we used code words to label the two different environments, but the explanation is simple. The *external* environment is what your senses register, such as light and noise. The *internal* environment refers to what is going on inside your body and, more importantly, your mind. It is extremely important that both environments be made as conducive to concentrating as possible.

The External Environment

Should the TV, Stereo, and Instant Messenger All Be on at the Same Time?

People differ in their ability to concentrate while lots of stuff is going on around them. Doug has been silly enough to have his television and IM fired up and talking on the phone while playing two tables. Your authors are in their mid-thirties and grew up before cable in three rooms of the house, the Internet, and video games were popular. The game we grew up loving was pinball. When we got introduced to video games, they weren't modern games like Halo 2, where things are so complex it boggles our minds. When we played a game, we were looking for two things: a joystick and a fire button. The SSX snowboarding game is really cool, but that's because to do the tricks when you jump you just randomly push buttons, at least that's what Doug does. Maybe that's why he always loses....

Anyway, the point is that people unaccustomed to having a lot of external stimuli around them while trying to concentrate will tend to be distracted if things they aren't used to are going on around them. Readers in their early and mid-twenties will perhaps not identify with this. Folks now legal to gamble have had computers and, more recently, the Internet in their lives since they can remember. The book *Growing Up Digital* (McGraw-Hill, 1999) describes how young children were able to carry on several IM sessions at the same time without becoming overwhelmed. Another thing to consider is what's going on around you. Do you have baby duty? If you do, concentrating may be difficult. Do you have noisy kids, neighbors, or housemates? Your authors grew up on 42 acres in Virginia's beautiful Shenandoah Valley. We fell asleep to the sounds of 18-wheelers rolling up and down Interstate 81, cows mooing, a donkey braying, insects chirping, and the occasional fox barking. People growing up in a city apartment will think nothing of having neighbors walking overhead, televisions and stereos from next door bleeding through the walls, and car horns and police/ambulance sirens going off at all times of the day and night. That would be distracting to some people. If you tend to need a lot of quiet when you play, consider playing early in the morning or late at night. If you live in a house, fire up a wireless network and play in the basement. This is all pretty obvious stuff, we realize, but it's worth noting.

Is Your Immediate Physical Environment Acceptable?

What we're talking about here are the computer, your chair, and the lighting you have to work with. If you have an old computer that keeps freezing up and forces you to shut down every hour, it may be time to get a new one. Computers are still expensive enough that many people can't just reach into their pocket and pull out the cash to buy one, but your major online computer retailers have payment plans available.

If you decide not to buy a new computer, there are several things you can do to make an aging computer work better. The first thing we suggest is to close all other programs while you're playing, because that takes up memory. The next step would be to see how much random access memory (RAM) you have in your computer. We talked early on in the book about minimum requirements to use the software, but if you only have 128 MB of RAM on your computer, we suggest putting a bunch more in. Luckily, memory is pretty cheap nowadays. Doing things like buying a new processor and monitor together would put you up to a cost where buying a new computer would be a much better idea. There are all sorts of ways to make your computer run more efficiently, such as removing programs you no longer use. We would also recommend you find a book, such as

Degunking Windows (Paraglyph Publishing, 2004) by Joli Ballew and Jeff Duntemann or search on the Web for free information on how to re-optimize your computer.

Another consideration is your physical comfort. If you're playing using a 14-inch screen, you are going to have one serious pair of tired eyes. And how about that chair you're sitting in? We're not saying you need to go out and buy some sort of NASA-engineered ergonomically perfect chaise lounge, but something with a little lumbar support wouldn't hurt. And do you need to lean over to see the screen? This is a *massive* strain on your neck. If you play for hours sitting in a rickety chair bending over to look at a small screen with a glare, you are going to be miserable soon enough. If nothing else, fit some sort of filter over the light bulb to make the light more gentle, put a small pillow behind your back for some support, and grab an outdated copy of the Yellow Pages or something you'll never use, like a calculus text or English literature anthology, and put the monitor on top of that.

The Internal Environment

How Was Your Day?

Assuming you're playing at night, how did today go? Did you get up at the normal time, have a normal or good day at work, get home at the regular time and eat dinner? Or did you have to go in early, deal with a crabby customer, co-worker, or boss, work through lunch, stay late, and get caught in traffic on the way home? Quite honestly, if the second scenario is what happened, you might want to think about doing something else tonight. When people are angry or otherwise not in their normal emotional state, they tend to act impulsively, which in the case of poker would be the wrong thing to do. Believe us, we're far from perfect on these things. We make the mistakes we warn you about all the time. The important thing to recognize is that they are indeed mistakes and that to be aware of them is a great first step in avoiding them as often as possible. Actually, writing this book has given us both fresh insight into our games. We are better off for having written it, and sincerely hope you're better off for reading it! If you do decide to play as a way to take your mind off something, we would suggest playing at a lower limit than you normally would play or, even better, enter an inexpensive tournament. Tournaments costing as little as $1 are out there. Hey, put down $10, and see what you can do. If you do well, you could play for a couple of hours. If you play well and get good cards, you could add a nice amount to your account. That would be a nice way to end a crappy day, wouldn't it? We provide a selection of titles for tournament and other poker books in the next chapter.

How Are You Feeling?

Aside from how any particular day went for you is the condition of your overall physical and emotional health. If you're sick as a dog and can barely keep your eyes open, it might be best to just take a hot shower to try to open up your sinuses, take some cold medicine, and crash in front of the television. If you haven't been sleeping well, or enough, recently your concentration and reasoning might not be as sharp as they are normally. If things are going poorly in a relationship or when there are other things weighing heavily on one's mind, this is when a lot of people turn to online poker or other risk-taking activities (yes, online poker is a risk-taking activity) for the prospective comfort of winning, and it is when they are likely to take chances they would not normally take. Sometimes they win, but often they lose, only making the situation worse. Most of the time this is a short-term thing; we all get a little depressed or upset now and then and blow a few bucks foolishly. No problem. Think of what else you could have used that money to do or buy, forgive yourself, and move on. If you think it may be more than a temporary thing, please talk to a professional. Gambling can be addictive, so please call a help line such as 1-800-GAMBLER if you feel your play is affecting your life negatively and are having trouble stopping.

The best thing about online poker is that there's always a game going on. The worst thing about online poker is that there's always a game going on.

Conclusion: A Good Environment Facilitates Good Poker

From the quality of the light you use to illuminate your room to how you're feeling that day, many non-poker factors contribute to how well or poorly you are likely to do in a playing session. If you're playing Stud and using the Excel spreadsheet to mark dead cards, does that mean you need to increase your screen resolution to allow it to be on the screen at the same time as your table? Does sitting in your computer chair for more than two hours at a time mean you need to visit the chiropractor? Did you have a bad day? Do the little things that help you concentrate, and play for lower stakes or not at all if you're not at your best. There will almost certainly be a game to play as soon as you log back in.

Conclusion

Well, here we are at the end! The novice player has gone from no knowledge to knowing how to go to an online poker Web site, establish an account, get set up, put money in their account, get on a table, and start playing with some detailed knowledge about how to go about it. The experienced player will have been exposed to some in-depth statistical analysis about where they stand in a hand. When we came up with the idea for this book, we broke down the concepts into three areas: data, draws, and discipline. To wrap up, we'll discuss each briefly.

Data

The amount of data available to an online poker player is staggering. First, a player is able to request hand histories for later study. Did you or your opponent get lucky, or did the winner, perhaps unknowingly, make a great play? Simulation software, such as that available from Wilson Software and other companies, enables the input of hands for repeatable play or simulations over perhaps 100,000 hands. And how about the data relating to your play? Do you tend to win consistently for the first three hours you're playing but trail off after that? Do you do better at a certain type of game or limit than others? If you're a favorite to win $12 an hour playing $3–$6 poker but are only a $10 an hour favorite playing $5–$10, play $3–$6 for gosh sakes! The downside of going bad at the lower limit isn't nearly as bad as at the higher one, and when you're winning, you'll tend to come out further ahead! An extremely important thing to remember is that most money is made in poker when losses are minimized as opposed to when wins are maximized.

Draws

The chapters on the pre-flop, flop, and turn provided an in-depth discussion of the possibilities myriad situations present a player. On average a player will only have the best cards 1/10 (board game) or 1/8 of the time (Stud), and realizing when you're likely beaten as early as possible is a key. Again, most money is lost in poker when a player stays in beyond when they have an acceptably high risk of winning. In limit poker, the damage is less than in no-limit, but if a player makes an average of $10 in incorrect bets per hour, they are throwing away $1,000 per 100 hours played. Over time, this becomes a massive drain on the bankroll. Not only knowing what you need to make your hand, but also having a feel for what your opponents have is crucial here. Are they solid players? Do they bluff a lot? Do they overplay weak hands? Do they not understand the game yet? As former World Champion Phil Hellmuth noted in a television interview, you have a limited amount of time to decide what your opponents have. Knowing the odds for your hand off the top of your head allows you to spend the majority of your thinking time figuring out what they have.

Discipline

An in-depth understanding of the underlying principles of any activity allows a person to go about pursuing it with discipline. Data does indeed facilitate discipline, but no less important is the role a person's internal and external environments play in putting all that knowledge to proper use. We're certainly not preaching, nor are we claiming any superiority over our readers. In reality, we learned from writing this book and hope you learned from reading it. On that note, all we have left to say is. . .

Thank you! And good luck! —Doug and Curt

Resources for Further Study

There are dozens of poker books and online resources out there, but a few stand out as being worthy of further study. Here are the books and resources we recommend.

Continuing Education: Hold 'Em

Doyle Brunson's Super System by Doyle Brunson and others (Cardoza, 1979).

Yes, *Super System* came out in 1979, but it's the classic no-limit Hold 'em reference and covers lots of other games as well. Can you afford *not* to have Chip Reese teach you seven-card Stud? We could have forgiven you for not buying it when it cost $60 and was only available from the Gambler's General Store and other Las Vegas establishments, but now it's a paperback that you can buy in most online and brick-and-mortar stores. If you remain ignorant, you have only yourself to blame.

Doyle Brunson's Super System II **by Doyle Brunson and others (Cardoza, 2005).**

An update of the classic that promises to deliver as much value as the original.

Hold'Em Poker for Advanced Players **by David Sklansky and Mason Malmuth (Two Plus Two Publishing, 1999).**

Another classic in the Hold 'em field. Some of the strategies and tactics, originally published in 1988, have been overtaken by events, but the basic concepts presented are all still valid.

Hold 'Em Excellence: From Beginner to Winner **by Lou Krieger (Conjelco, 2nd edition, 2000).**

Lou Krieger is a successful player who makes a bundle playing Hold 'em in California. This book, which updates some of the concepts in *Hold 'Em Poker for Advanced Players*, is filled to the brim with specific Hold 'em advice.

Winning Low Limit Hold'Em **by Lee Jones (Conjelco, 2nd edition, 2000).**

The low-limit game, played at $4–$8 and below, is a different animal than $10–$20 and above. Lee Jones offers advice on how to beat loose-aggressive games often found in California card rooms.

Small Stakes Hold 'em: Winning Big With Expert Play **by Ed Miller, David Sklansky, and Mason Malmuth (Two Plus Two Publishing, 2004).**

This book is a comprehensive examination of most situations you will encounter in lower-limit Hold 'em games. As opposed to *Hold 'Em Poker for Advanced Players*, this book talks about what you are facing when you are against a couple of solid players but at least a few loose players as well. Several in-hand situations are covered.

Play Poker Like the Pros **by Phil Hellmuth, Jr. (Harper Resource, 2003).**

The 1989 World Series of Poker main event champion takes players through beginning, intermediate, and advanced discussions on playing poker. Hellmuth spends the first half of the book on Hold 'em and the rest on the Stud and Omaha games. Recommended reading for any up-and-coming poker player.

Championship No-Limit & Pot-Limit Hold 'Em **by T.J. Cloutier and Tom McEvoy (Cardoza, 2004).**

Back in the early days of casino poker, you had to sit down with $10,000 to play no-limit, but now there are games available online where you can buy in for as little as $60. If you want to learn about big bet poker, listen to T.J. Cloutier. He's one of the best all-around poker players in the world. The only reason he hasn't won the World Series of Poker main event is bad luck. If you plan to play no-limit or pot-limit poker, this book will save you a lot of money.

Continuing Education: Seven-Card Stud

Seven Card Stud for Advanced Players **by David Sklansky, Mason Malmuth, and Ray Zee (Two Plus Two Publishing, 1999).**

Just as *Hold 'em Poker for Advanced Players* is part of the Hold 'em canon, this book, originally published in 1989, is an indispensable reference for the serious seven-card Stud player. The concepts in this book have aged better than some of the Hold 'em books' prescriptions.

7-Card Stud : 42 Lessons How to Win at Medium & Lower Limits **by Roy West (Cardoza, 2004).**

West writes in a more approachable style than the *Advanced Players* gang, which makes it easier to absorb the lessons he teaches. We use the strategies in *42 Lessons* as the basis of our seven-card Stud play, to very good results.

Continuing Education: Omaha and High-Low Games

The Best of Cappelletti on Omaha **by Mike Cappelletti (self-published, 1998).**

Mike Cappelletti is one of the best Omaha players in the world. This book, a collection of his best columns, should form the basis of any Omaha player's library. You'll have to order this book from the Gambler's General Store, which you can find on the Web at www.gamblersgeneralstore.com.

High-Low-Split Poker: Seven-Card Stud and Omaha Eight-or-Better for Advanced Players **by Ray Zee (Two Plus Two Publishing, 1992).**

Seven-card Stud high-low is a tricky game to learn and an easy game to play poorly. Ray Zee discusses starting hand requirements and how this game differs from high-only seven-card Stud. Zee doesn't offer an Omaha point count system of the sort developed by Ed Hutchison, but there's still a lot of good information on Omaha high-low in this book.

How to Win at Omaha High-Low Poker **by Mike Cappelletti (Cardoza, 2003).**

No apologies for listing two books by the same guy; Cappelletti's the man when it comes to all forms of Omaha. Buy this book if you play Omaha high-low. Seriously.

Continuing Education: Tournaments

Tournament Poker **by Tom McEvoy (Cardsmith Publishing, 1995).**

Tournament poker, particularly no-limit Hold 'em tournaments, is a breed apart from limit poker. In this book, McEvoy tells you what to expect each step of the way in a big tournament, how to think about putting yourself in a position to win, and how to avoid playing yourself out of contention for a huge payday.

Championship Satellite Strategy **by Tom McEvoy and Brad Dougherty (Cardsmith Publishing, 2003).**

Most players try to enter big tournaments on the cheap by winning a satellite, a minitournament where the prizes are seats in the main event. This book describes each stage of the satellite so you know what to do from the start instead of having to figure it out after the satellite's over.

Tournament Poker for Advanced Players **by David Sklansky (Two Plus Two Publishing, 2002).**

With examples from Hold 'em and Stud, Sklansky helps tournament players gain perspective on important tournament concepts. Sklansky advocates a strategy minimizing toss-up situations for all or most of your chips in the early stages of a tournament. He also gives the reader several analytical tools with which to work in determining the correct action at a given time.

Continuing Education: Online

The Mike Caro University of Poker

Mike Caro, "Poker's Mad Genius," is one of the most insightful writers and players out there. You can find all sorts of fun and interesting articles at his University of Poker found online atwww.poker1.com/mcup.asp.

The Poker Source

The Poker Source, which you can find online at www.thepokersource.com/, has a lot of advertisements on the front page, but it also offers a number of interesting articles and charts. The best of those resources is the Hold 'em odds chart, found at www.thepokersource.com/holdem_odds.shtml. Want to know the odds of a pocket pair improving to trips after the flop? It's there. The odds that none of nine players holds an Ace? Ditto.

The Gambler's General Store

If you can't find a poker-related pamphlet on Amazon, be sure to visit the Gambler's General Store in Las Vegas. If you can't get to Vegas, you can visit them online at www.gamblers generalstore.com. They also stock all manner of gaming equipment and accessories.

The Gambler's Book Shop

The Gambler's Book Shop is the other major Vegas gaming institution. If you're looking for a hard-to-find book, try here as well. You can find them on the Web at www.gamblersbook.com.

Ed Hutchison's Point Count System

You can find updated versions of Ed Hutchison's Omaha high-low point count system at http://ehutchison.homestead.com/omahasystem.html. That page also has links to his Omaha high and Hold 'em point count systems.

About the Authors

Dr. Douglas Frye is a longtime incorrigible poker player who has played extensively online and in brick-and-mortar card rooms, mostly in Atlantic City. Doug has spent most of his professional career in policy and academic research surrounding information and space technologies. Additionally, he has taught Communication and Government classes at the university level for several years. Doug is currently a consultant for a company providing enterprise integration services to U.S. Government clients. He lives in Virginia.

Curtis Frye is a professional writer living and working in Portland, Oregon. He has more than 20 books and online courses to his credit, most recently having written *Excel Annoyances* for O'Reilly Media and *Microsoft Office Excel 2003 Step By Step* for Microsoft Press. He has played casino poker seriously since 1992 and competed in several of the early World Rec.Gambling Poker Tournaments, which were run by electronic mail. When he isn't writing or playing poker, Curt is a professional improvisational comedian with ComedySportz Portland.

Index

A

Index

OpenOffice, 166. *See also* spreadsheets
operating system
system requirements, 10-11, 235-236
spreadsheets, 166
optimizing hardware, 235-236
outs (discovered outs), 134-135
overcards
hands, analyzing, 104
Hold 'Em
flops, 104-105
turns, 135-136
overpair
hands, analyzing, 104
Hold 'Em
flops, 104
turns, 134-135

P

pair, 17
Aces
hands, analyzing, 108-109, 136-137
Hold 'Em flops, 108-109
Hold 'Em turns, 136-137
Seven-Card Stud river, 158
overpair
hands, analyzing, 104
Hold 'Em flops, 104
Hold 'Em turns, 134-135
Seven-Card Stud river, 158
two pair, 17
Hold 'Em flops, 104
Hold 'Em turns, 132-133
Seven-Card Stud river, 156-158
statistics, 45-46
pair of Aces
hands, analyzing, 108-109, 136-137
Hold 'Em
flops, 108-109
turns, 136-137
Seven-Card Stud river, 158
Paradise Poker site, 12
Party Poker site, 12-13

payout structure (Poker Stars site), 50-51
PayPal site, 14
perfect-perfect hands, 110
perks (sites), 13-14
Pineapple
high-low split, 38
practice hands, 40-41
starting hands, 94
overview, 33
playing, 33
river, 144
starting hands, 93-94
players
analyzing strategies, 231-233
lineups (Turbo Poker), 204-206, 214-215, 217
number
online, 3-4
Turbo Poker, 203-204, 212-213
professionals, sites, 13
Turbo Poker
lineups (Turbo Poker), 204-206, 214-215, 217
number , 203-204, 212-213
profiles, 206-207
point count system, 81-93, 242
points (sites), 13-14
poker
games. *See* games
hands. *See* hands
legal issues. *See* legal issues
number of players, 3-4
online advantages, 4-5
online disadvantages, 5-6
online history, 2-4
online popularity, 3-4
problem gambling, 14, 236-237
sites. *See* sites
Poker Inspector site, 66-67
Poker Odds Calculator site, 196-197
Poker Probe, 82
Poker Pulse site, 3-4, 12
Poker Source site, 242